V. E. SCHWAB
EXTRAORDINARY

TITANCOMICS®

ALSO AVAILABLE FROM V.E. SCHWAB
AND TITAN BOOKS

THE NEAR WITCH
VICIOUS | VENGEFUL
THIS SAVAGE SONG | OUR DARK DUET
A DARKER SHADE OF MAGIC | A GATHERING OF SHADOWS | A CONJURING OF LIGHT
THE DARK VAULT

ALSO AVAILABLE FROM V.E. SCHWAB
AND TITAN COMICS

SHADES OF MAGIC: THE STEEL PRINCE
SHADES OF MAGIC: THE STEEL PRINCE: NIGHT OF KNIVES
SHADES OF MAGIC: THE STEEL PRINCE: THE REBEL ARMY

EDITOR
DAVID LEACH

SENIOR DESIGNER
ANDREW LEUNG

TITAN COMICS

MANAGING EDITOR / **MARTIN EDEN**
ASSISTANT EDITOR / **PHOEBE HEDGES**
SENIOR EDITOR / **JAKE DEVINE**
PRODUCTION CONTROLLERS / **CATERINA FALQUI & KELLY FENLON**
PRODUCTION MANAGER / **JACKIE FLOOK**
ART DIRECTOR / **OZ BROWNE**
SALES & CIRCULATION MANAGER / **STEVE TOTHILL**
MARKETING AND ADVERTISEMENT ASSISTANT / **LAUREN NODING**
SALES AND MARKETING COORDINATOR / **GEORGE WICKENDEN**
PUBLICIST / **PHOEBE TRILLO**
HEAD OF RIGHTS / **JENNY BOYCE**
ACQUISITIONS EDITOR / **DUNCAN BAIZLEY**
PUBLISHING DIRECTORS / **RICKY CLAYDON & JOHN DZIEWIATKOWSKI**
OPERATIONS DIRECTOR / **LEIGH BAULCH**
PUBLISHERS / **VIVIAN CHEUNG & NICK LANDAU**

Published by Titan Comics, a division of Titan Publishing Group, Ltd.
Titan Comics is a registered trademark of Titan Publishing Group, Ltd.
144 Southwark Street, London SE1 0UP

STANDARD EDITION ISBN 9781785865886
FORBIDDEN PLANET A EDITION ISBN 9781787738218
FORBIDDEN PLANET B EDITION ISBN 9781787738270
WATERSTONES EDITION ISBN 9781787738386
DIAMOND EXCLUSIVE EDITION ISBN 9781787738393
CONVENTION EDITION ISBN 9781787738409
BARNES & NOBLE EDITION ISBN 9781787738201
2022 ANNIVERSARY EDITION ISBN 9781787738195

A CIP catalogue for this title is available from the British Library.

First edition: December 2021
10 9 8 7 6 5 4 3 2 1
Printed in Italy.

DISTRIBUTION: Direct Sales Diamond Comic Distributors
NEWSSTAND DISTRIBUTION: Total Publishers Services Inc, John Dziewiatkowski, 610-851-7683
For information on advertising, contact adinfo@titanemail.com or call +44 20 7620 0200
For international rights information, contact Jenny Boyce: jenny.boyce@titanemail.com

V. E. SCHWAB

ExtraOrdinary

WRITER
V.E. SCHWAB

ARTIST
ENID BALÁM

COLORIST
JORDI ESCUIN LIORACH

LETTERER
ROB STEEN

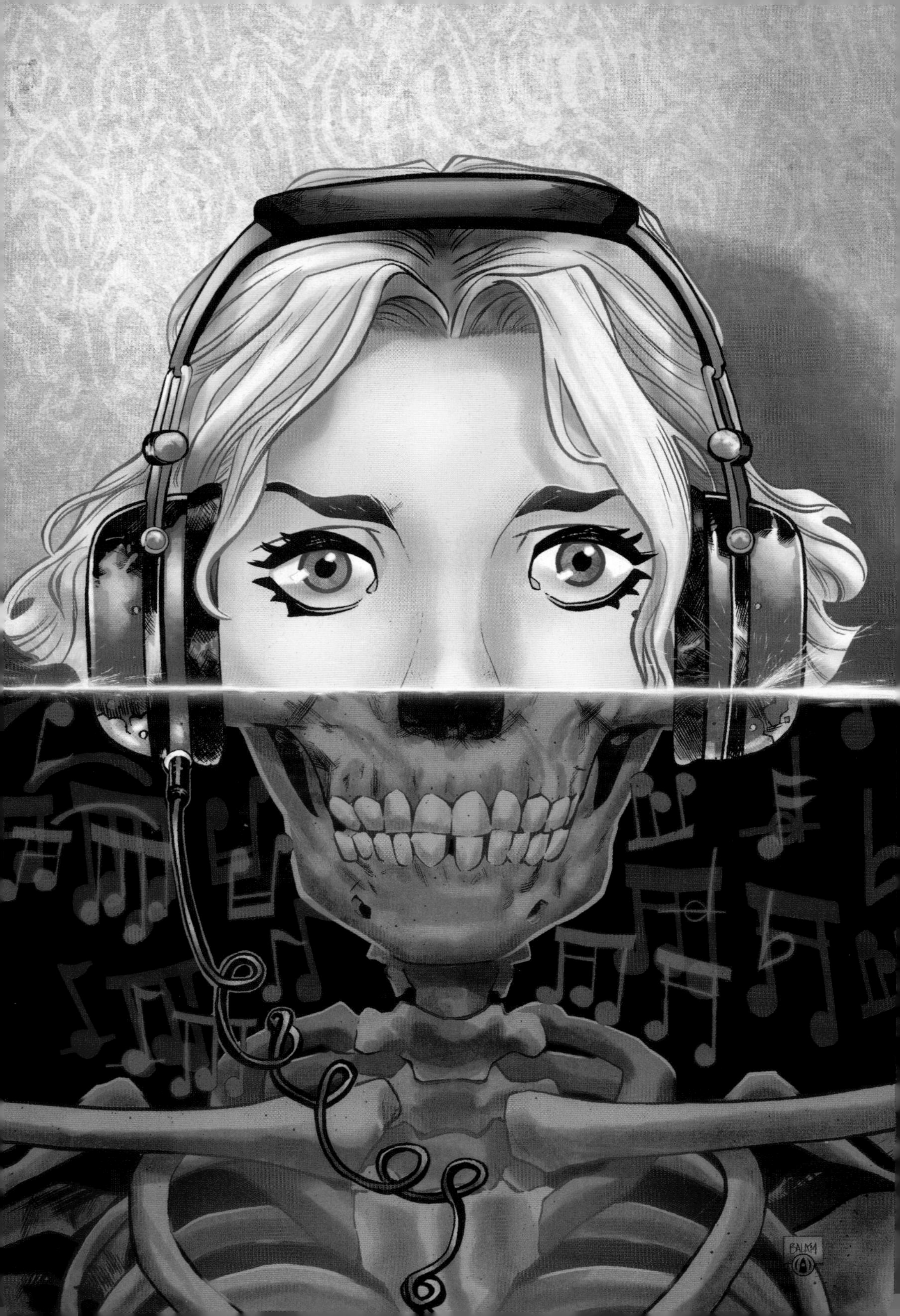

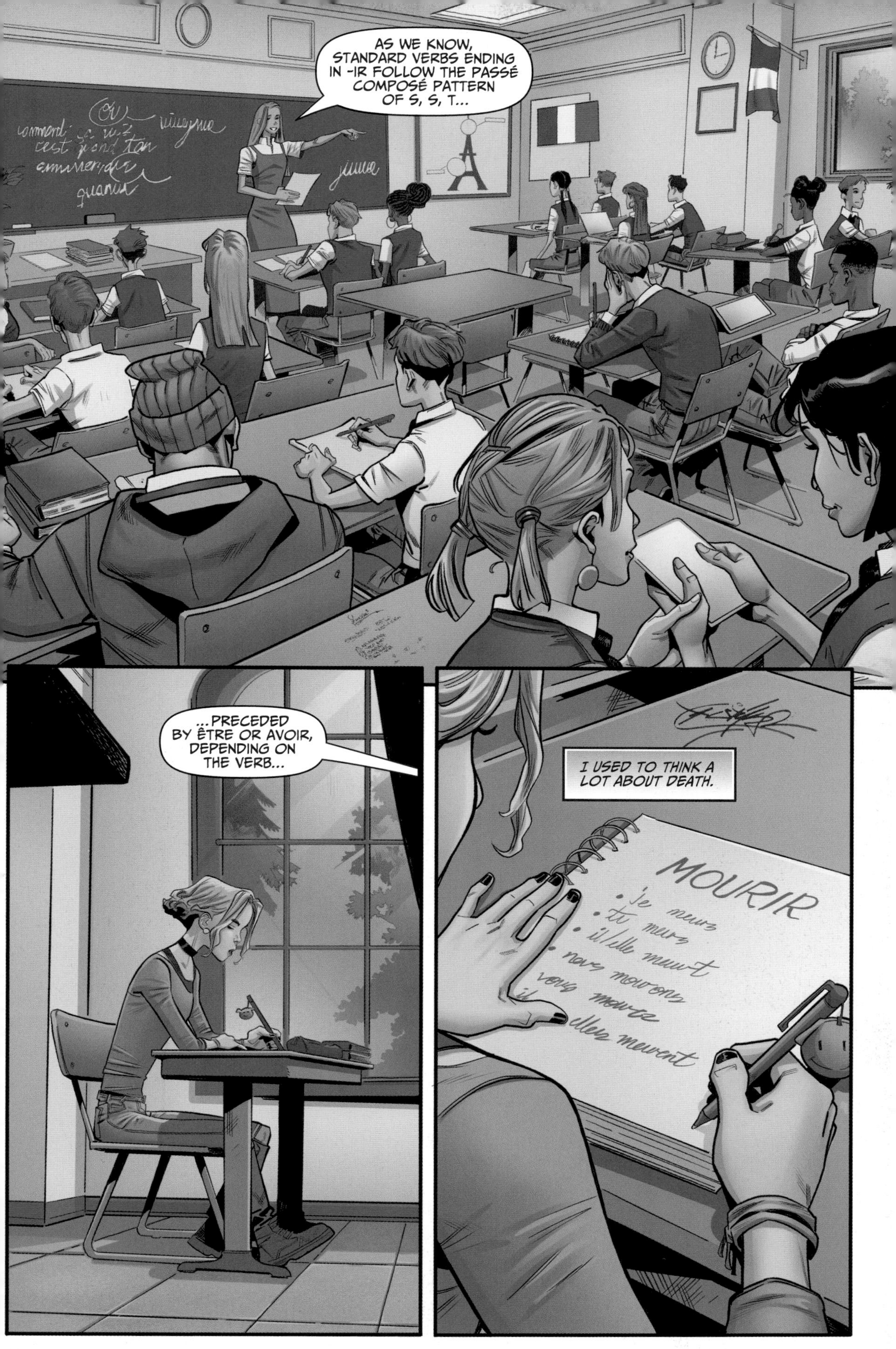
AS WE KNOW, STANDARD VERBS ENDING IN -IR FOLLOW THE PASSÉ COMPOSÉ PATTERN OF S, S, T...
...PRECEDED BY ÊTRE OR AVOIR, DEPENDING ON THE VERB...
I USED TO THINK A LOT ABOUT DEATH.
MOURIR
• je meurs
• tu meurs
• il/elle meurt
• nous mourons
vous mourez
ils/elles meurent

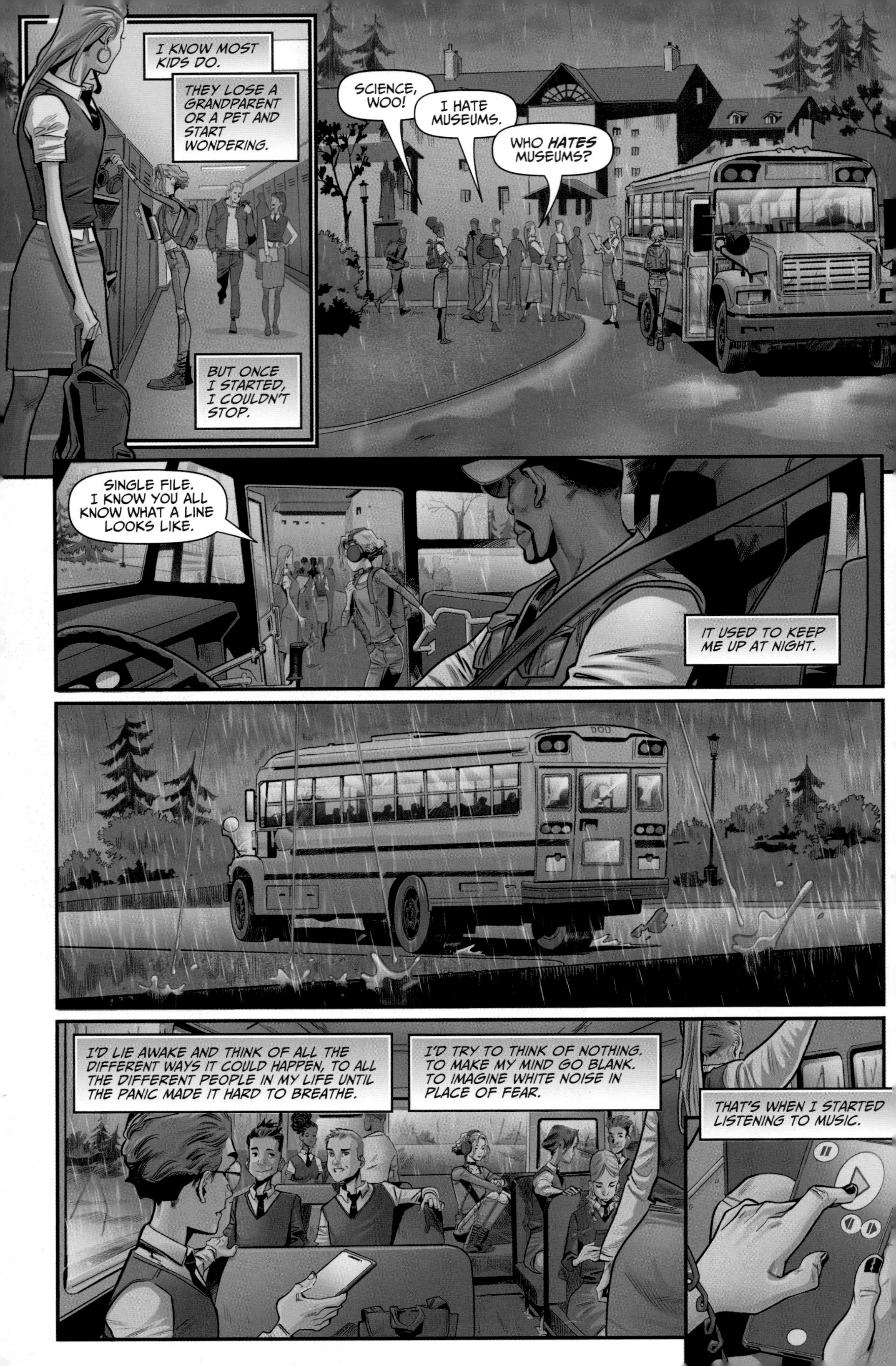
I KNOW MOST KIDS DO.
THEY LOSE A GRANDPARENT OR A PET AND START WONDERING.
BUT ONCE I STARTED, I COULDN'T STOP.
SCIENCE, WOO!
I HATE MUSEUMS.
WHO HATES MUSEUMS?
SINGLE FILE. I KNOW YOU ALL KNOW WHAT A LINE LOOKS LIKE.
IT USED TO KEEP ME UP AT NIGHT.
I'D LIE AWAKE AND THINK OF ALL THE DIFFERENT WAYS IT COULD HAPPEN, TO ALL THE DIFFERENT PEOPLE IN MY LIFE UNTIL THE PANIC MADE IT HARD TO BREATHE.
I'D TRY TO THINK OF NOTHING. TO MAKE MY MIND GO BLANK. TO IMAGINE WHITE NOISE IN PLACE OF FEAR.
THAT'S WHEN I STARTED LISTENING TO MUSIC.

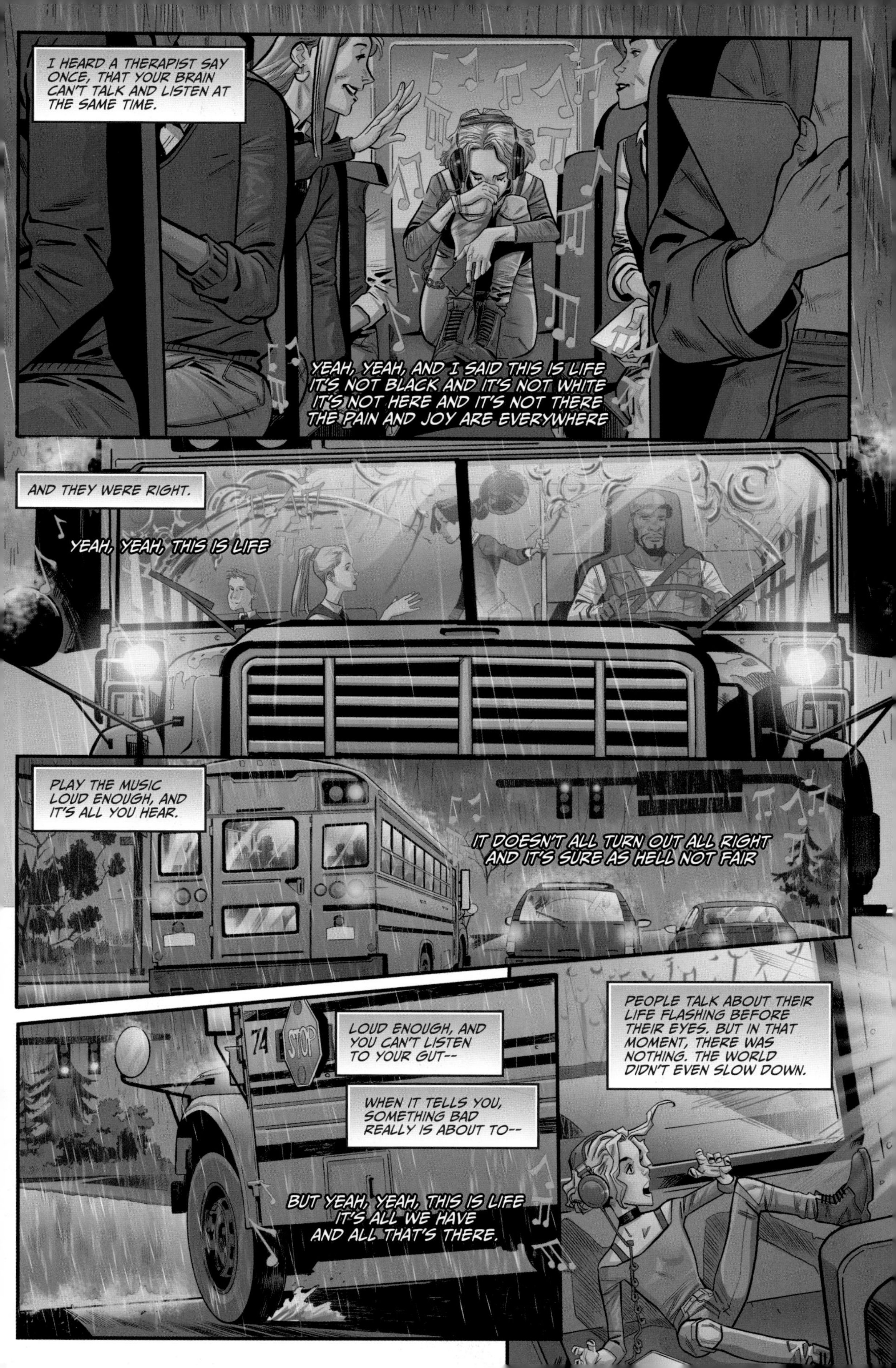
I HEARD A THERAPIST SAY ONCE, THAT YOUR BRAIN CAN'T TALK AND LISTEN AT THE SAME TIME.
YEAH, YEAH, AND I SAID THIS IS LIFE
IT'S NOT BLACK AND IT'S NOT WHITE
IT'S NOT HERE AND IT'S NOT THERE
THE PAIN AND JOY ARE EVERYWHERE
AND THEY WERE RIGHT.
YEAH, YEAH, THIS IS LIFE
PLAY THE MUSIC LOUD ENOUGH, AND IT'S ALL YOU HEAR.
IT DOESN'T ALL TURN OUT ALL RIGHT
AND IT'S SURE AS HELL NOT FAIR
74
STOP
LOUD ENOUGH, AND YOU CAN'T LISTEN TO YOUR GUT--
WHEN IT TELLS YOU, SOMETHING BAD REALLY IS ABOUT TO--
BUT YEAH, YEAH, THIS IS LIFE
IT'S ALL WE HAVE
AND ALL THAT'S THERE.
PEOPLE TALK ABOUT THEIR LIFE FLASHING BEFORE THEIR EYES. BUT IN THAT MOMENT, THERE WAS NOTHING. THE WORLD DIDN'T EVEN SLOW DOWN.

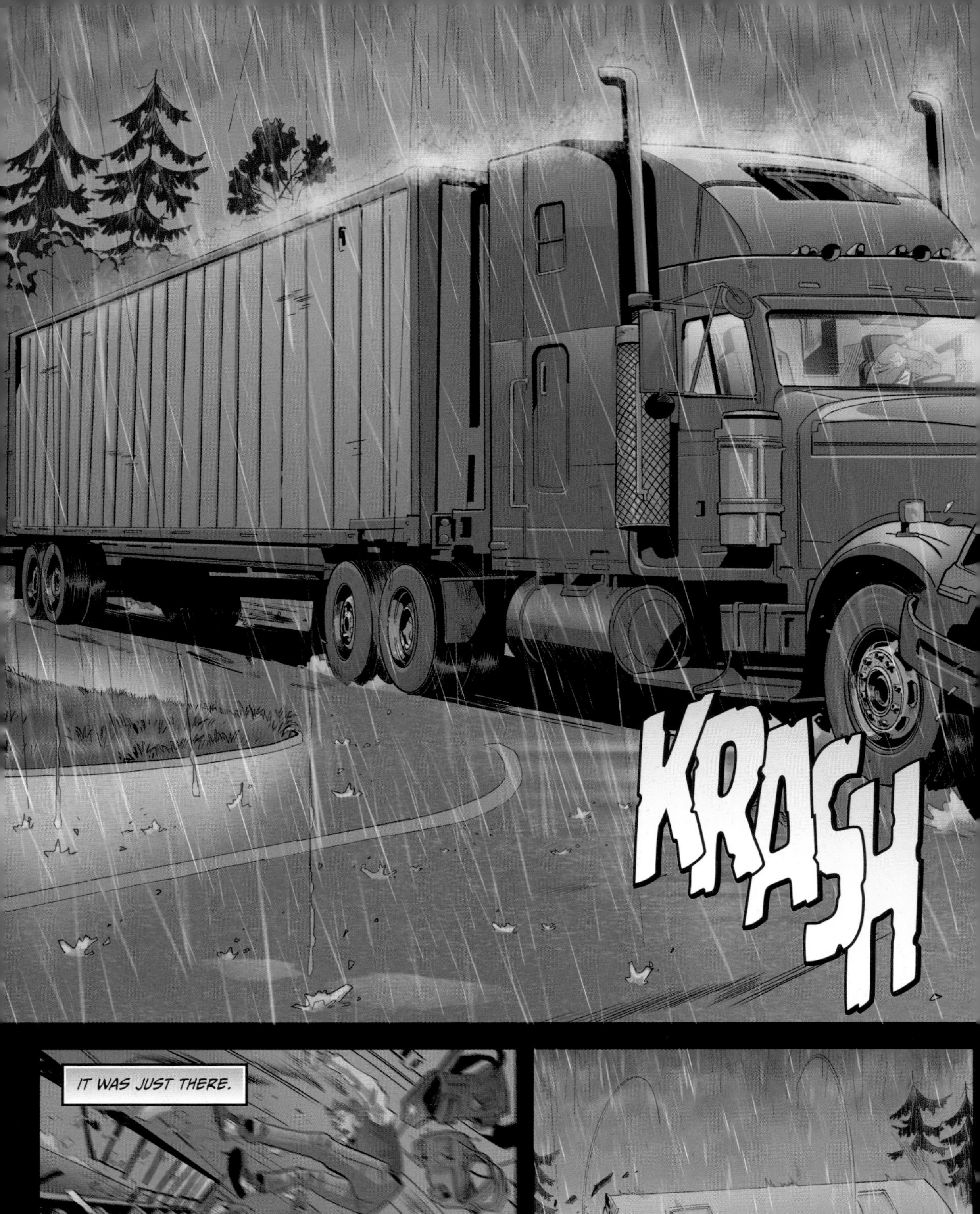
KRASH

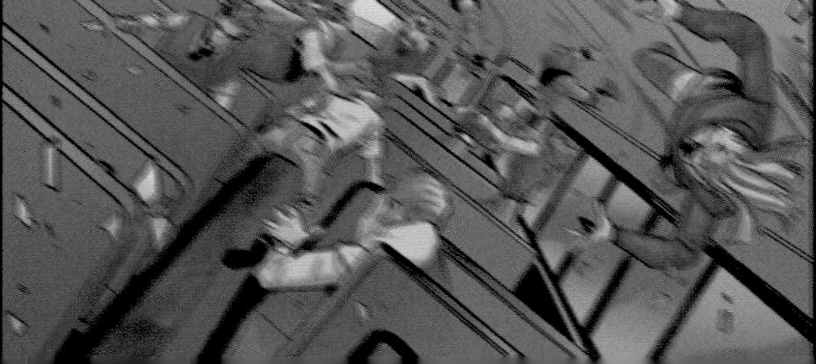
IT WAS JUST THERE.

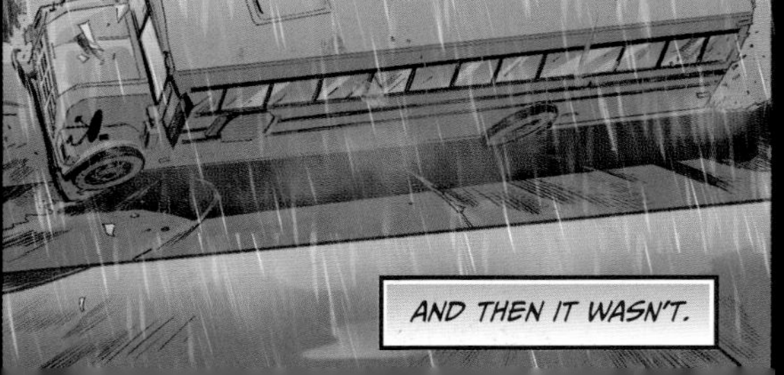
AND THEN IT WASN'T.

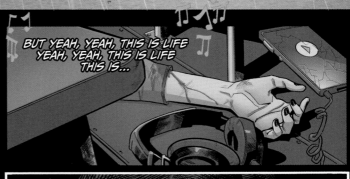

BUT YEAH, YEAH, THIS IS LIFE
YEAH, YEAH, THIS IS LIFE
THIS IS...

I ALWAYS THOUGHT OF DEATH AS THE END OF EVERYTHING. A ONE-WAY STREET. NO COMING BACK.

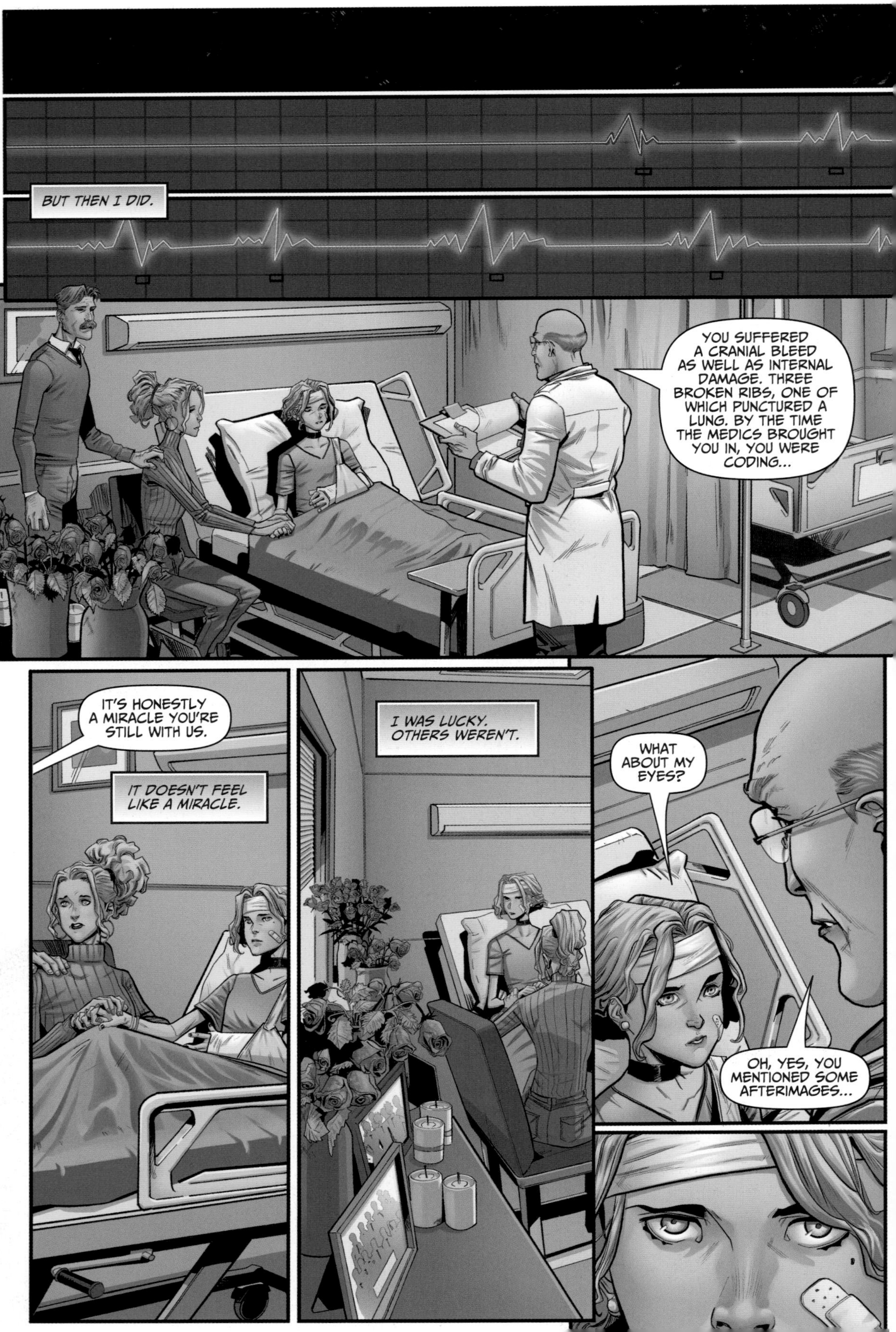
BUT THEN I DID.
YOU SUFFERED A CRANIAL BLEED AS WELL AS INTERNAL DAMAGE. THREE BROKEN RIBS, ONE OF WHICH PUNCTURED A LUNG. BY THE TIME THE MEDICS BROUGHT YOU IN, YOU WERE CODING...
IT'S HONESTLY A MIRACLE YOU'RE STILL WITH US.
IT DOESN'T FEEL LIKE A MIRACLE.
I WAS LUCKY. OTHERS WEREN'T.
WHAT ABOUT MY EYES?
OH, YES, YOU MENTIONED SOME AFTERIMAGES...

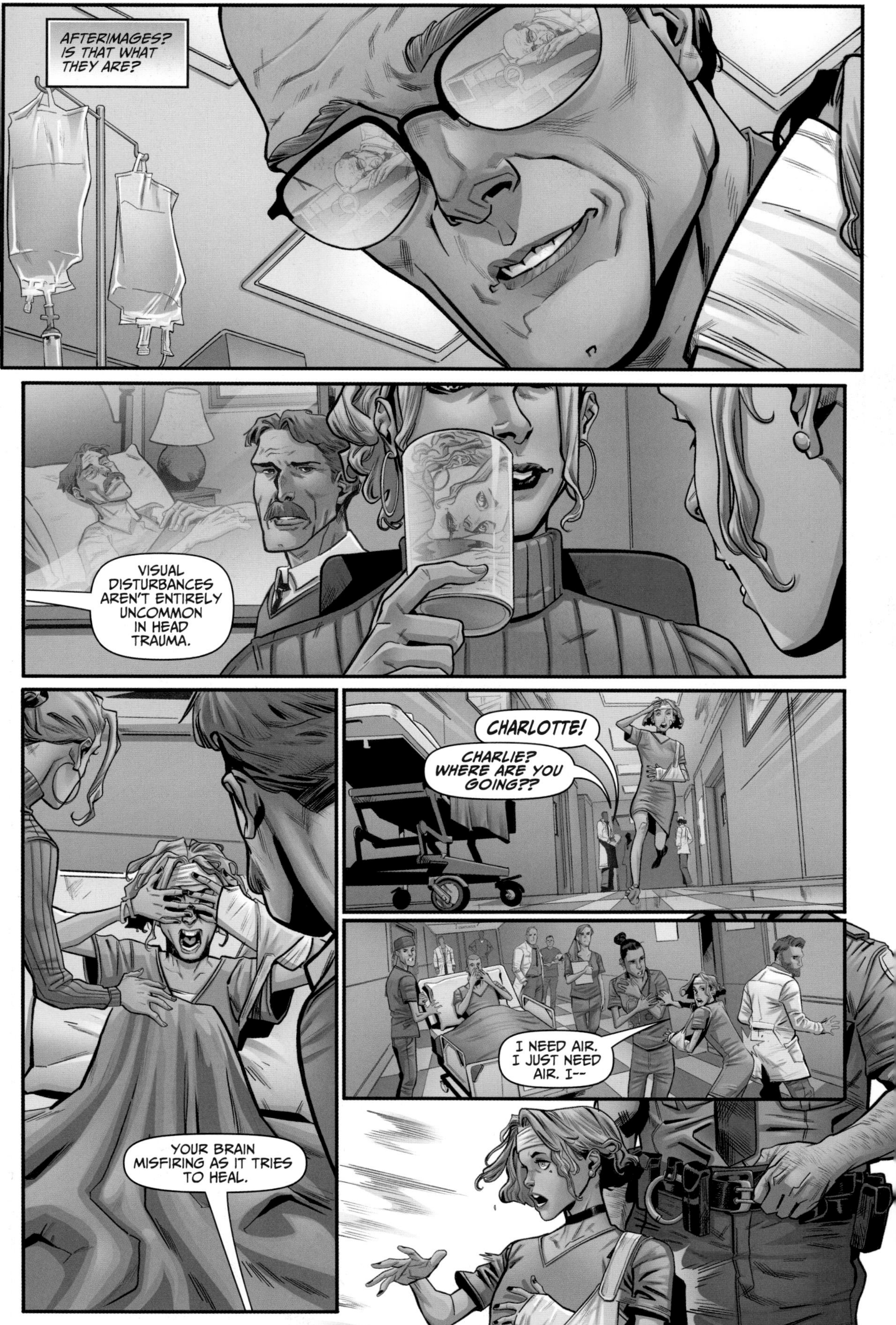
AFTERIMAGES? IS THAT WHAT THEY ARE?
VISUAL DISTURBANCES AREN'T ENTIRELY UNCOMMON IN HEAD TRAUMA.
YOUR BRAIN MISFIRING AS IT TRIES TO HEAL.
CHARLOTTE!
CHARLIE? WHERE ARE YOU GOING??
I NEED AIR. I JUST NEED AIR. I--

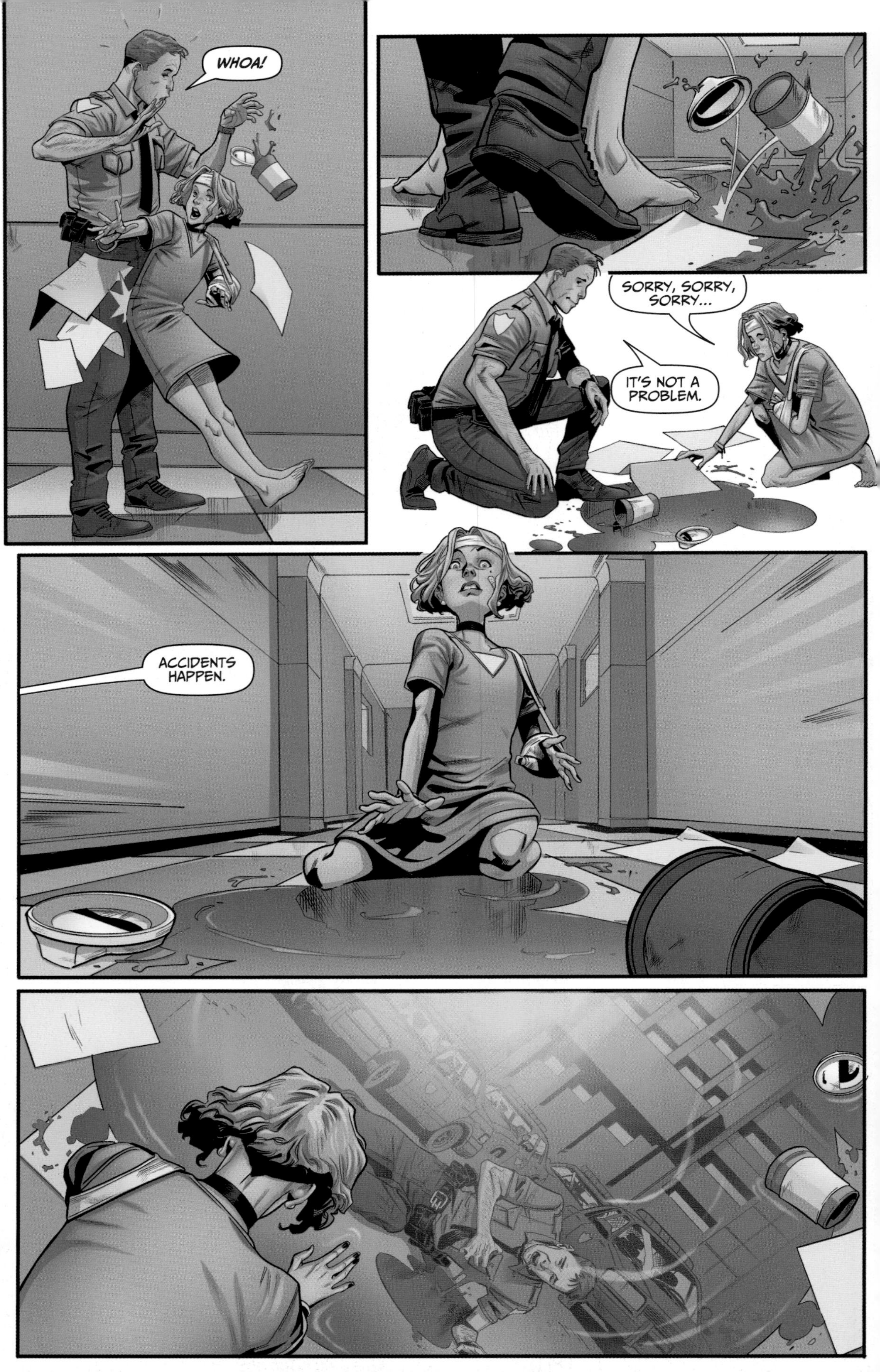
WHOA!
SORRY, SORRY, SORRY...
IT'S NOT A PROBLEM.
ACCIDENTS HAPPEN.

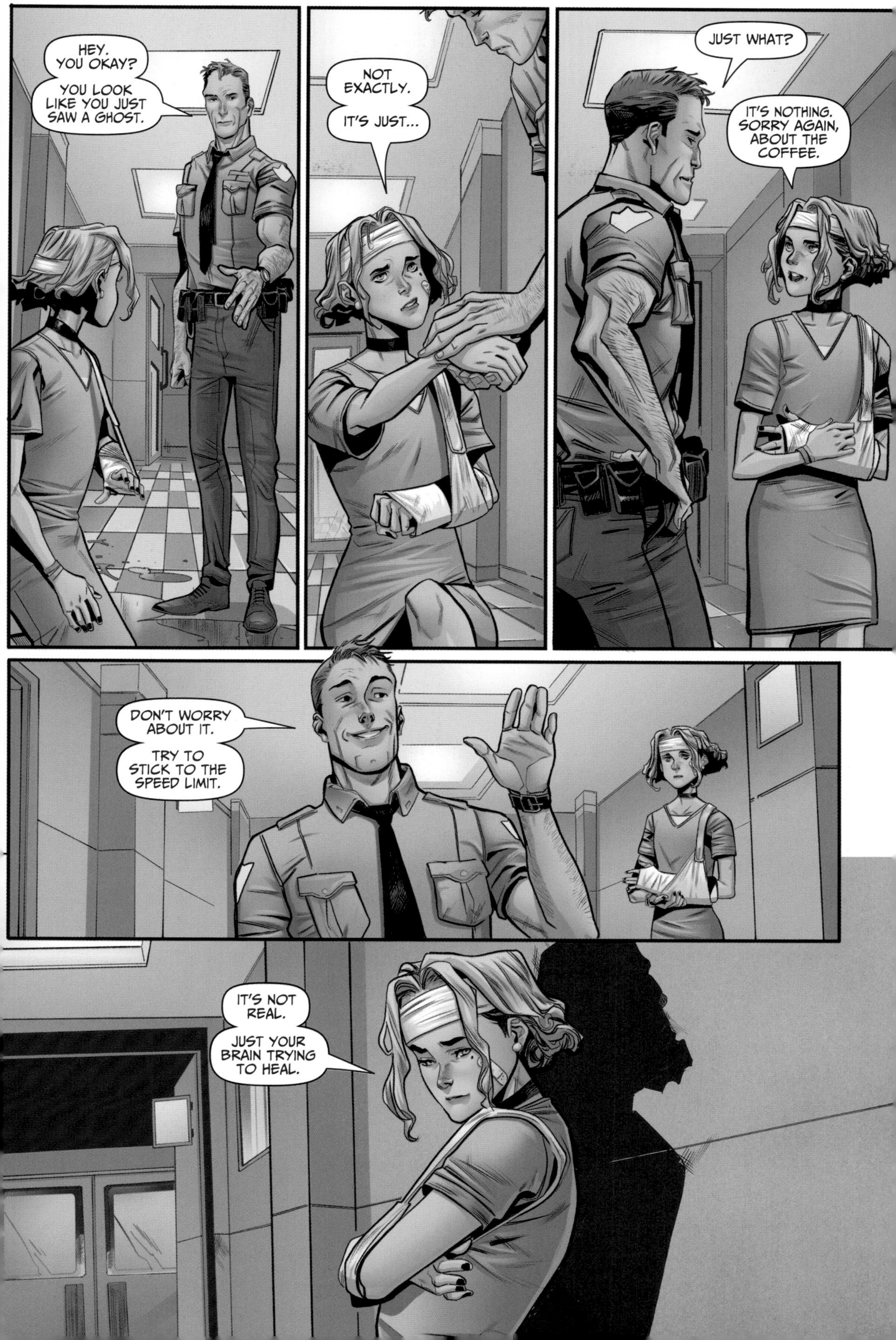
HEY. YOU OKAY?
YOU LOOK LIKE YOU JUST SAW A GHOST.
NOT EXACTLY.
IT'S JUST...
JUST WHAT?
IT'S NOTHING. SORRY AGAIN, ABOUT THE COFFEE.
DON'T WORRY ABOUT IT.
TRY TO STICK TO THE SPEED LIMIT.
IT'S NOT REAL.
JUST YOUR BRAIN TRYING TO HEAL.

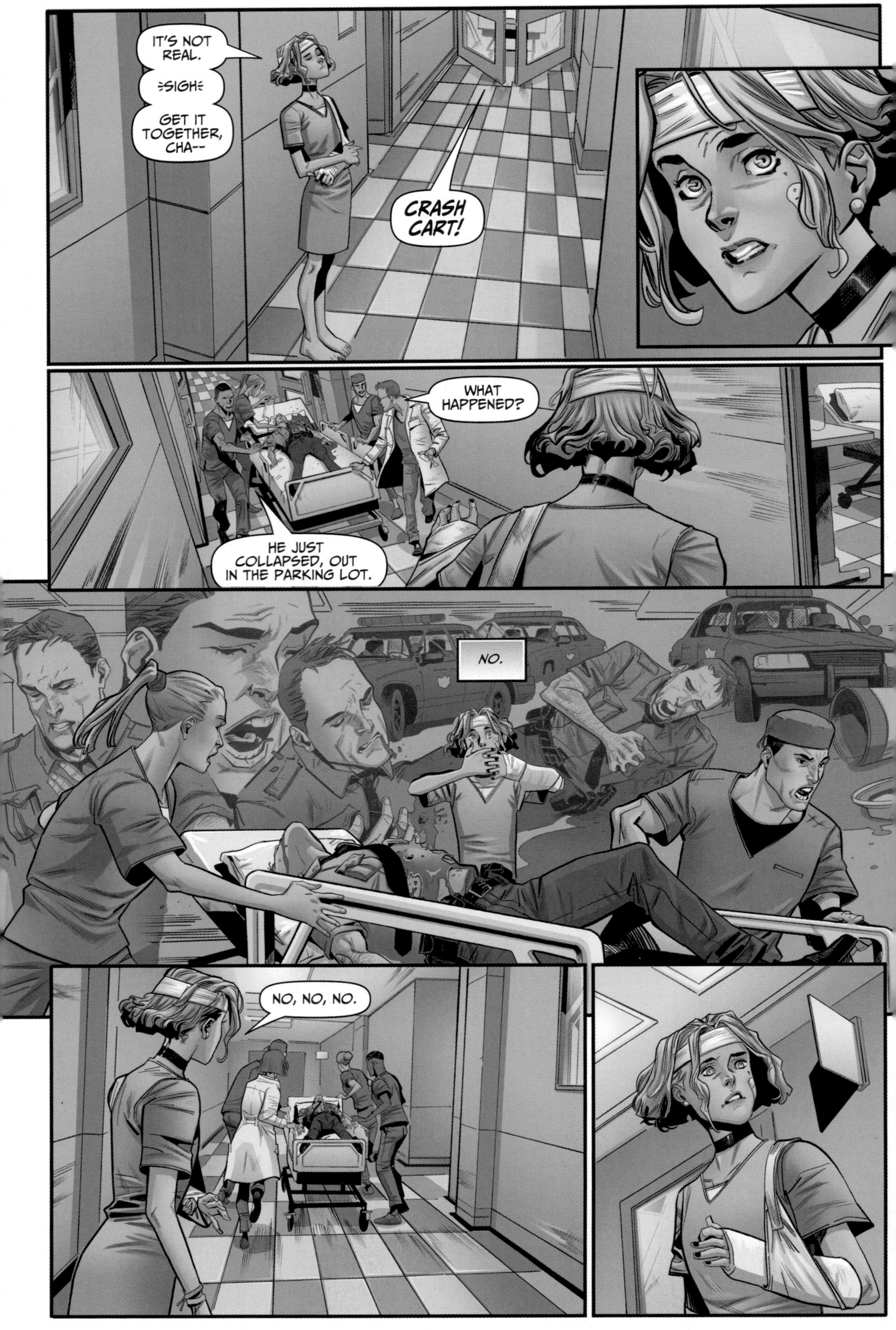
IT'S NOT REAL.
=SIGH=
GET IT TOGETHER, CHA--
CRASH CART!
WHAT HAPPENED?
HE JUST COLLAPSED, OUT IN THE PARKING LOT.
NO.
NO, NO, NO.

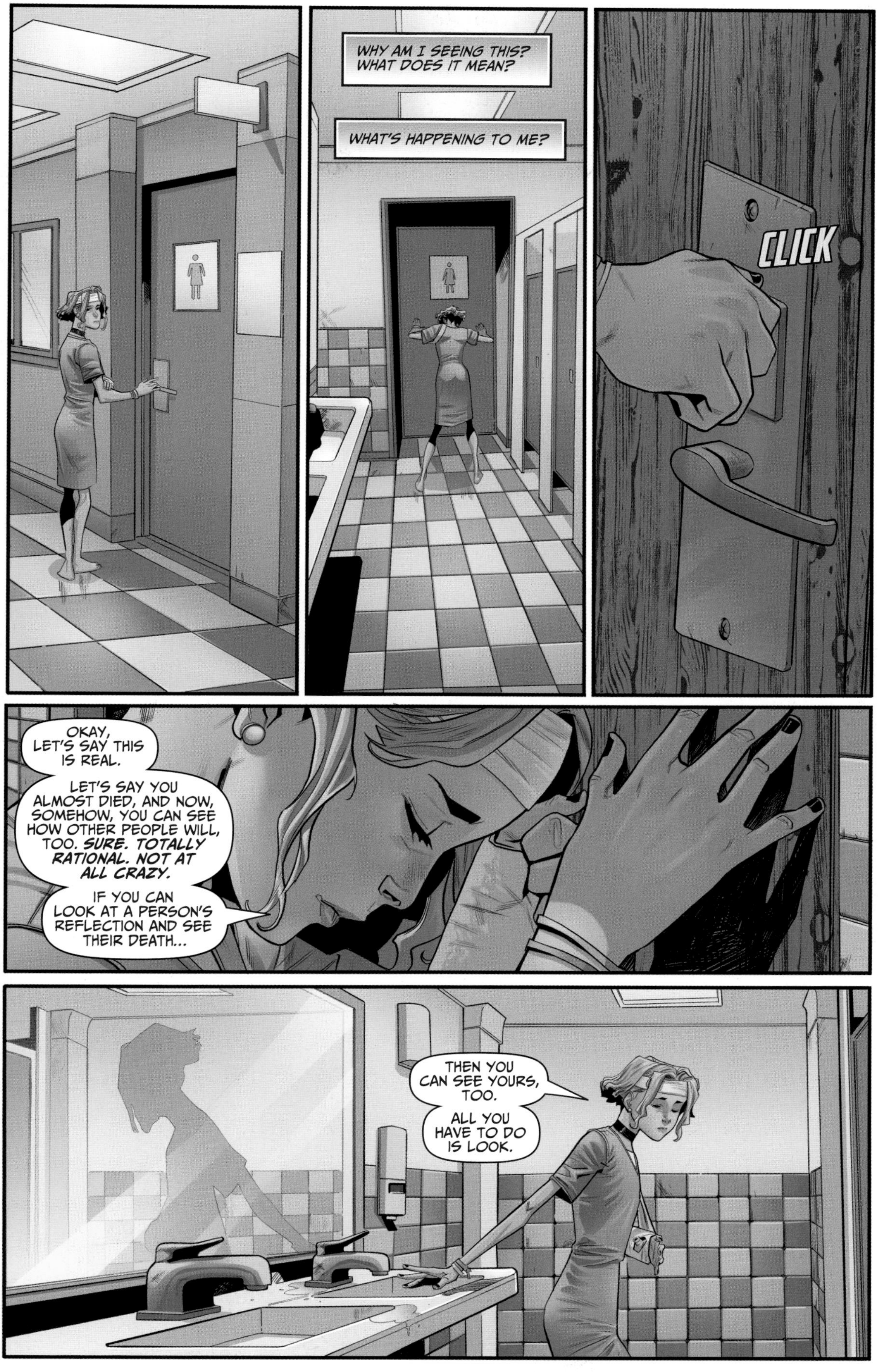
WHY AM I SEEING THIS? WHAT DOES IT MEAN?
WHAT'S HAPPENING TO ME?
CLICK
OKAY, LET'S SAY THIS IS REAL.
LET'S SAY YOU ALMOST DIED, AND NOW, SOMEHOW, YOU CAN SEE HOW OTHER PEOPLE WILL, TOO. SURE. TOTALLY RATIONAL. NOT AT ALL CRAZY.
IF YOU CAN LOOK AT A PERSON'S REFLECTION AND SEE THEIR DEATH...
THEN YOU CAN SEE YOURS, TOO.
ALL YOU HAVE TO DO IS LOOK.

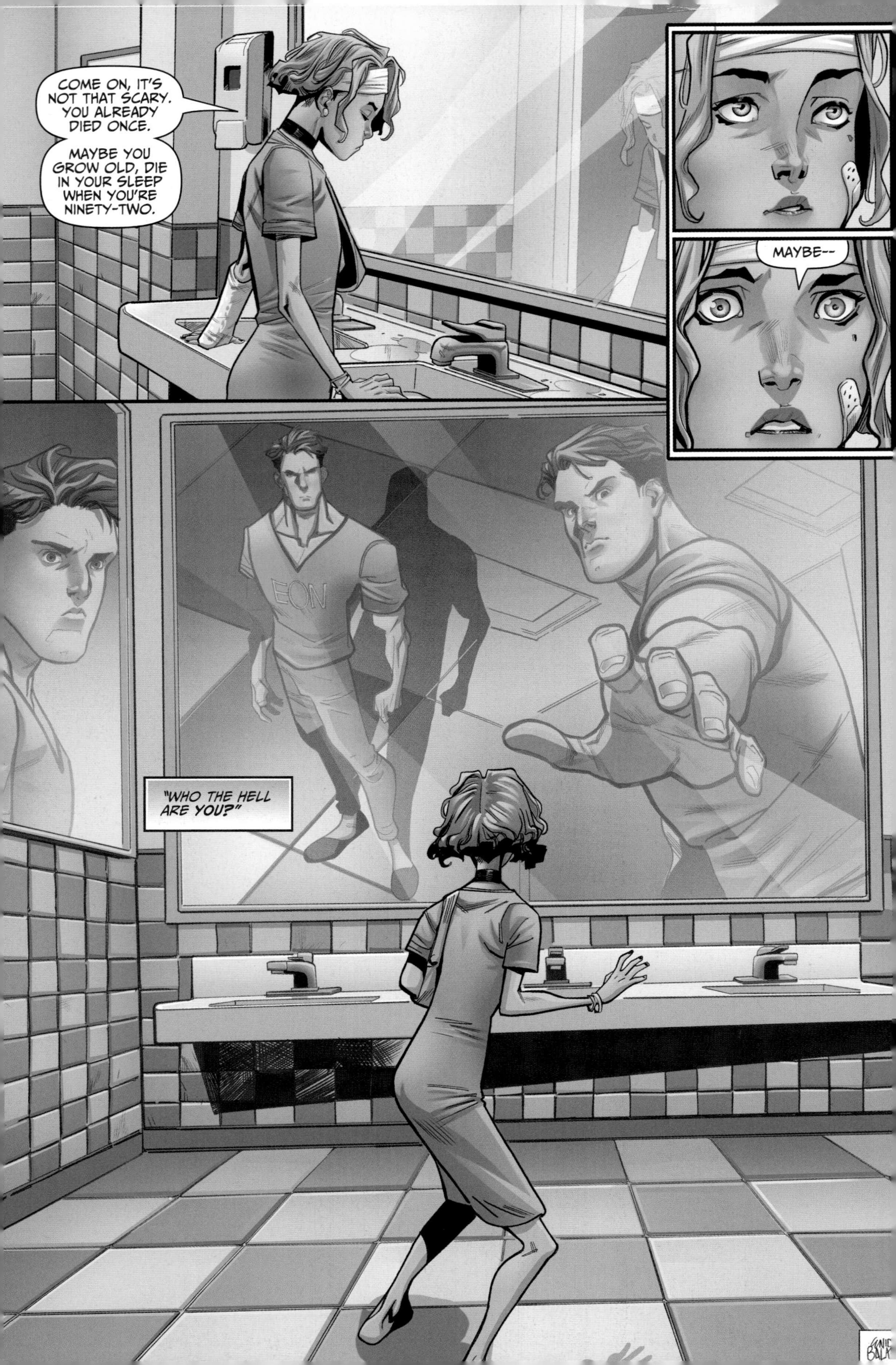
COME ON, IT'S NOT THAT SCARY. YOU ALREADY DIED ONCE.
MAYBE YOU GROW OLD, DIE IN YOUR SLEEP WHEN YOU'RE NINETY-TWO.
MAYBE--
"WHO THE HELL ARE YOU?"

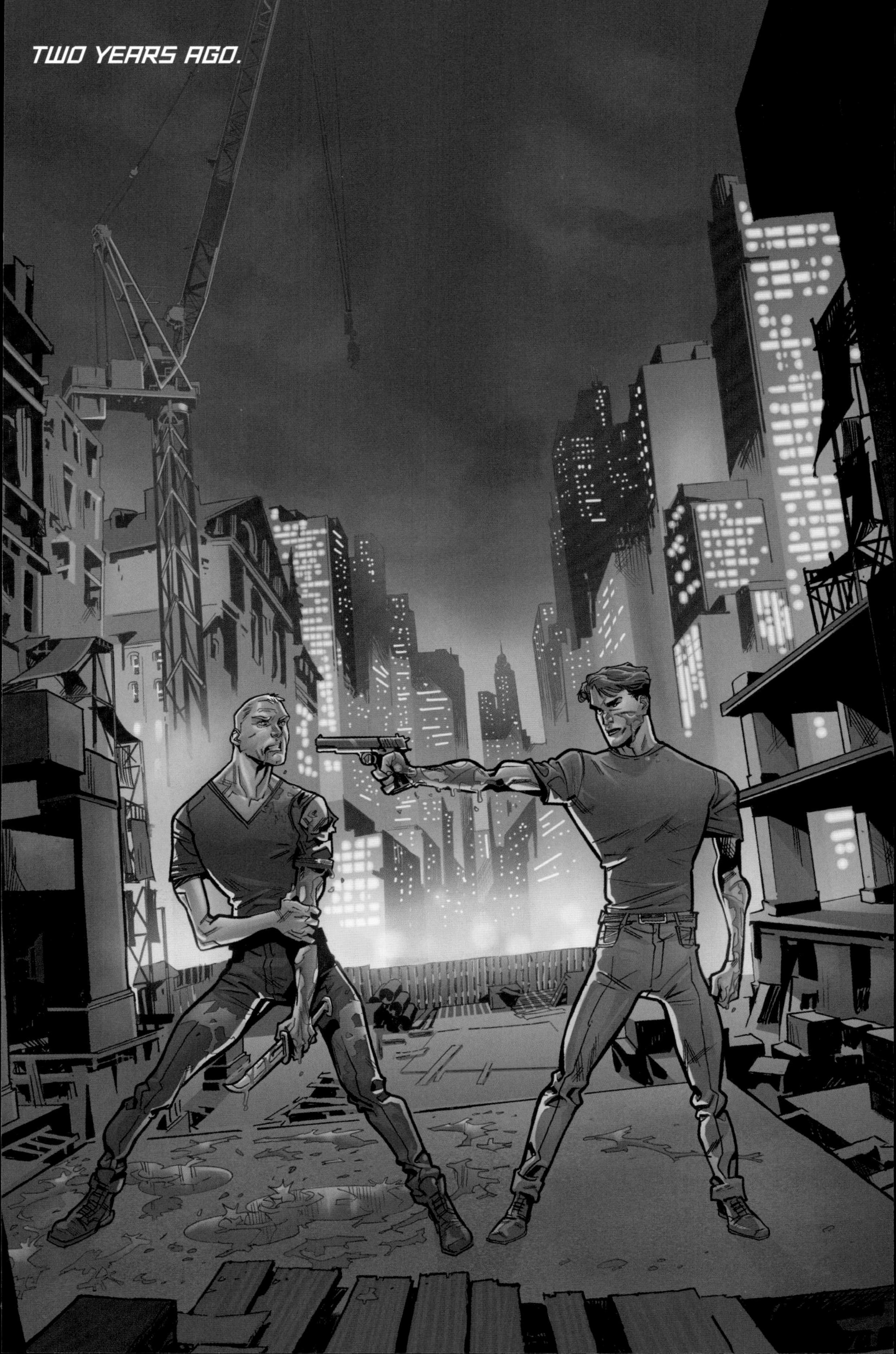
TWO YEARS AGO.

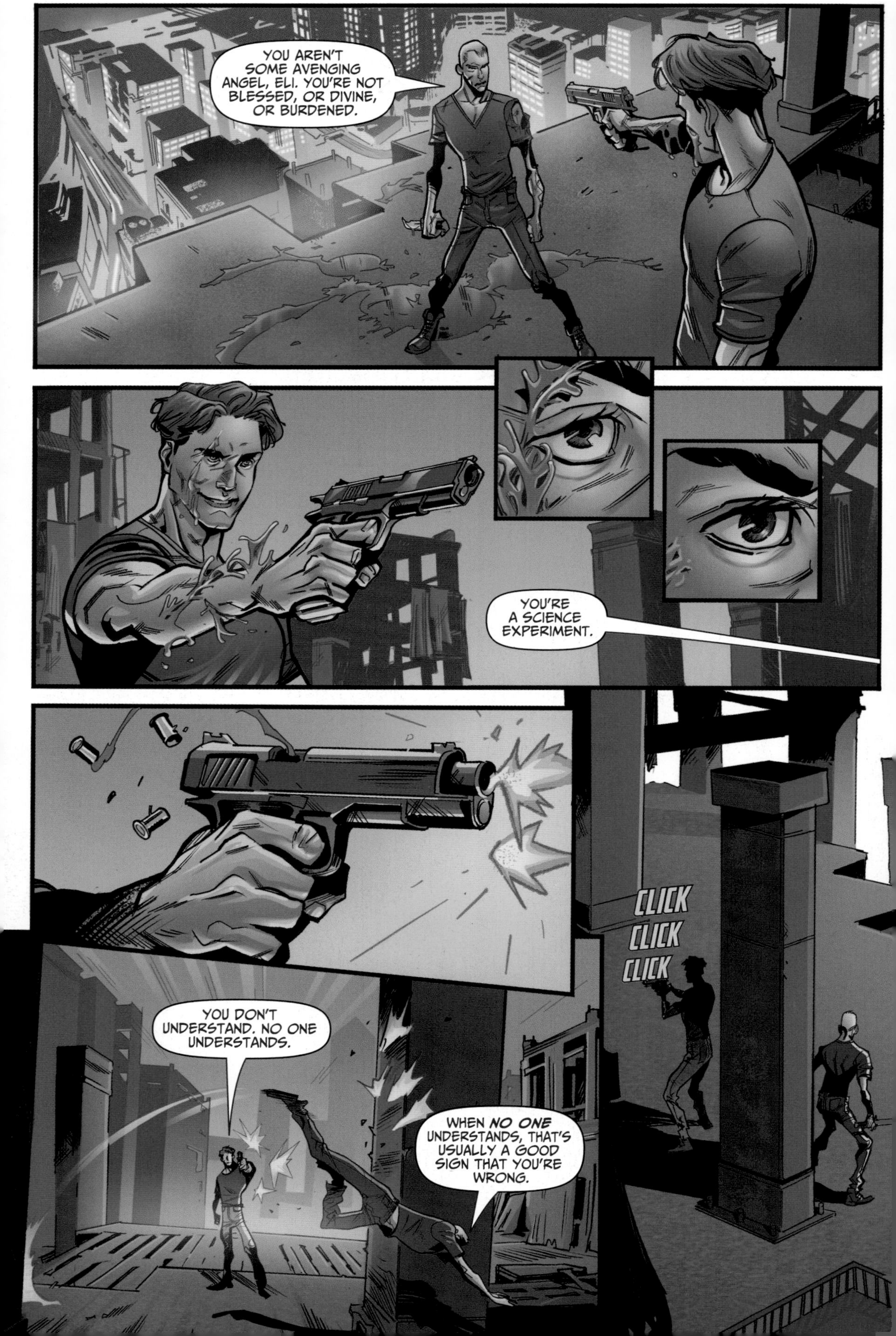
YOU AREN'T SOME AVENGING ANGEL, ELI. YOU'RE NOT BLESSED, OR DIVINE, OR BURDENED.
YOU'RE A SCIENCE EXPERIMENT.
CLICK
CLICK
CLICK
YOU DON'T UNDERSTAND. NO ONE UNDERSTANDS.
WHEN *NO ONE* UNDERSTANDS, THAT'S USUALLY A GOOD SIGN THAT YOU'RE WRONG.

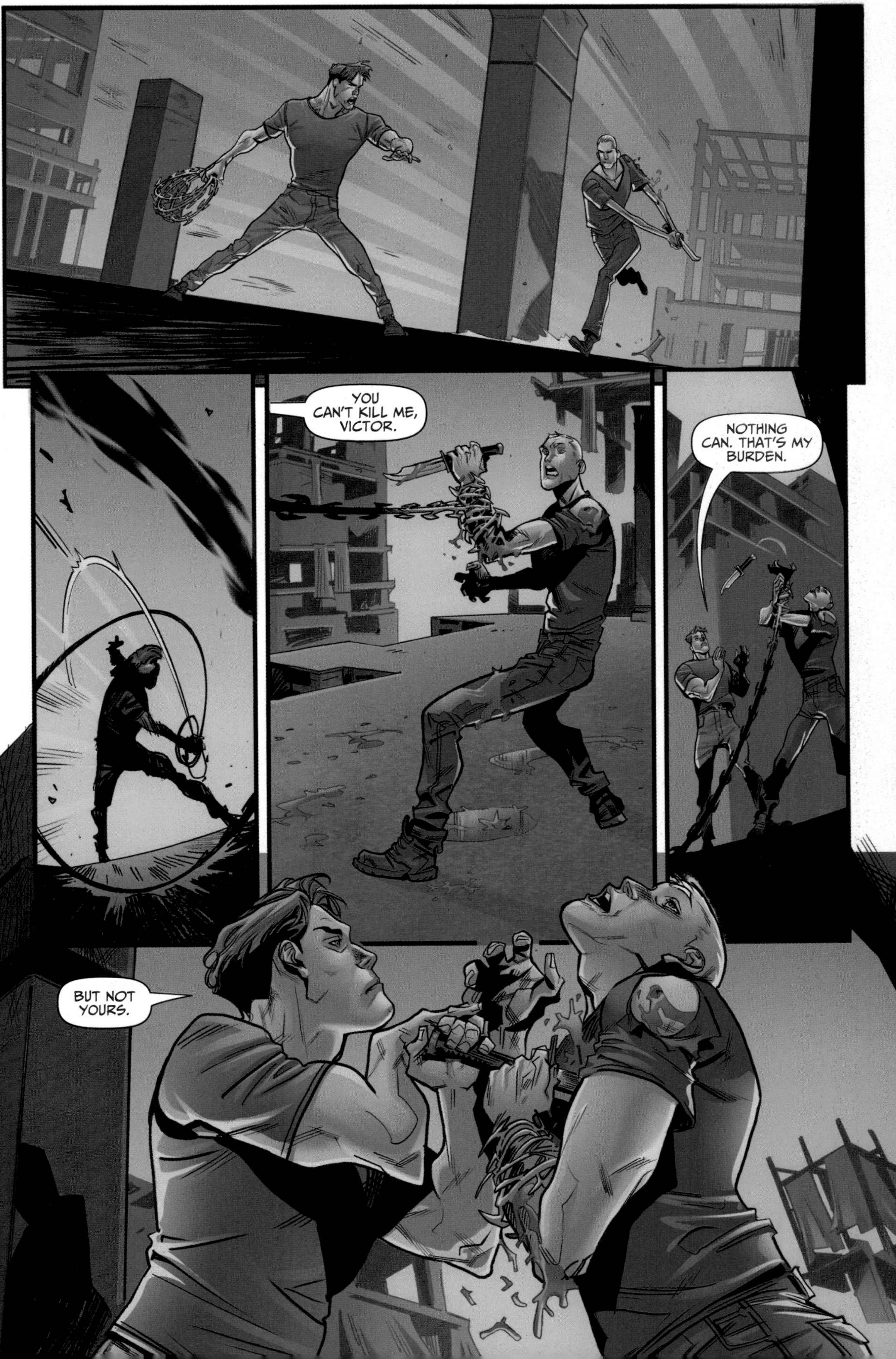
YOU CAN'T KILL ME, VICTOR.
NOTHING CAN. THAT'S MY BURDEN.
BUT NOT YOURS.

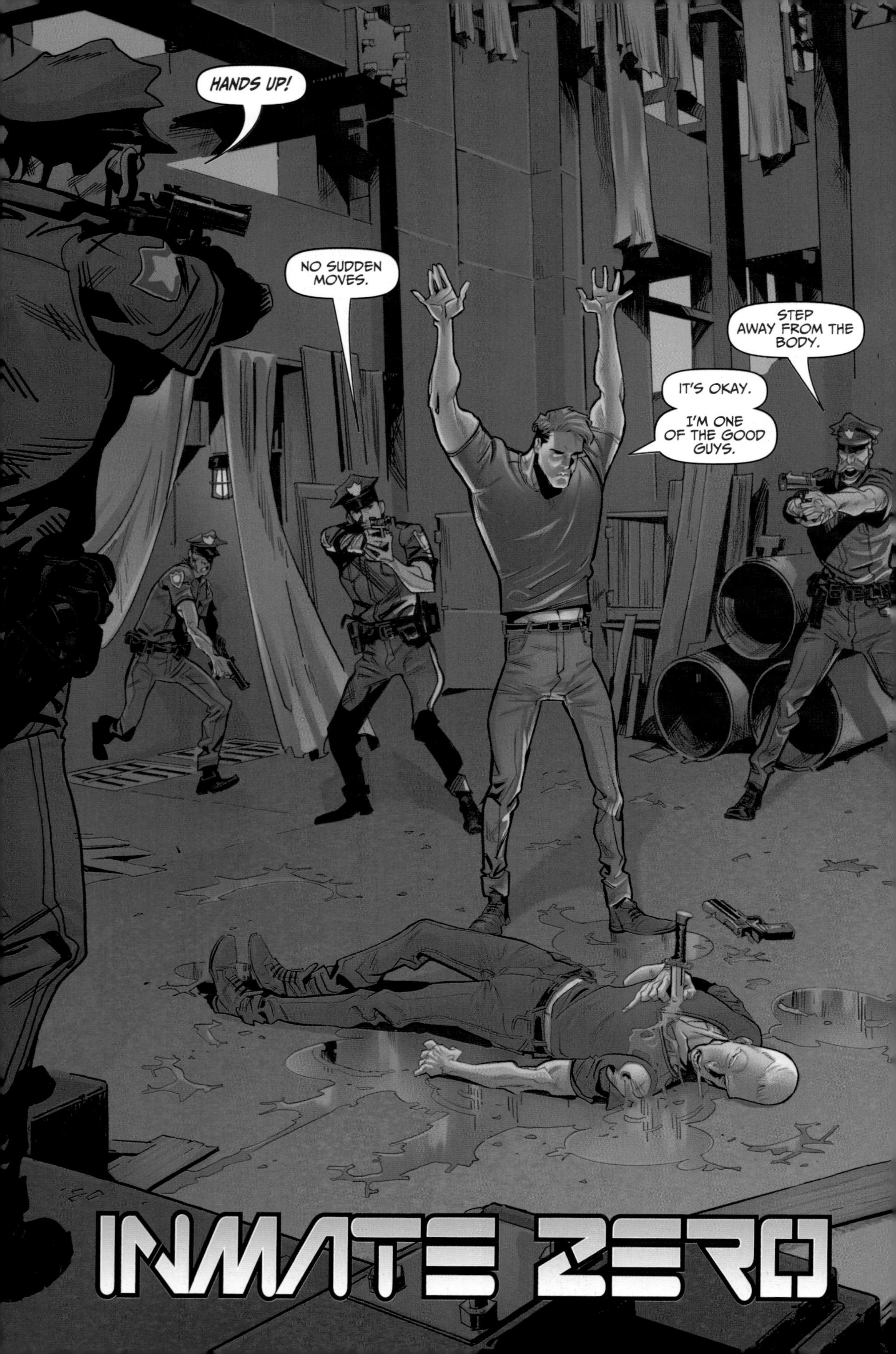
HANDS UP!
NO SUDDEN MOVES.
STEP AWAY FROM THE BODY.
IT'S OKAY.
I'M ONE OF THE GOOD GUYS.
INMATE ZERO

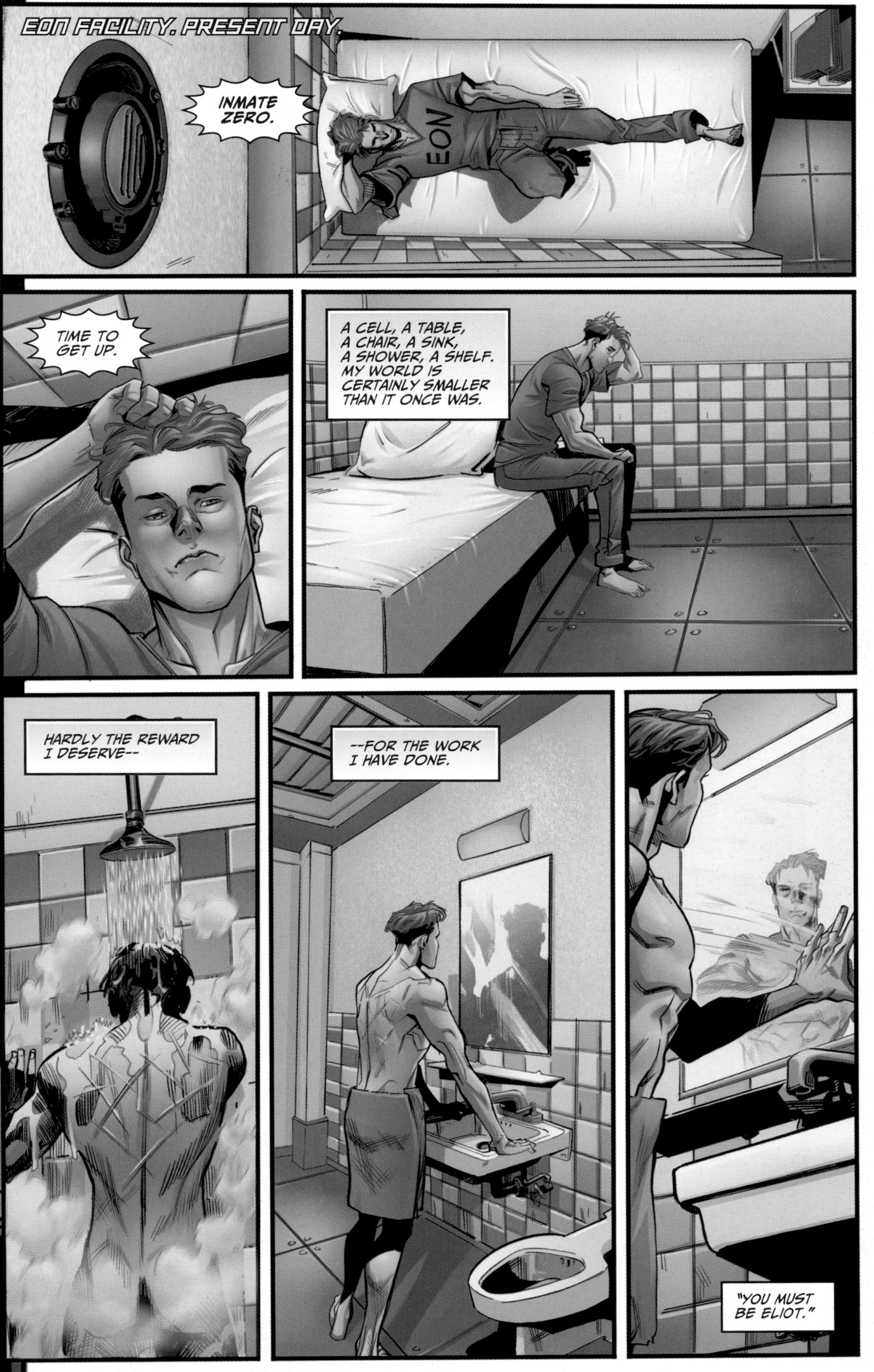
EON FACILITY. PRESENT DAY.
INMATE ZERO.
EON
TIME TO GET UP.
A CELL, A TABLE, A CHAIR, A SINK, A SHOWER, A SHELF. MY WORLD IS CERTAINLY SMALLER THAN IT ONCE WAS.
HARDLY THE REWARD I DESERVE--
--FOR THE WORK I HAVE DONE.
"YOU MUST BE ELIOT."

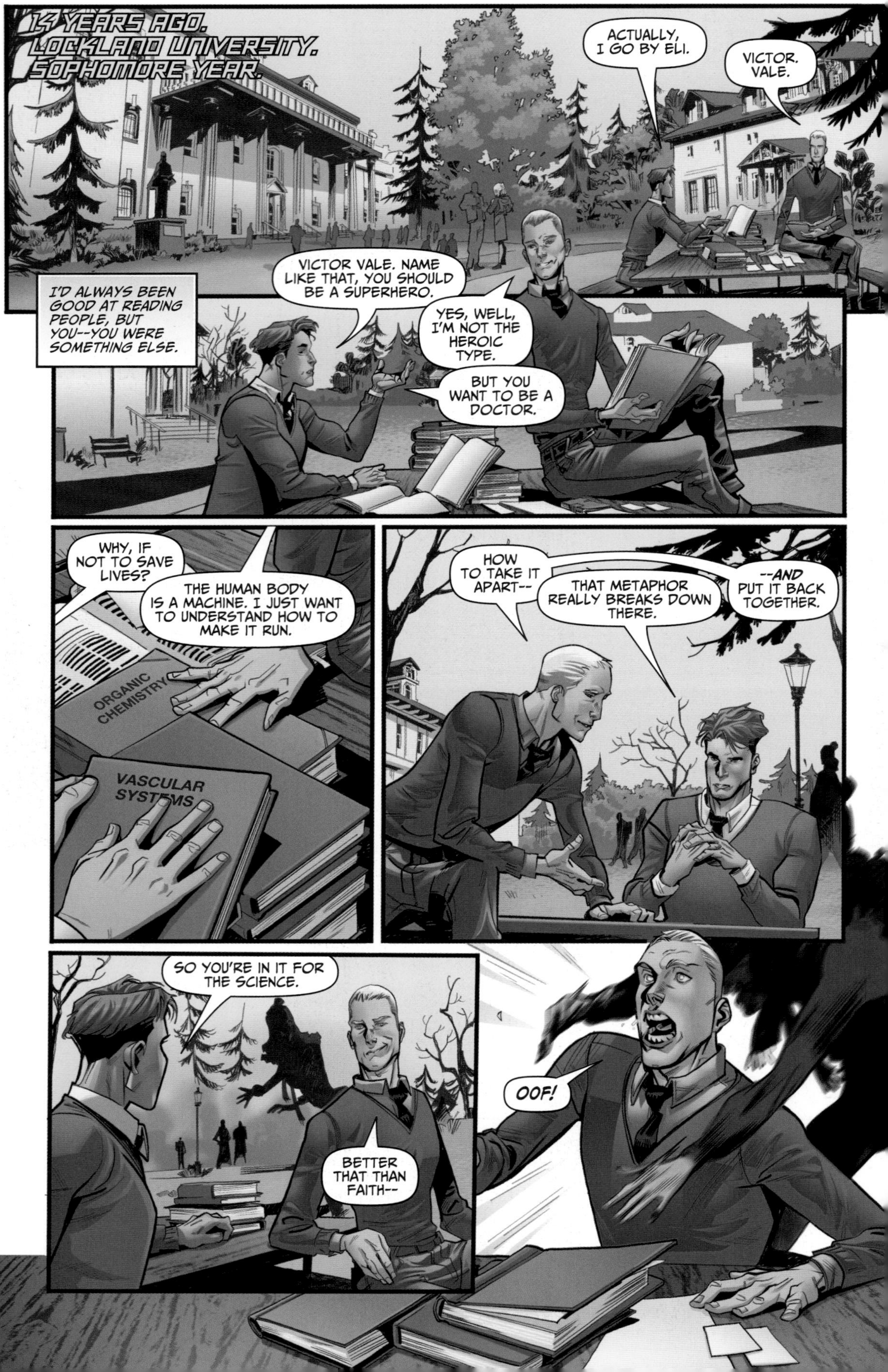
14 YEARS AGO. LOCKLAND UNIVERSITY. SOPHOMORE YEAR.
ACTUALLY, I GO BY ELI.
VICTOR. VALE.
I'D ALWAYS BEEN GOOD AT READING PEOPLE, BUT YOU--YOU WERE SOMETHING ELSE.
VICTOR VALE. NAME LIKE THAT, YOU SHOULD BE A SUPERHERO.
YES, WELL, I'M NOT THE HEROIC TYPE.
BUT YOU WANT TO BE A DOCTOR.
WHY, IF NOT TO SAVE LIVES?
THE HUMAN BODY IS A MACHINE. I JUST WANT TO UNDERSTAND HOW TO MAKE IT RUN.
ORGANIC CHEMISTRY
VASCULAR SYSTEMS
HOW TO TAKE IT APART--
--AND PUT IT BACK TOGETHER.
THAT METAPHOR REALLY BREAKS DOWN THERE.
SO YOU'RE IN IT FOR THE SCIENCE.
BETTER THAN FAITH--
OOF!

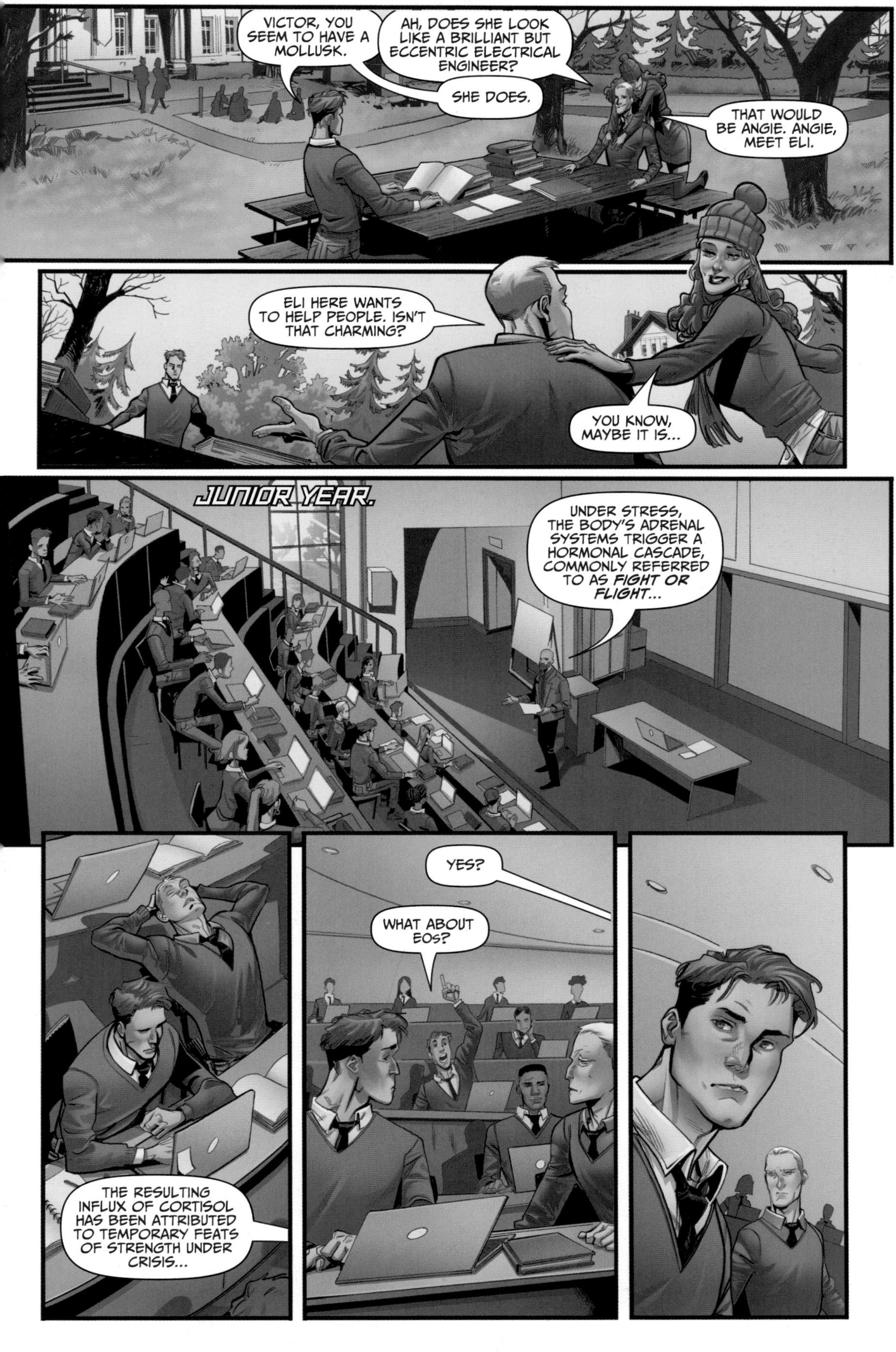
VICTOR, YOU SEEM TO HAVE A MOLLUSK.
AH, DOES SHE LOOK LIKE A BRILLIANT BUT ECCENTRIC ELECTRICAL ENGINEER?
SHE DOES.
THAT WOULD BE ANGIE. ANGIE, MEET ELI.
ELI HERE WANTS TO HELP PEOPLE. ISN'T THAT CHARMING?
YOU KNOW, MAYBE IT IS...
JUNIOR YEAR.
UNDER STRESS, THE BODY'S ADRENAL SYSTEMS TRIGGER A HORMONAL CASCADE, COMMONLY REFERRED TO AS *FIGHT OR FLIGHT*...
THE RESULTING INFLUX OF CORTISOL HAS BEEN ATTRIBUTED TO TEMPORARY FEATS OF STRENGTH UNDER CRISIS...
YES?
WHAT ABOUT EOs?

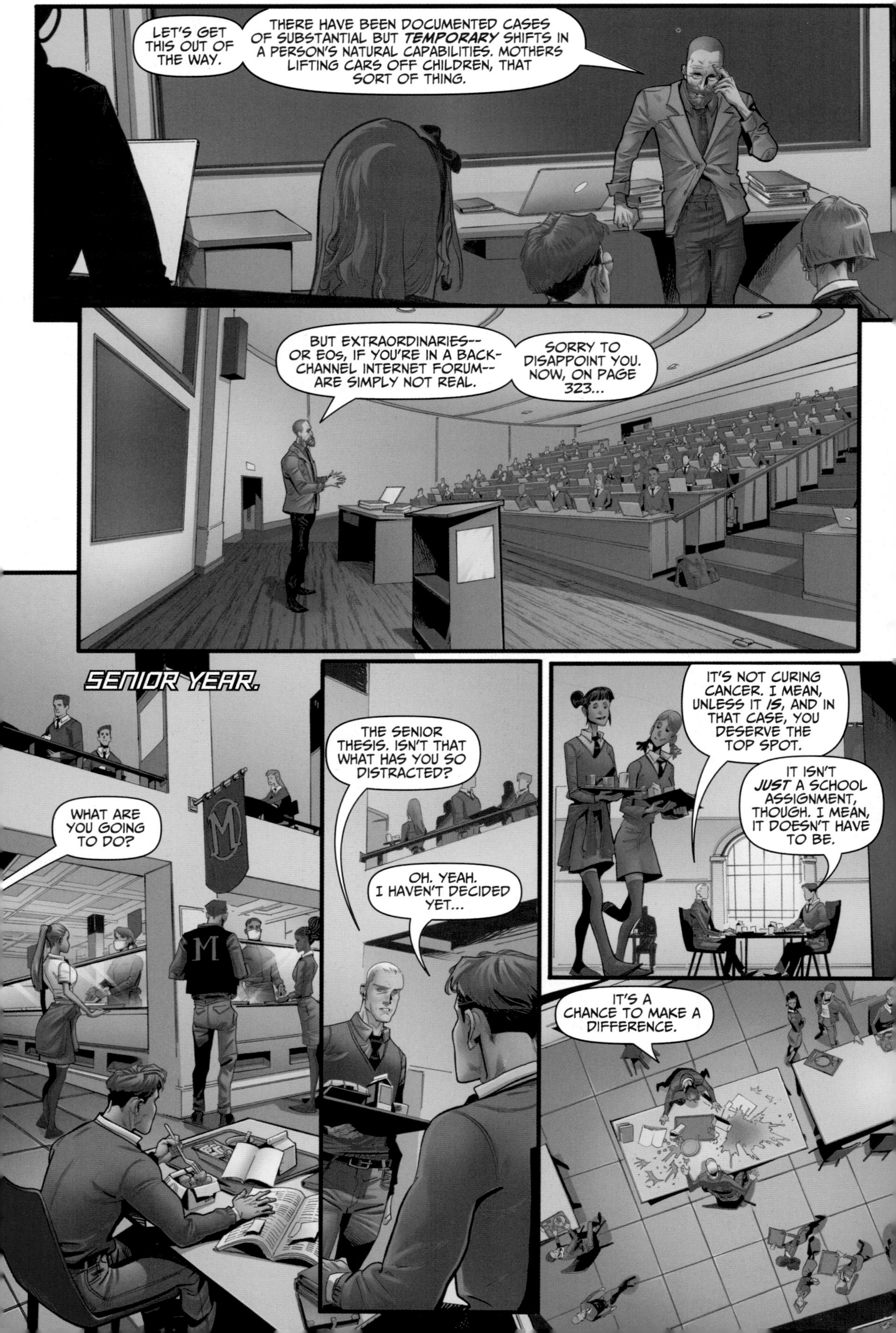

LET'S GET THIS OUT OF THE WAY.
THERE HAVE BEEN DOCUMENTED CASES OF SUBSTANTIAL BUT *TEMPORARY* SHIFTS IN A PERSON'S NATURAL CAPABILITIES. MOTHERS LIFTING CARS OFF CHILDREN, THAT SORT OF THING.
BUT EXTRAORDINARIES-- OR EOs, IF YOU'RE IN A BACK-CHANNEL INTERNET FORUM-- ARE SIMPLY NOT REAL.
SORRY TO DISAPPOINT YOU. NOW, ON PAGE 323...
SENIOR YEAR.
WHAT ARE YOU GOING TO DO?
THE SENIOR THESIS. ISN'T THAT WHAT HAS YOU SO DISTRACTED?
OH. YEAH. I HAVEN'T DECIDED YET...
IT'S NOT CURING CANCER. I MEAN, UNLESS IT *IS*, AND IN THAT CASE, YOU DESERVE THE TOP SPOT.
IT ISN'T *JUST* A SCHOOL ASSIGNMENT, THOUGH. I MEAN, IT DOESN'T HAVE TO BE.
IT'S A CHANCE TO MAKE A DIFFERENCE.

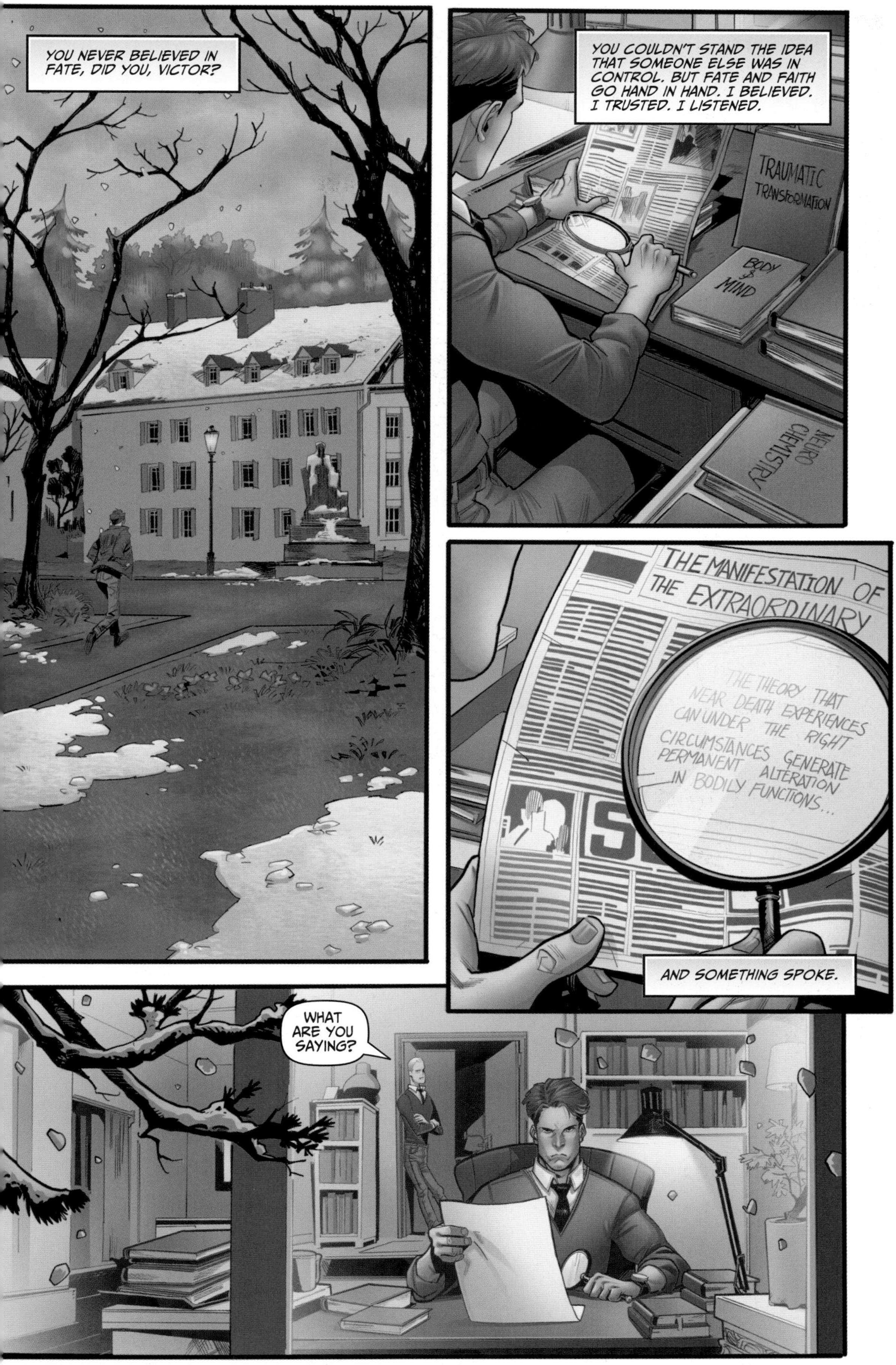
YOU NEVER BELIEVED IN FATE, DID YOU, VICTOR?
YOU COULDN'T STAND THE IDEA THAT SOMEONE ELSE WAS IN CONTROL. BUT FATE AND FAITH GO HAND IN HAND. I BELIEVED. I TRUSTED. I LISTENED.
TRAUMATIC TRANSFORMATION
BODY & MIND
NEURO CHEMISTRY
THE MANIFESTATION OF THE EXTRAORDINARY
THE THEORY THAT NEAR DEATH EXPERIENCES CAN UNDER THE RIGHT CIRCUMSTANCES GENERATE PERMANENT ALTERATION IN BODILY FUNCTIONS...
AND SOMETHING SPOKE.
WHAT ARE YOU SAYING?

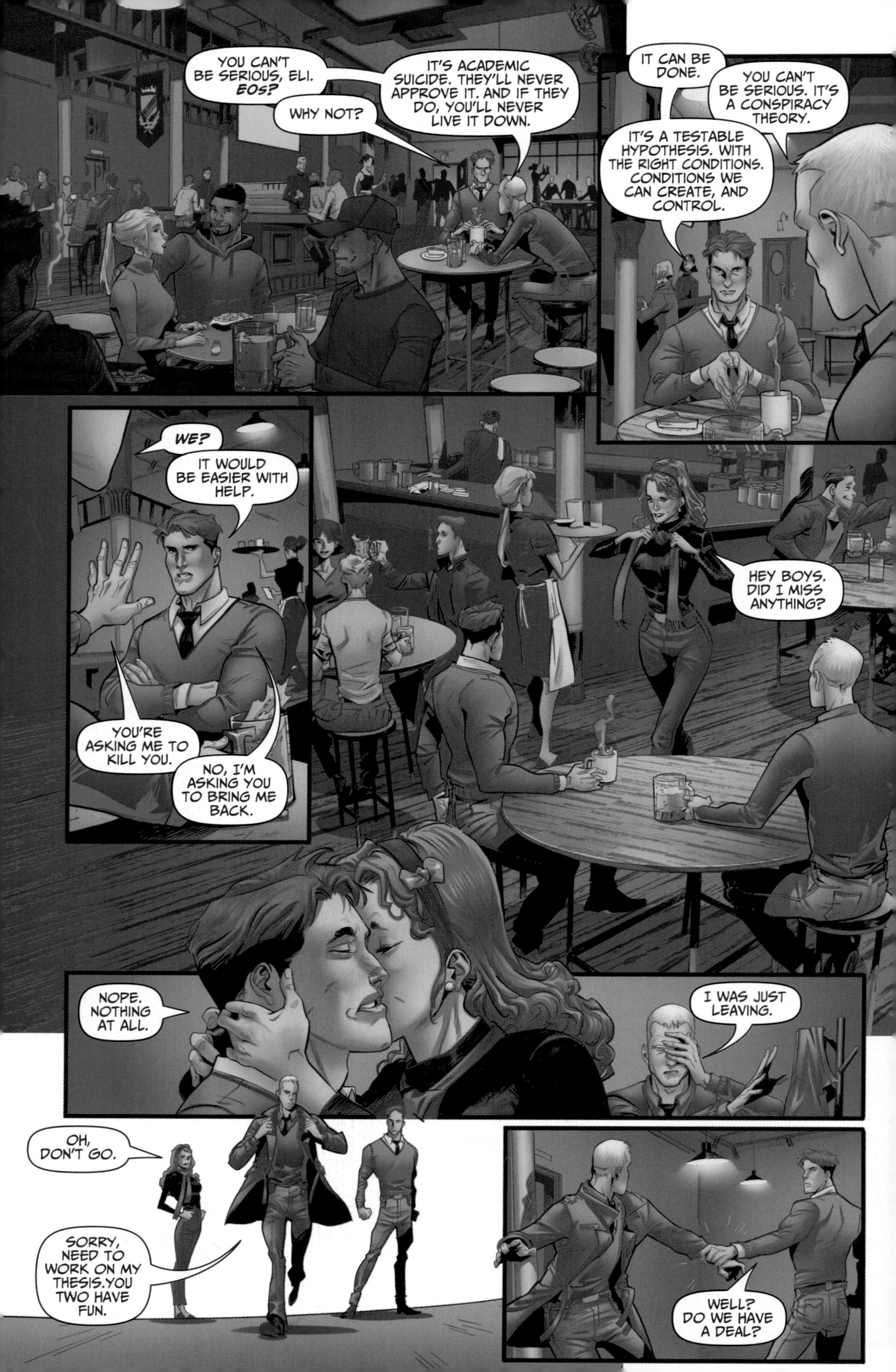
YOU CAN'T BE SERIOUS, ELI. EOS?
WHY NOT?
IT'S ACADEMIC SUICIDE. THEY'LL NEVER APPROVE IT. AND IF THEY DO, YOU'LL NEVER LIVE IT DOWN.
IT CAN BE DONE.
YOU CAN'T BE SERIOUS. IT'S A CONSPIRACY THEORY.
IT'S A TESTABLE HYPOTHESIS. WITH THE RIGHT CONDITIONS. CONDITIONS WE CAN CREATE, AND CONTROL.
WE?
IT WOULD BE EASIER WITH HELP.
YOU'RE ASKING ME TO KILL YOU.
NO, I'M ASKING YOU TO BRING ME BACK.
HEY BOYS. DID I MISS ANYTHING?
NOPE. NOTHING AT ALL.
I WAS JUST LEAVING.
OH, DON'T GO.
SORRY, NEED TO WORK ON MY THESIS.YOU TWO HAVE FUN.
WELL? DO WE HAVE A DEAL?

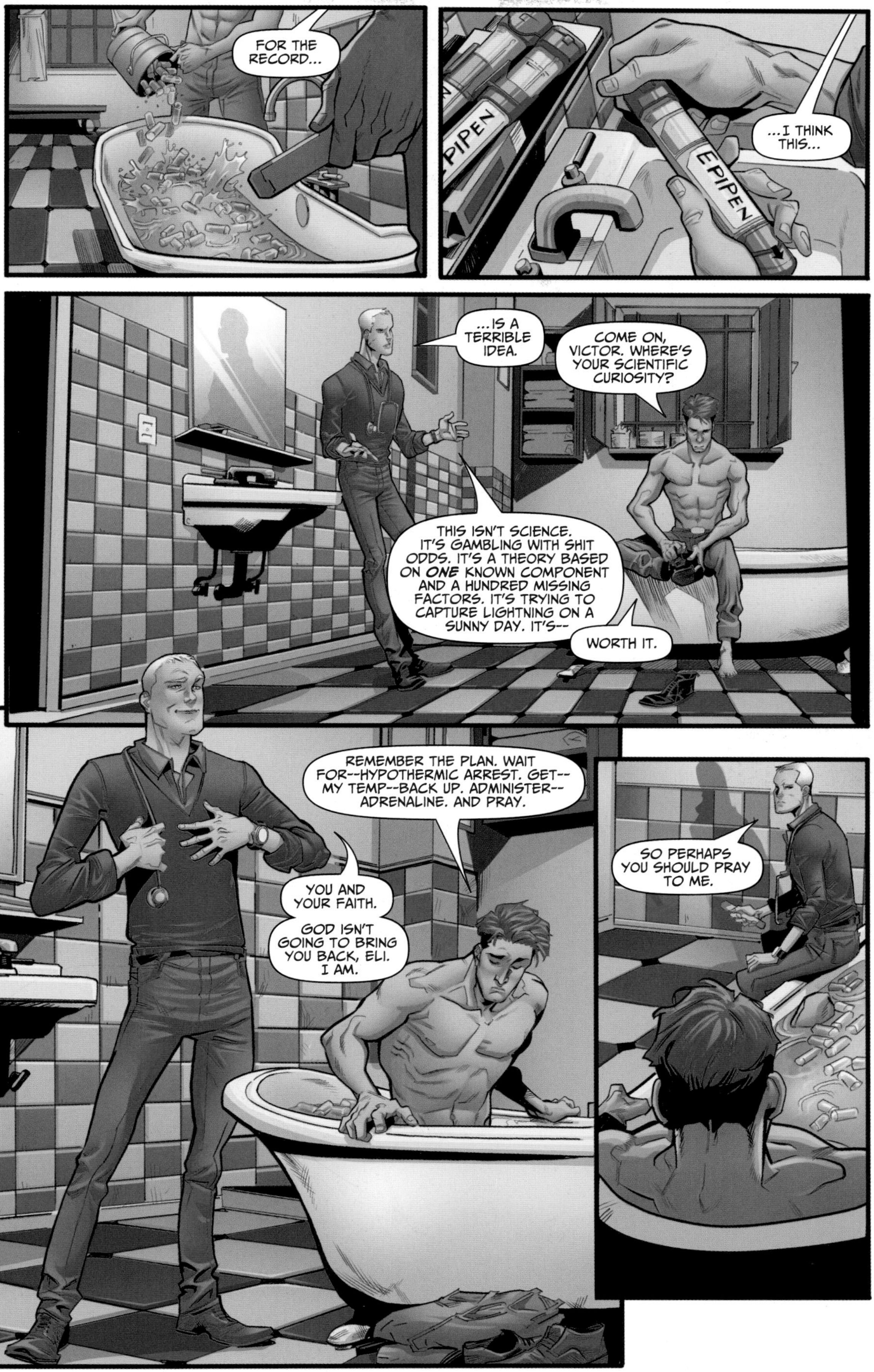
FOR THE RECORD...
...I THINK THIS...
...IS A TERRIBLE IDEA.
COME ON, VICTOR. WHERE'S YOUR SCIENTIFIC CURIOSITY?
THIS ISN'T SCIENCE. IT'S GAMBLING WITH SHIT ODDS. IT'S A THEORY BASED ON **ONE** KNOWN COMPONENT AND A HUNDRED MISSING FACTORS. IT'S TRYING TO CAPTURE LIGHTNING ON A SUNNY DAY. IT'S--
WORTH IT.
REMEMBER THE PLAN. WAIT FOR--HYPOTHERMIC ARREST. GET--MY TEMP--BACK UP. ADMINISTER--ADRENALINE. AND PRAY.
YOU AND YOUR FAITH.
GOD ISN'T GOING TO BRING YOU BACK, ELI. I AM.
SO PERHAPS YOU SHOULD PRAY TO ME.

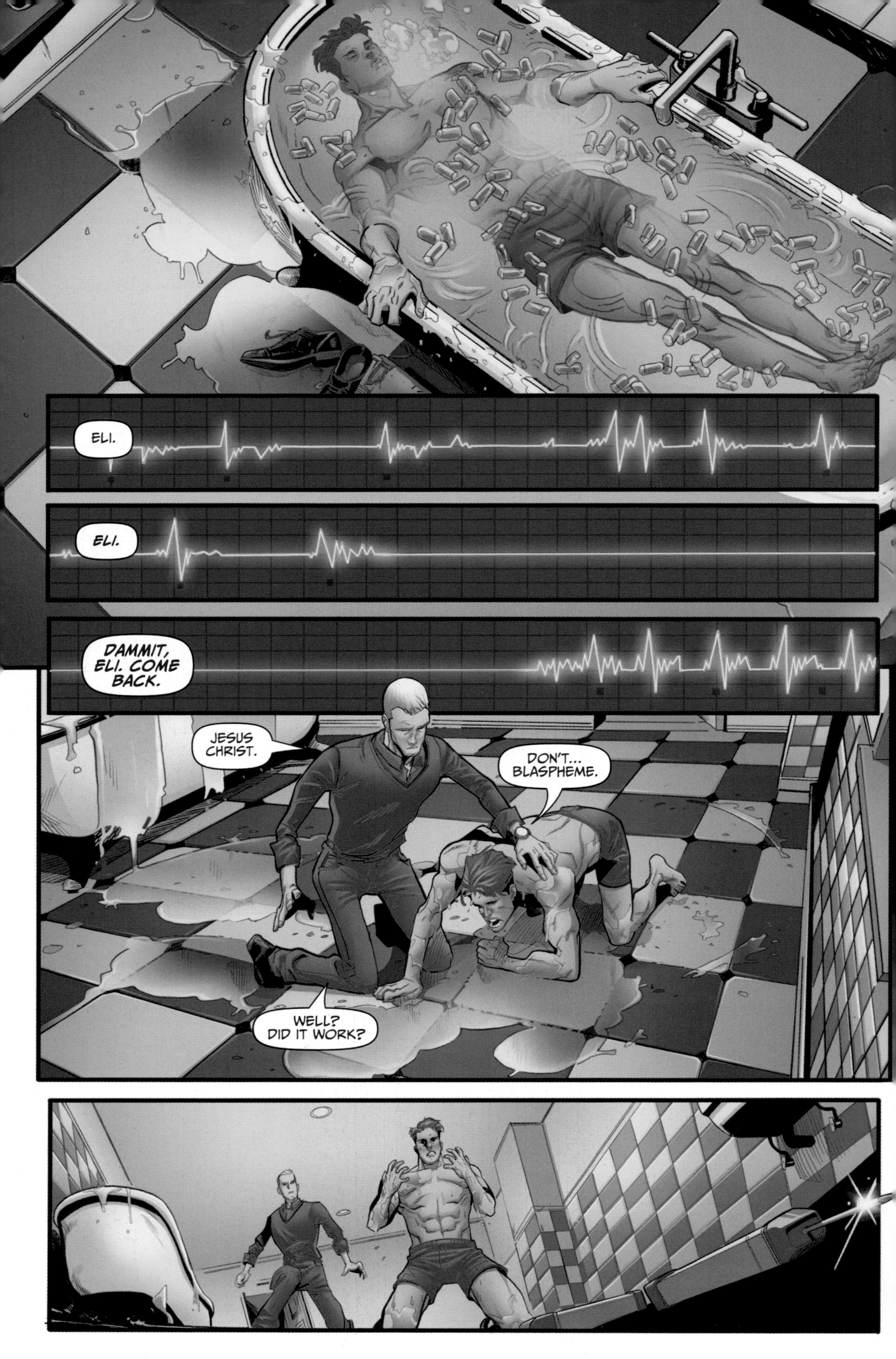
ELI.
ELI.
DAMMIT, ELI. COME BACK.
JESUS CHRIST.
DON'T... BLASPHEME.
WELL? DID IT WORK?

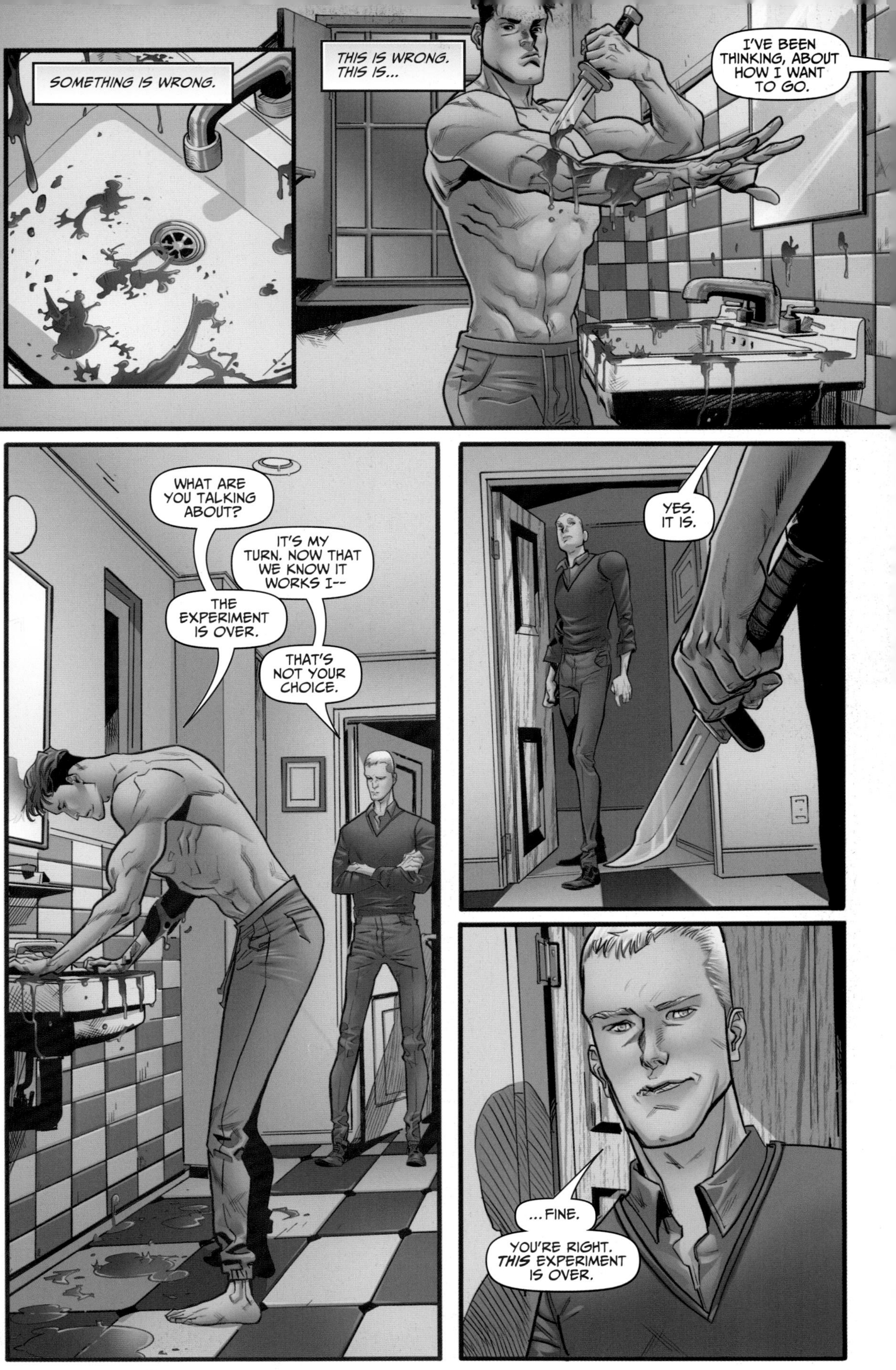
SOMETHING IS WRONG.
THIS IS WRONG. THIS IS...
I'VE BEEN THINKING, ABOUT HOW I WANT TO GO.
WHAT ARE YOU TALKING ABOUT?
IT'S MY TURN. NOW THAT WE KNOW IT WORKS I--
THE EXPERIMENT IS OVER.
THAT'S NOT YOUR CHOICE.
YES. IT IS.
...FINE.
YOU'RE RIGHT. *THIS* EXPERIMENT IS OVER.

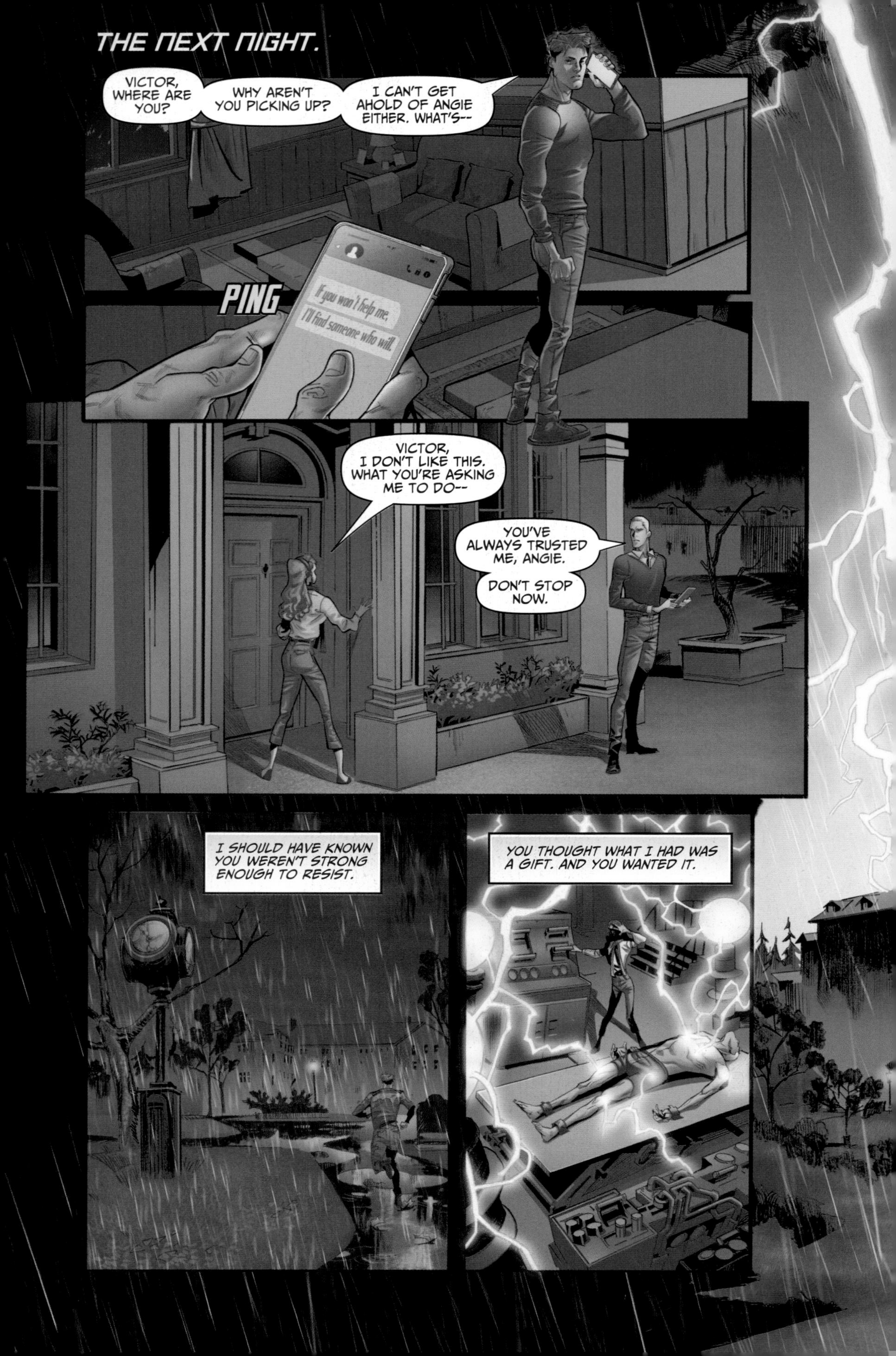
THE NEXT NIGHT.
VICTOR, WHERE ARE YOU?
WHY AREN'T YOU PICKING UP?
I CAN'T GET AHOLD OF ANGIE EITHER. WHAT'S--
PING
If you won't help me, I'll find someone who will.
VICTOR, I DON'T LIKE THIS. WHAT YOU'RE ASKING ME TO DO--
YOU'VE ALWAYS TRUSTED ME, ANGIE.
DON'T STOP NOW.
I SHOULD HAVE KNOWN YOU WEREN'T STRONG ENOUGH TO RESIST.
YOU THOUGHT WHAT I HAD WAS A GIFT. AND YOU WANTED IT.

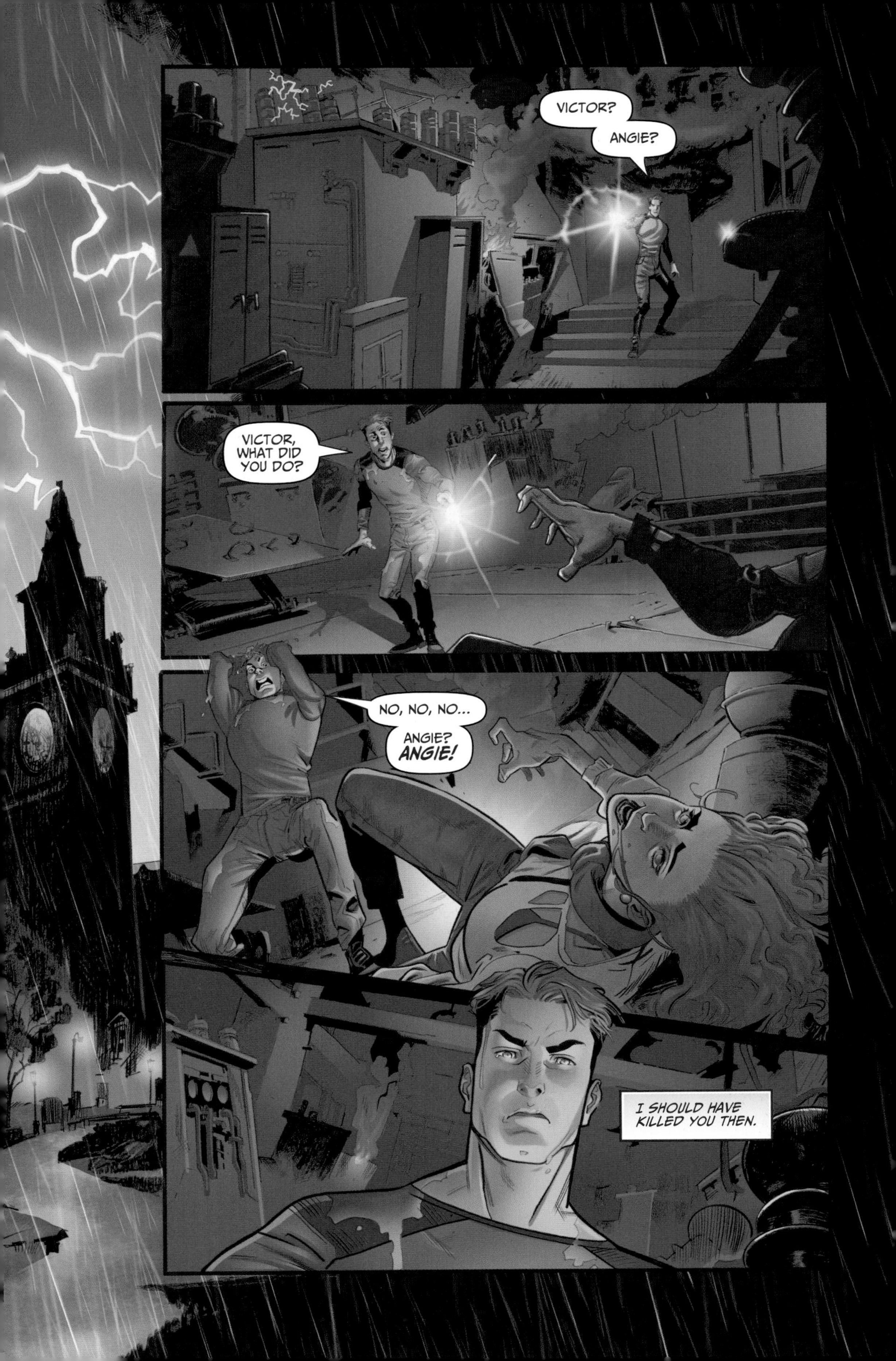
VICTOR?
ANGIE?
VICTOR, WHAT DID YOU DO?
NO, NO, NO...
ANGIE? ANGIE!
I SHOULD HAVE KILLED YOU THEN.

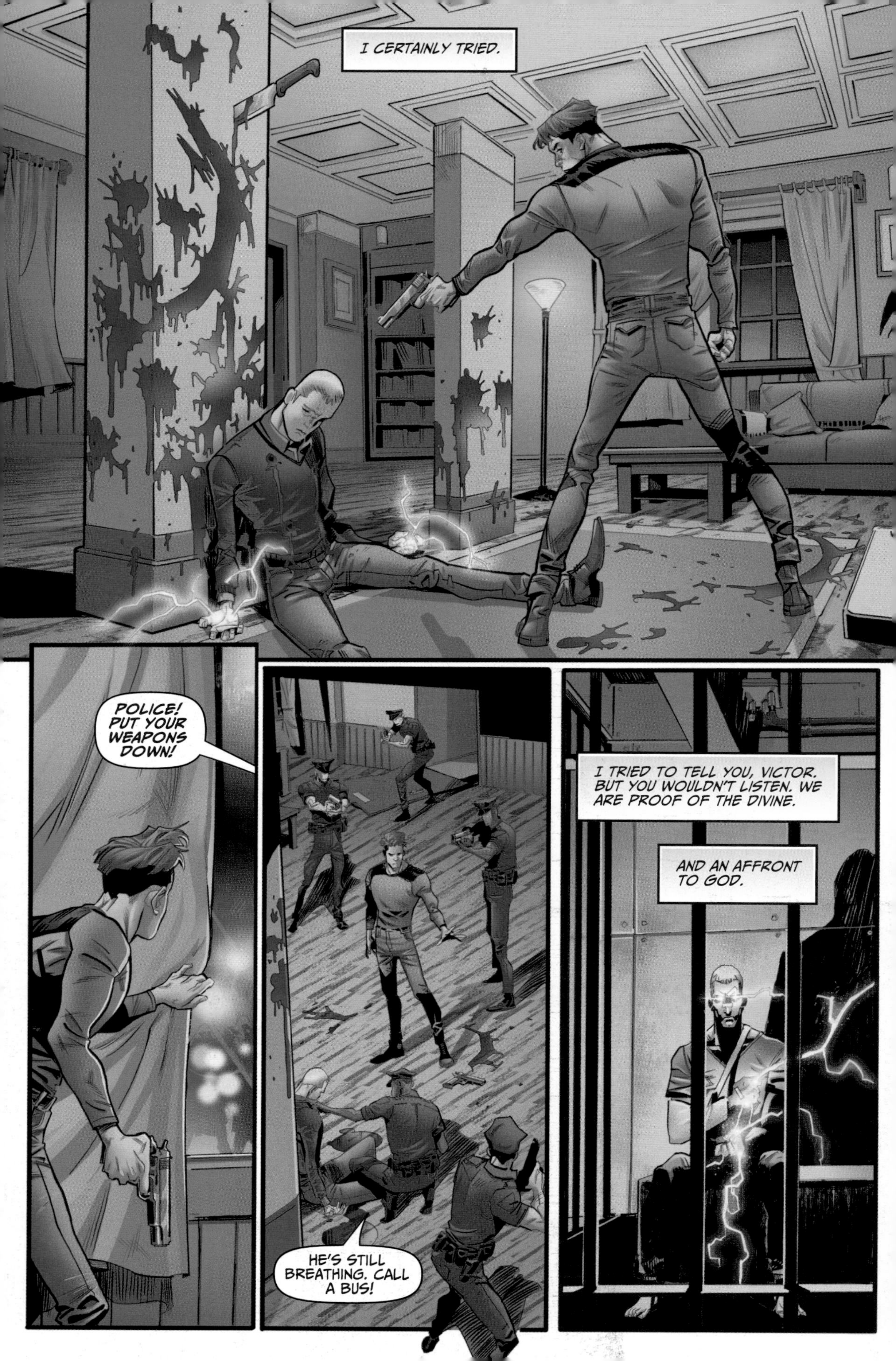
I CERTAINLY TRIED.
POLICE! PUT YOUR WEAPONS DOWN!
HE'S STILL BREATHING. CALL A BUS!
I TRIED TO TELL YOU, VICTOR. BUT YOU WOULDN'T LISTEN. WE ARE PROOF OF THE DIVINE.
AND AN AFFRONT TO GOD.

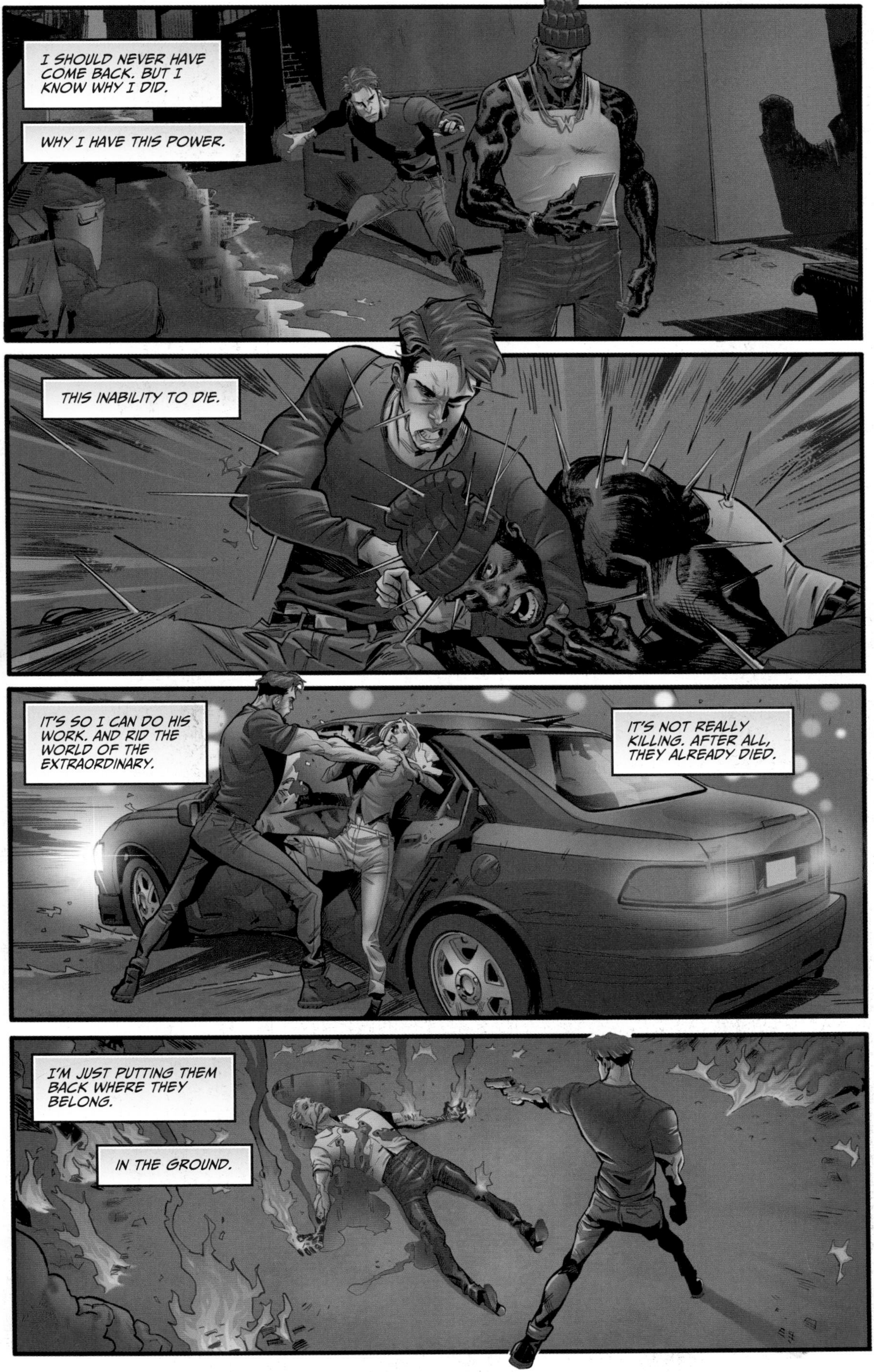
I SHOULD NEVER HAVE COME BACK. BUT I KNOW WHY I DID.
WHY I HAVE THIS POWER.
THIS INABILITY TO DIE.
IT'S SO I CAN DO HIS WORK. AND RID THE WORLD OF THE EXTRAORDINARY.
IT'S NOT REALLY KILLING. AFTER ALL, THEY ALREADY DIED.
I'M JUST PUTTING THEM BACK WHERE THEY BELONG.
IN THE GROUND.

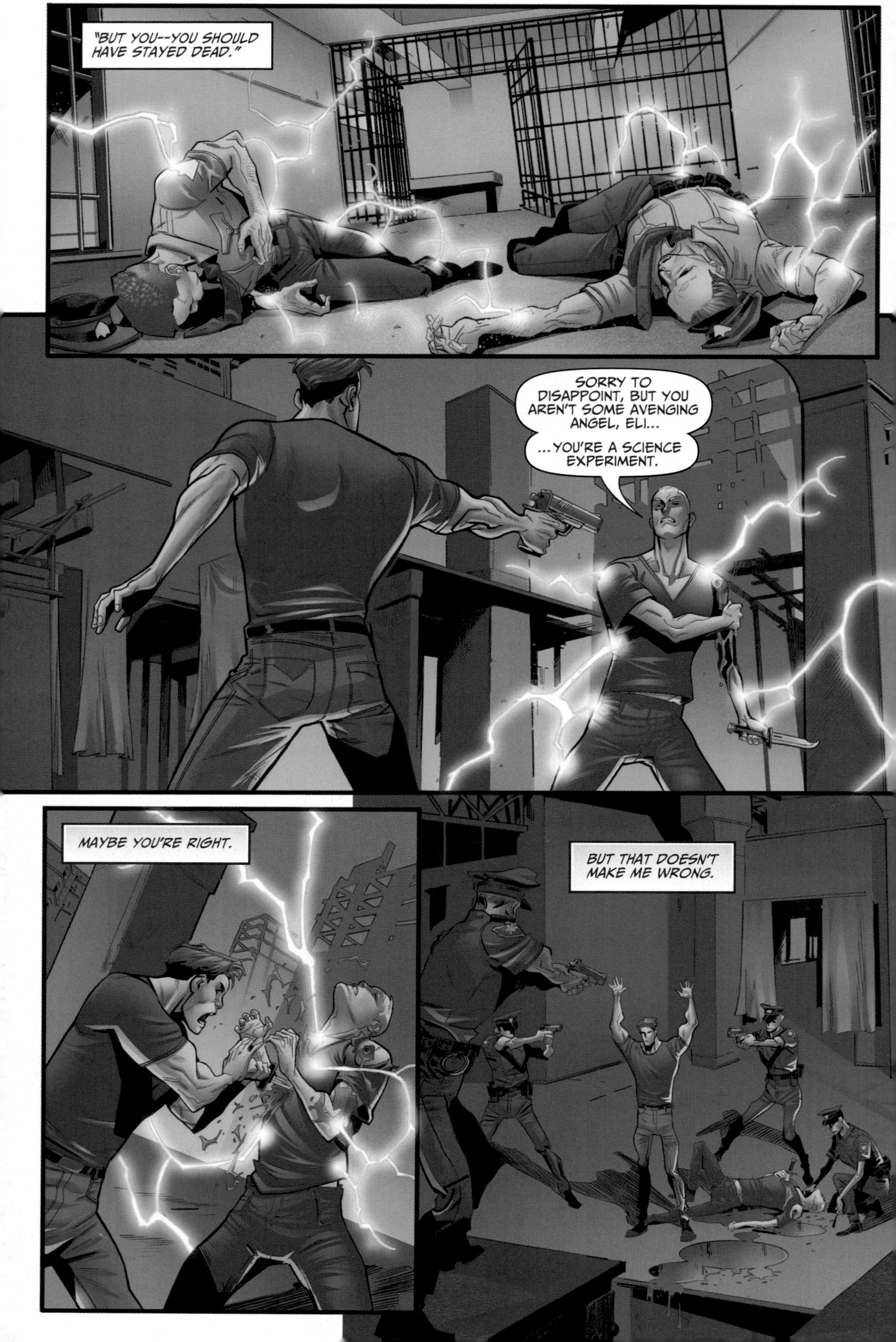
"BUT YOU--YOU SHOULD HAVE STAYED DEAD."
SORRY TO DISAPPOINT, BUT YOU AREN'T SOME AVENGING ANGEL, ELI...
...YOU'RE A SCIENCE EXPERIMENT.
MAYBE YOU'RE RIGHT.
BUT THAT DOESN'T MAKE ME WRONG.

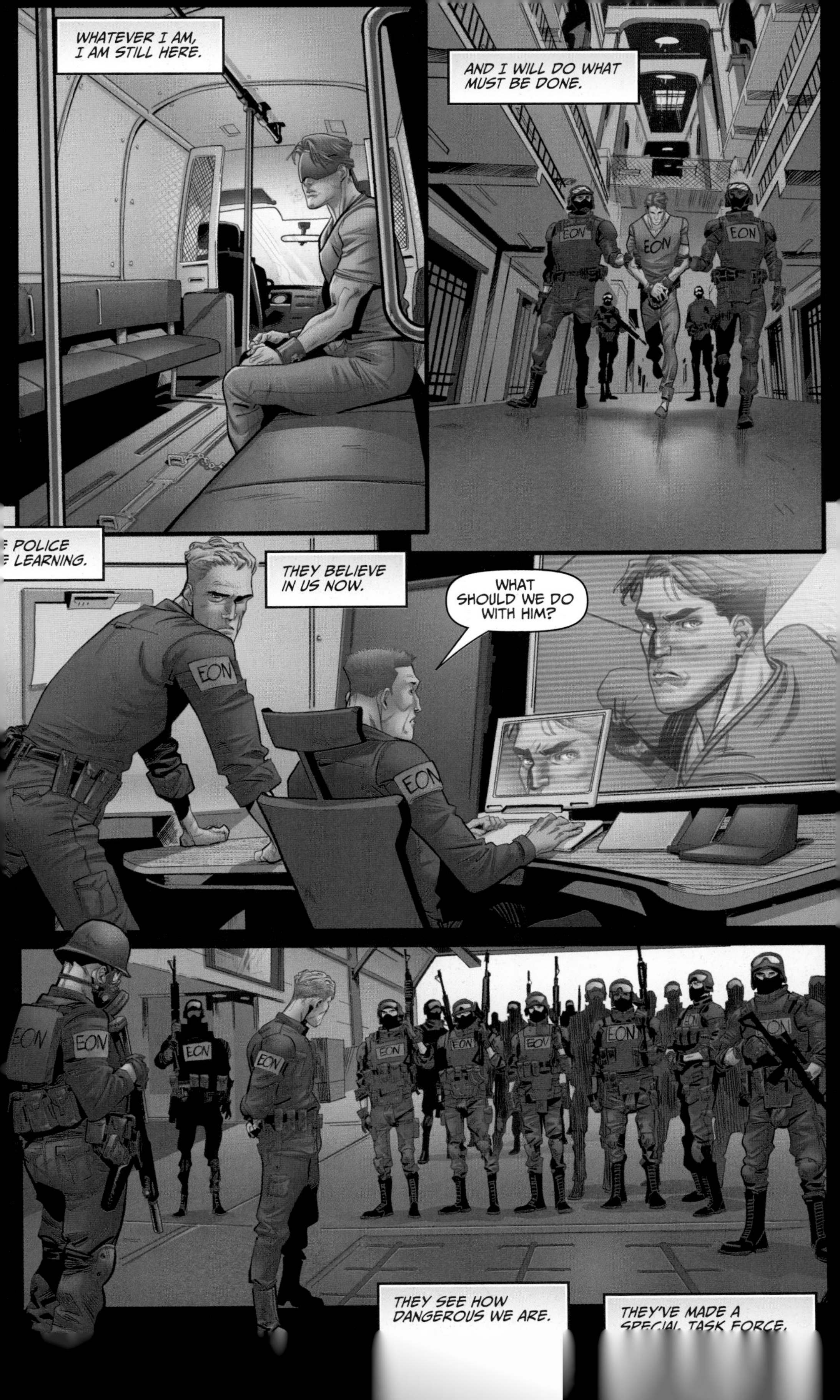
WHATEVER I AM, I AM STILL HERE.
AND I WILL DO WHAT MUST BE DONE.
POLICE
LEARNING.
THEY BELIEVE IN US NOW.
WHAT SHOULD WE DO WITH HIM?
THEY SEE HOW DANGEROUS WE ARE.
THEY'VE MADE A SPECIAL TASK FORCE.

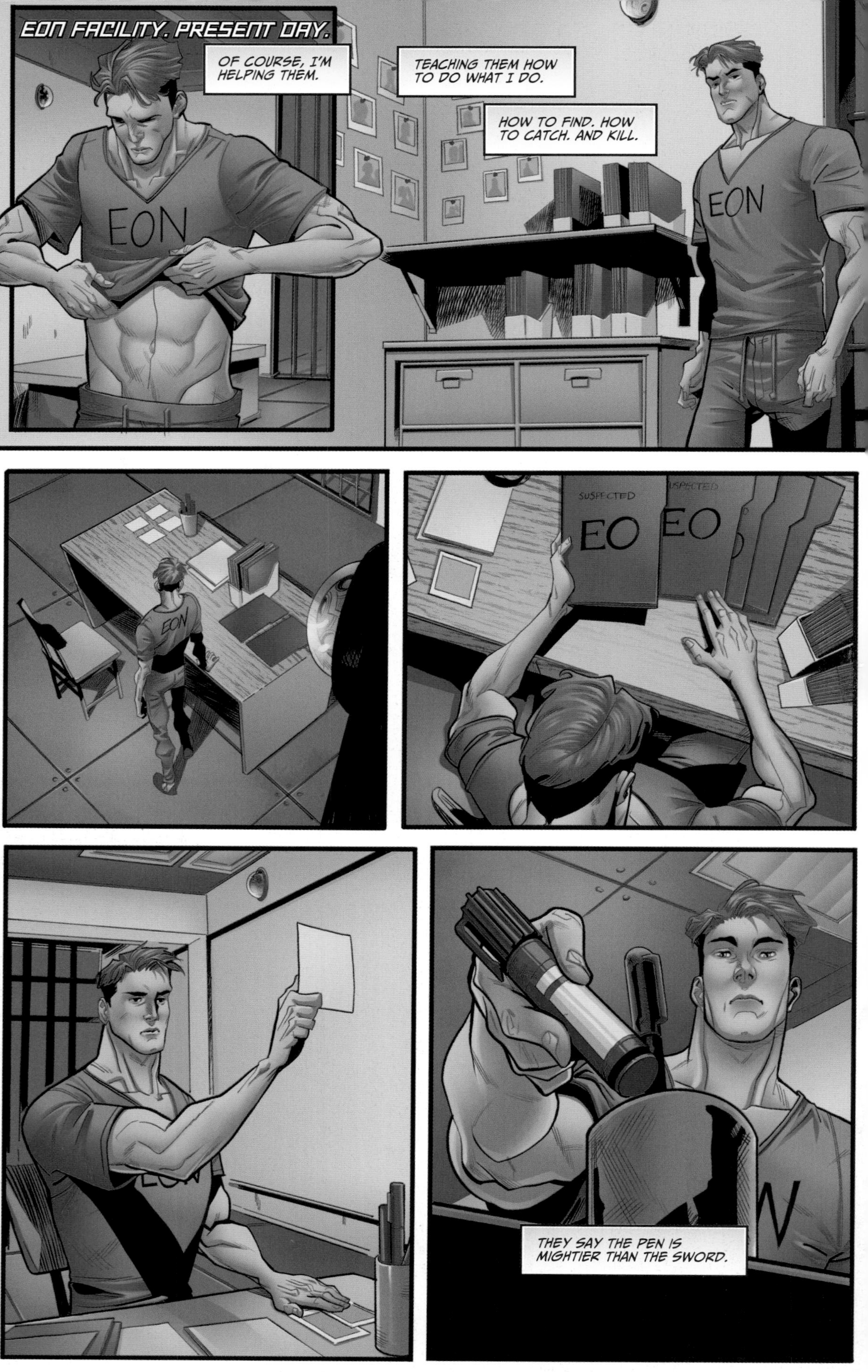
EON FACILITY. PRESENT DAY.
OF COURSE, I'M HELPING THEM.
TEACHING THEM HOW TO DO WHAT I DO.
HOW TO FIND. HOW TO CATCH. AND KILL.
EON
EON
THEY SAY THE PEN IS MIGHTIER THAN THE SWORD.

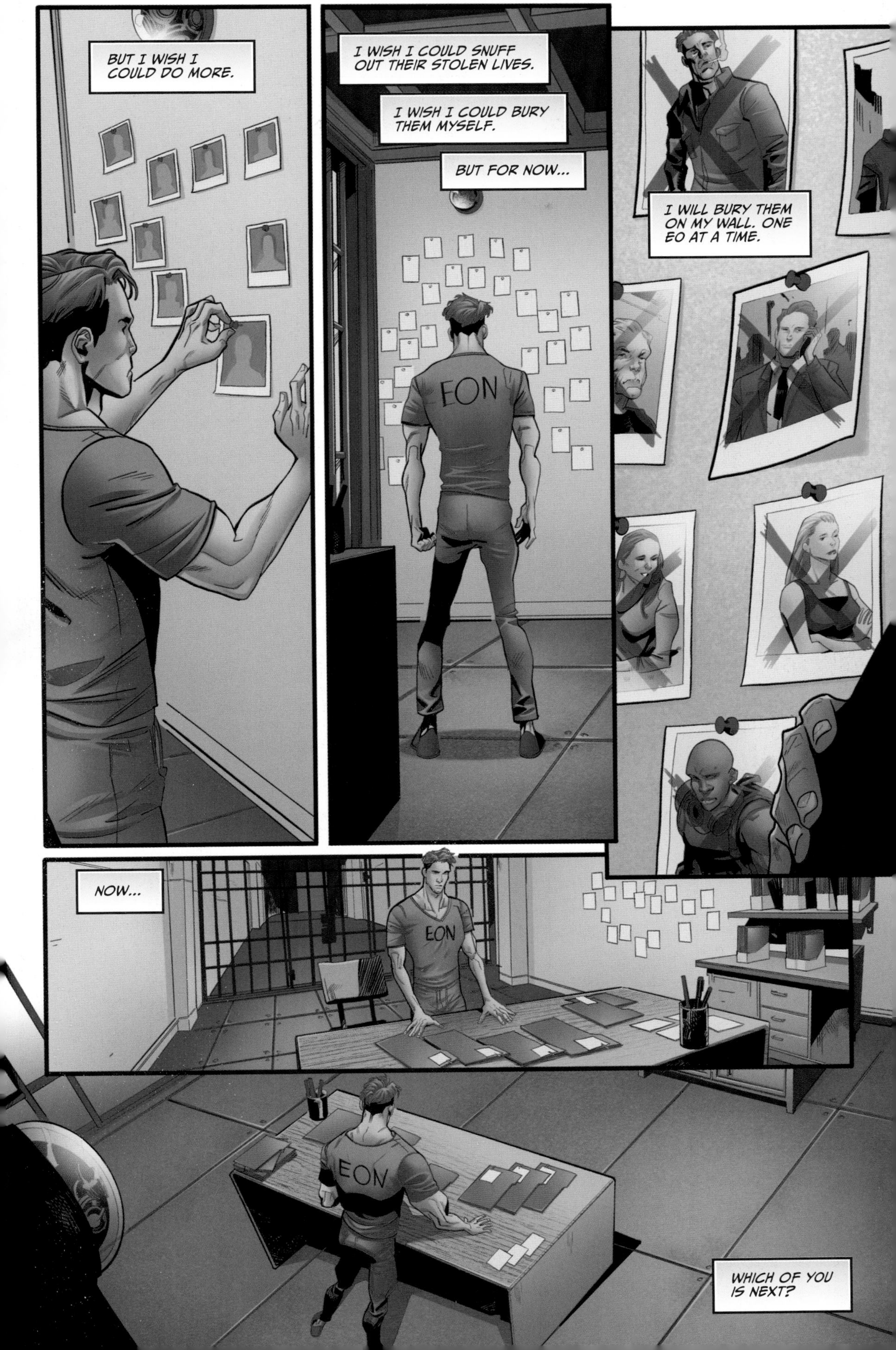
BUT I WISH I COULD DO MORE.
I WISH I COULD SNUFF OUT THEIR STOLEN LIVES.
I WISH I COULD BURY THEM MYSELF.
BUT FOR NOW...
EON
I WILL BURY THEM ON MY WALL. ONE EO AT A TIME.
NOW...
EON
EON
WHICH OF YOU IS NEXT?

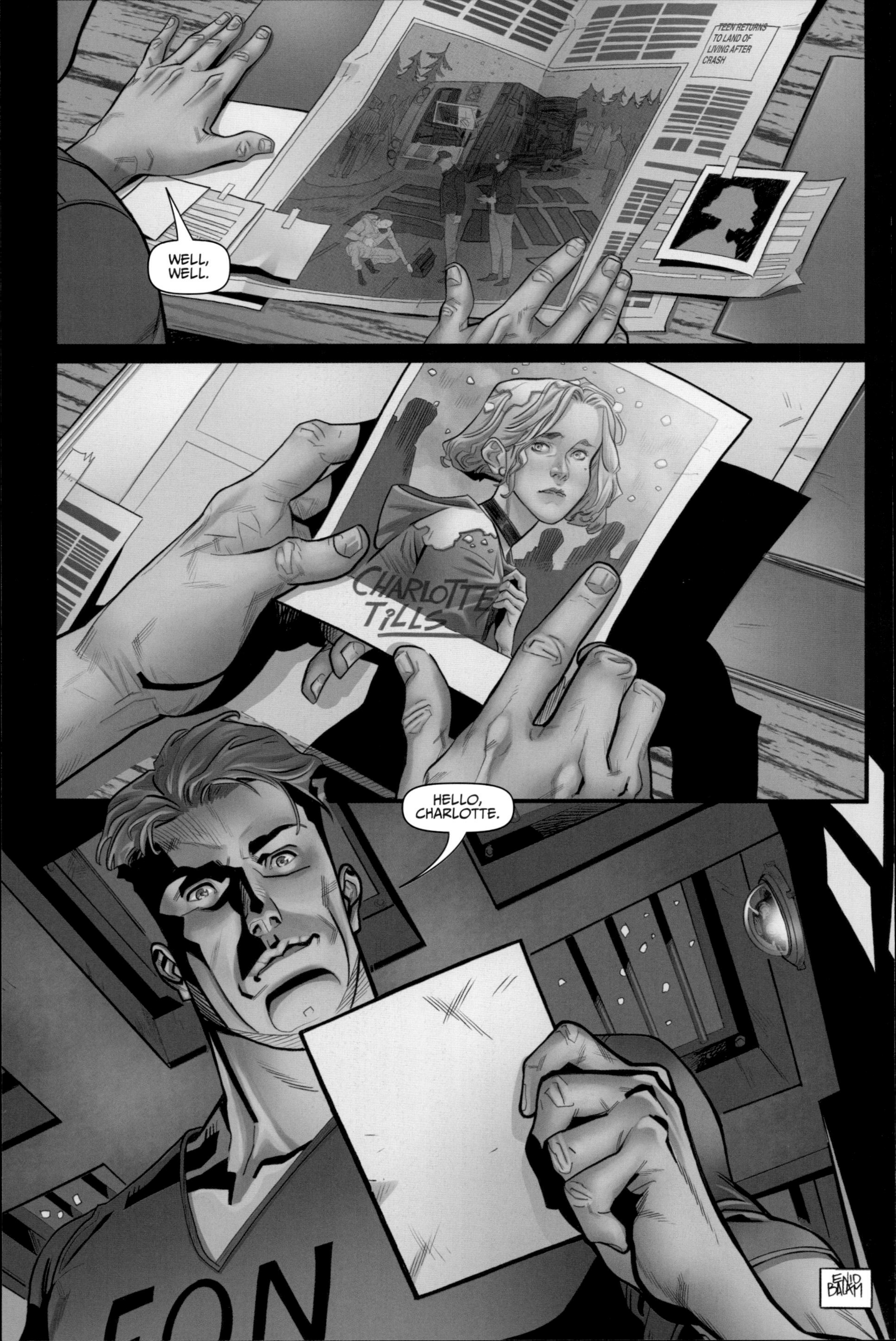
TEEN RETURNS TO LAND OF LIVING AFTER CRASH
WELL, WELL.
CHARLOTTE TILLS
HELLO, CHARLOTTE.
ENID BALAM

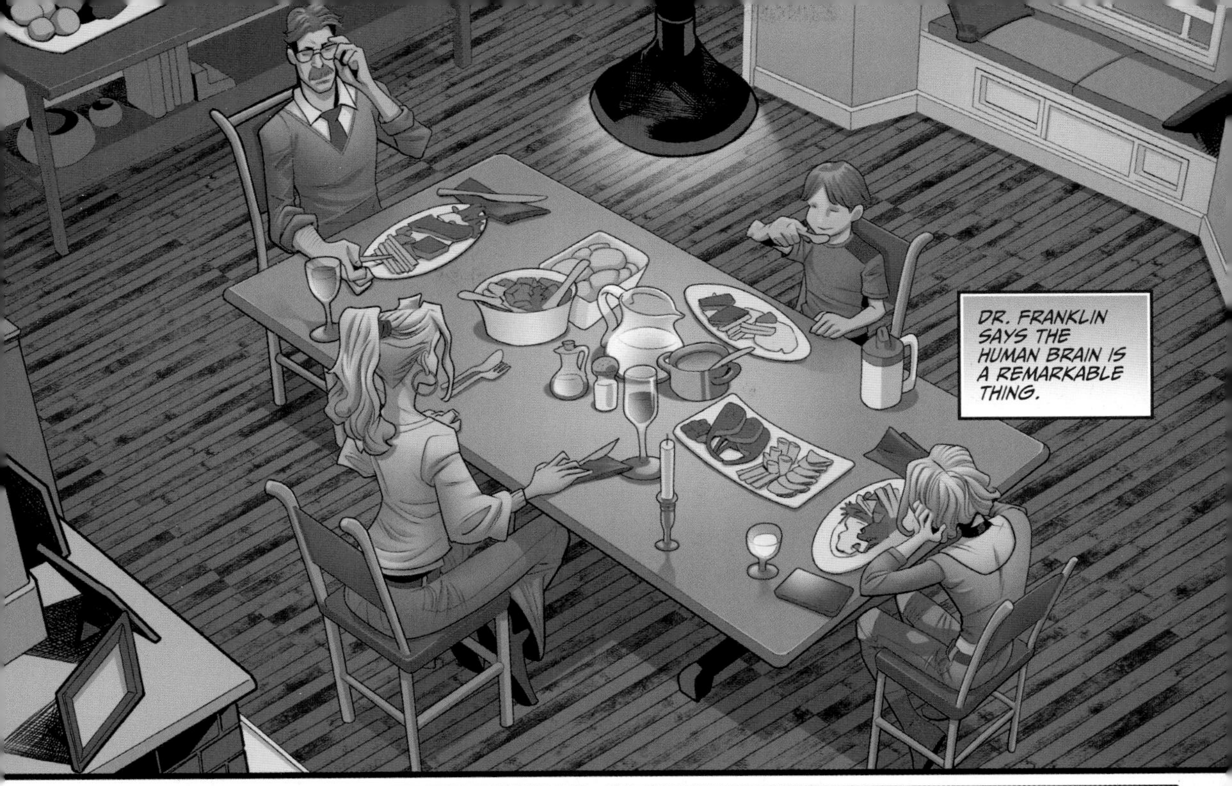
DR. FRANKLIN SAYS THE HUMAN BRAIN IS A REMARKABLE THING.
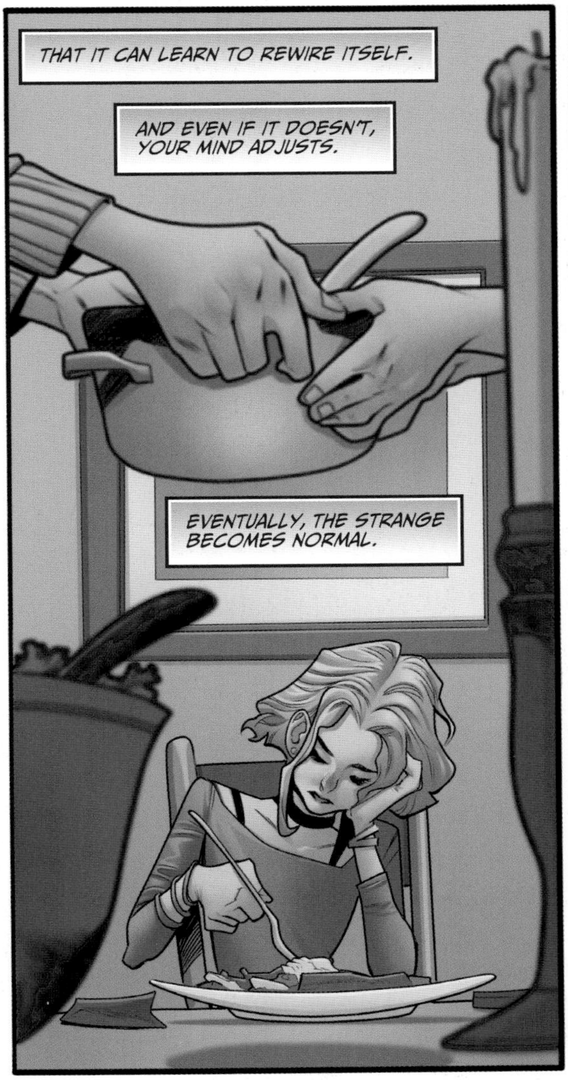
THAT IT CAN LEARN TO REWIRE ITSELF.
AND EVEN IF IT DOESN'T, YOUR MIND ADJUSTS.
EVENTUALLY, THE STRANGE BECOMES NORMAL.
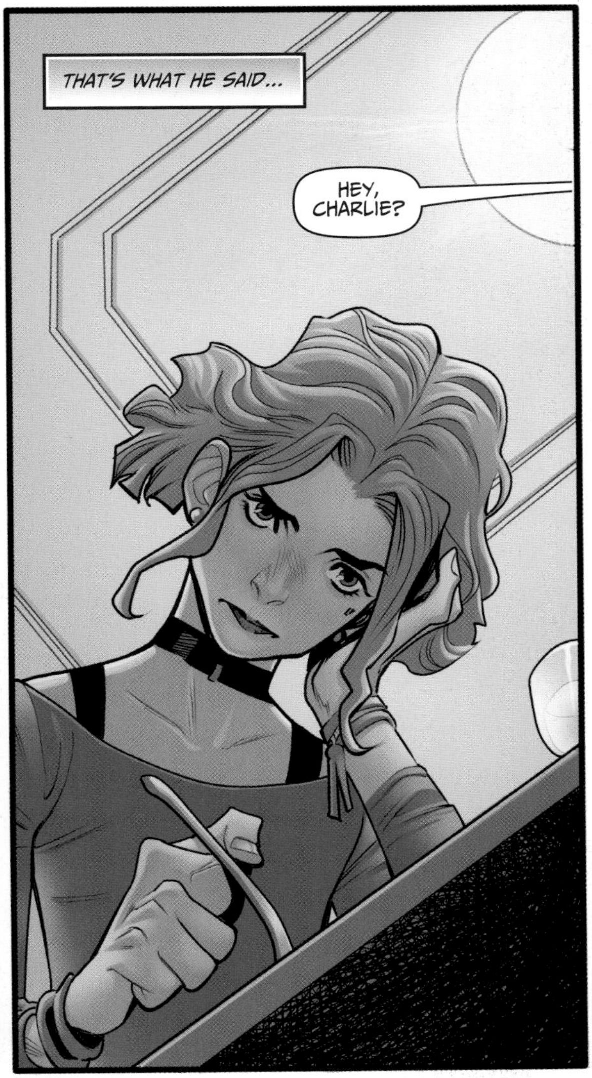
THAT'S WHAT HE SAID...
HEY, CHARLIE?

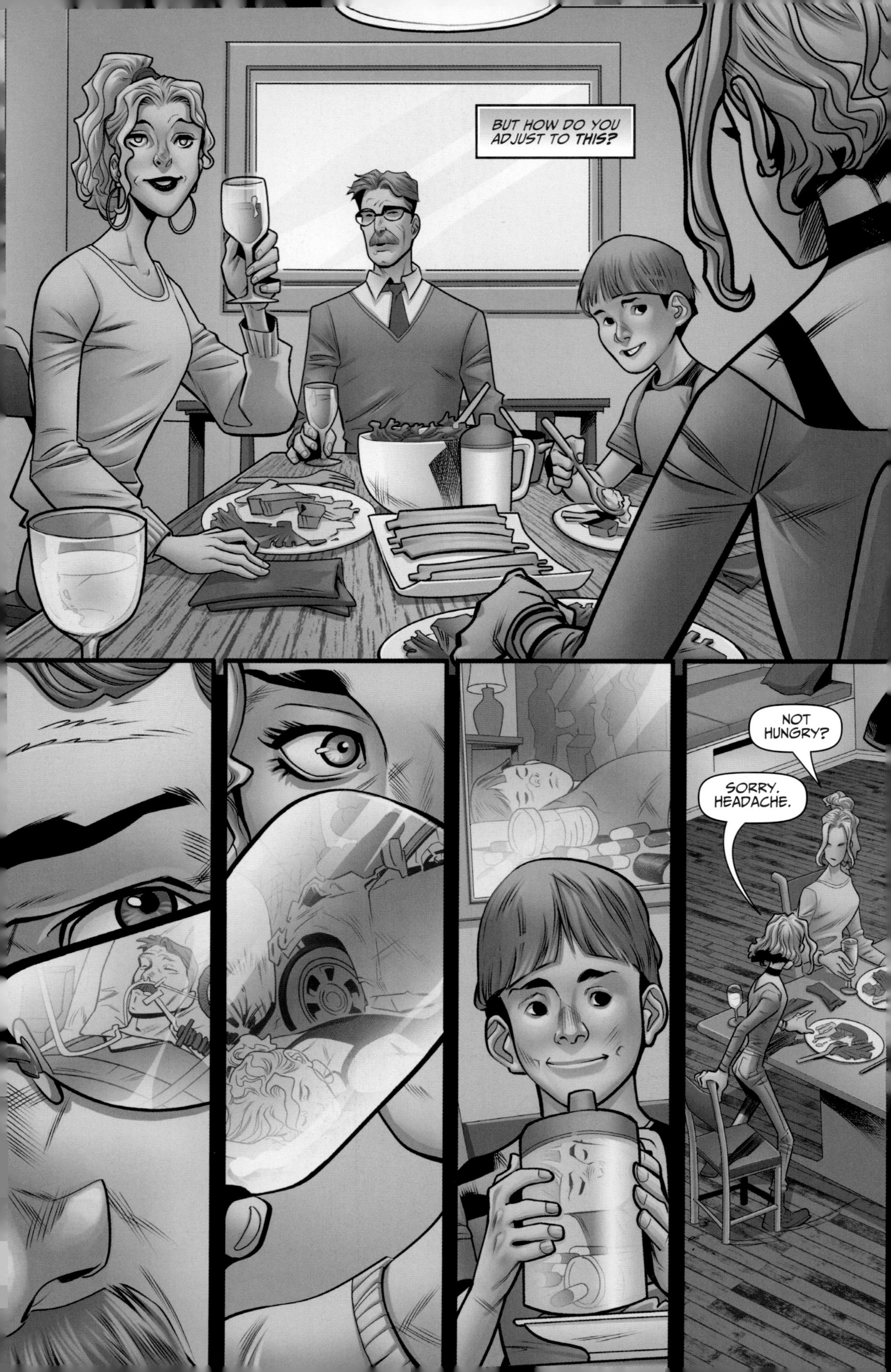
BUT HOW DO YOU ADJUST TO THIS?
NOT HUNGRY?
SORRY. HEADACHE.

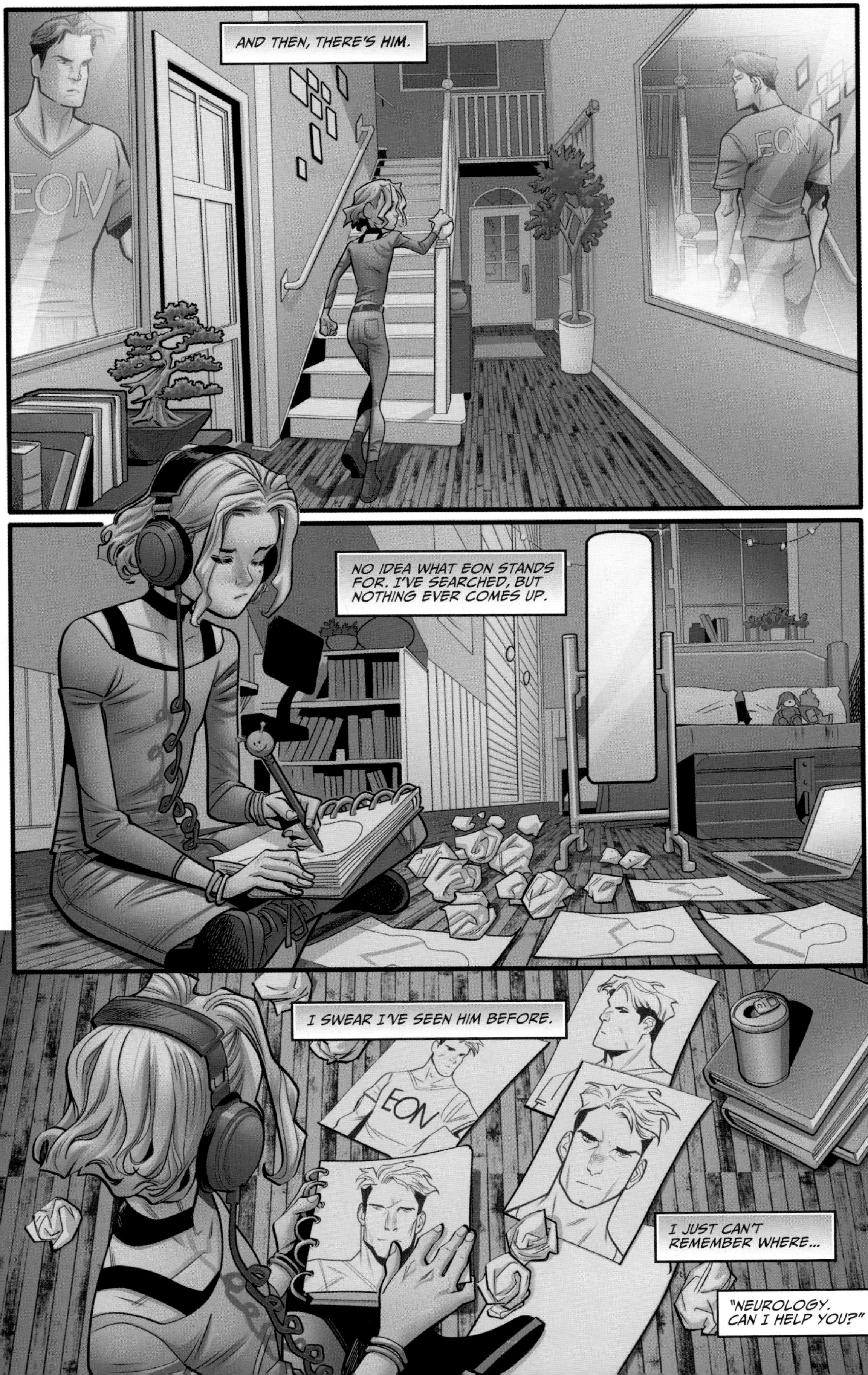
AND THEN, THERE'S HIM.
EON
EON
NO IDEA WHAT EON STANDS FOR. I'VE SEARCHED, BUT NOTHING EVER COMES UP.
I SWEAR I'VE SEEN HIM BEFORE.
EON
I JUST CAN'T REMEMBER WHERE...
"NEUROLOGY. CAN I HELP YOU?"

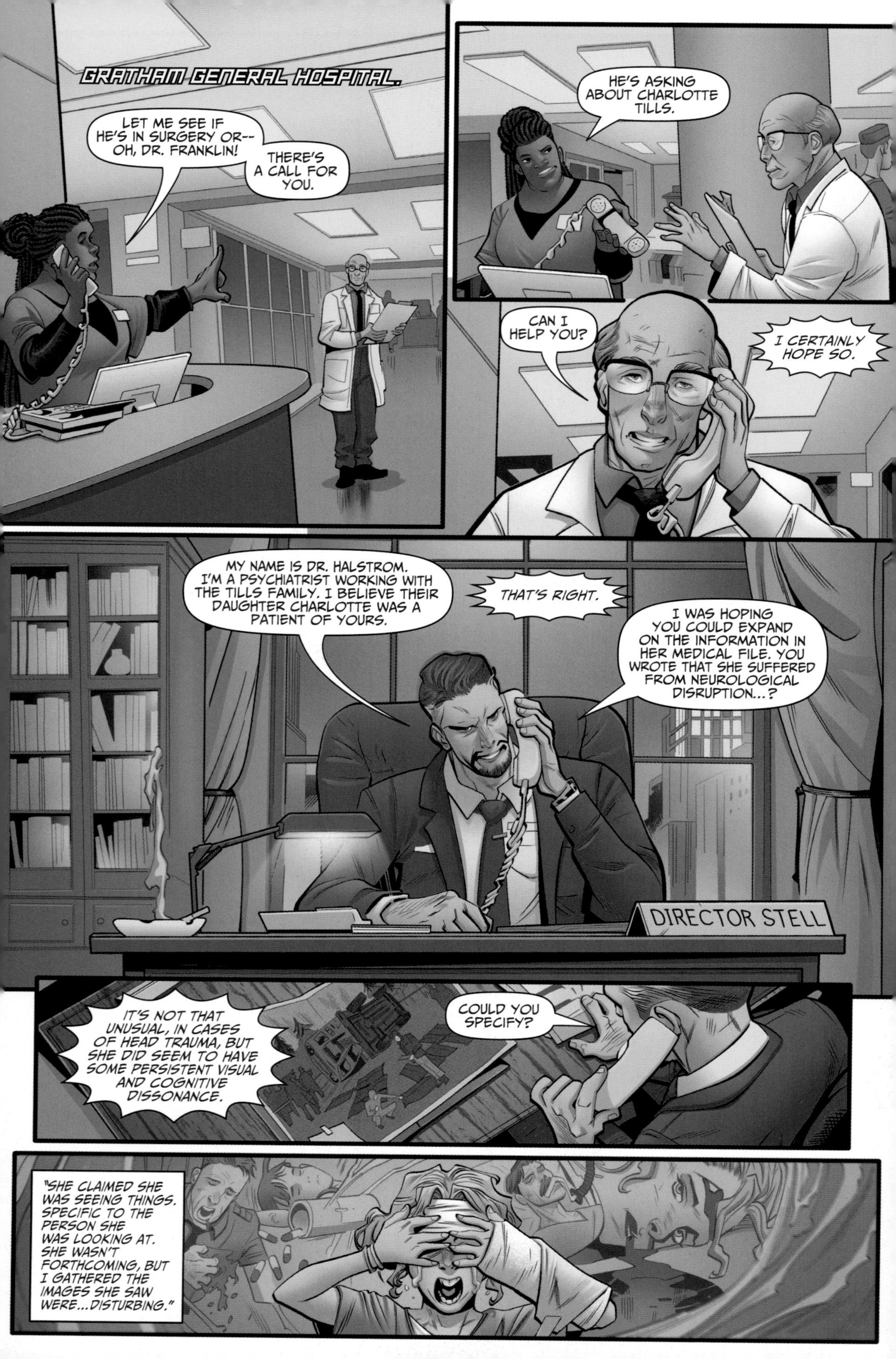
GRATHAM GENERAL HOSPITAL.
LET ME SEE IF HE'S IN SURGERY OR-- OH, DR. FRANKLIN!
THERE'S A CALL FOR YOU.
HE'S ASKING ABOUT CHARLOTTE TILLS.
CAN I HELP YOU?
I CERTAINLY HOPE SO.
MY NAME IS DR. HALSTROM. I'M A PSYCHIATRIST WORKING WITH THE TILLS FAMILY. I BELIEVE THEIR DAUGHTER CHARLOTTE WAS A PATIENT OF YOURS.
THAT'S RIGHT.
I WAS HOPING YOU COULD EXPAND ON THE INFORMATION IN HER MEDICAL FILE. YOU WROTE THAT SHE SUFFERED FROM NEUROLOGICAL DISRUPTION...?
DIRECTOR STELL
IT'S NOT THAT UNUSUAL, IN CASES OF HEAD TRAUMA, BUT SHE DID SEEM TO HAVE SOME PERSISTENT VISUAL AND COGNITIVE DISSONANCE.
COULD YOU SPECIFY?
"SHE CLAIMED SHE WAS SEEING THINGS. SPECIFIC TO THE PERSON SHE WAS LOOKING AT. SHE WASN'T FORTHCOMING, BUT I GATHERED THE IMAGES SHE SAW WERE...DISTURBING."

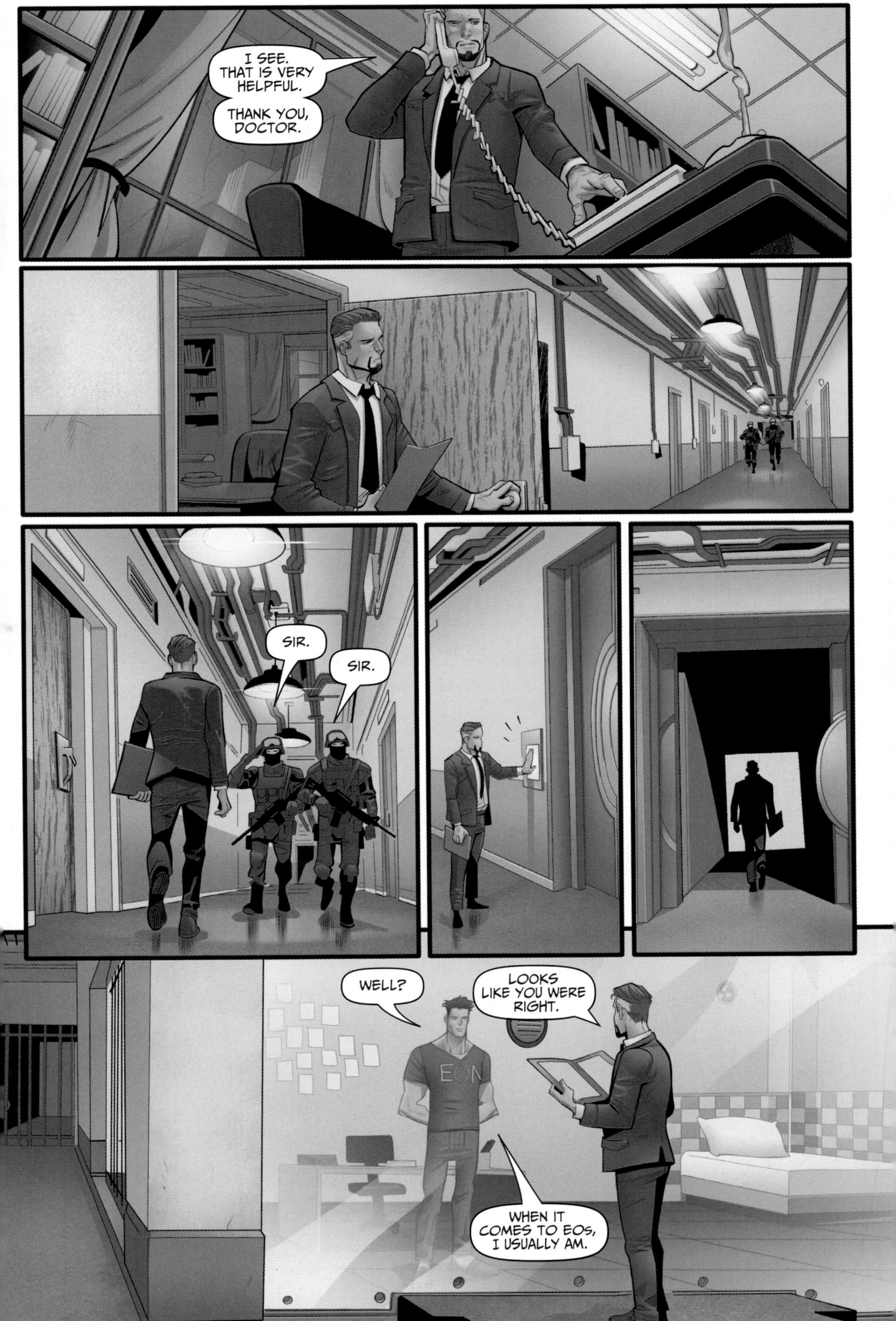
I SEE. THAT IS VERY HELPFUL.
THANK YOU, DOCTOR.
SIR.
SIR.
WELL?
LOOKS LIKE YOU WERE RIGHT.
WHEN IT COMES TO EOS, I USUALLY AM.

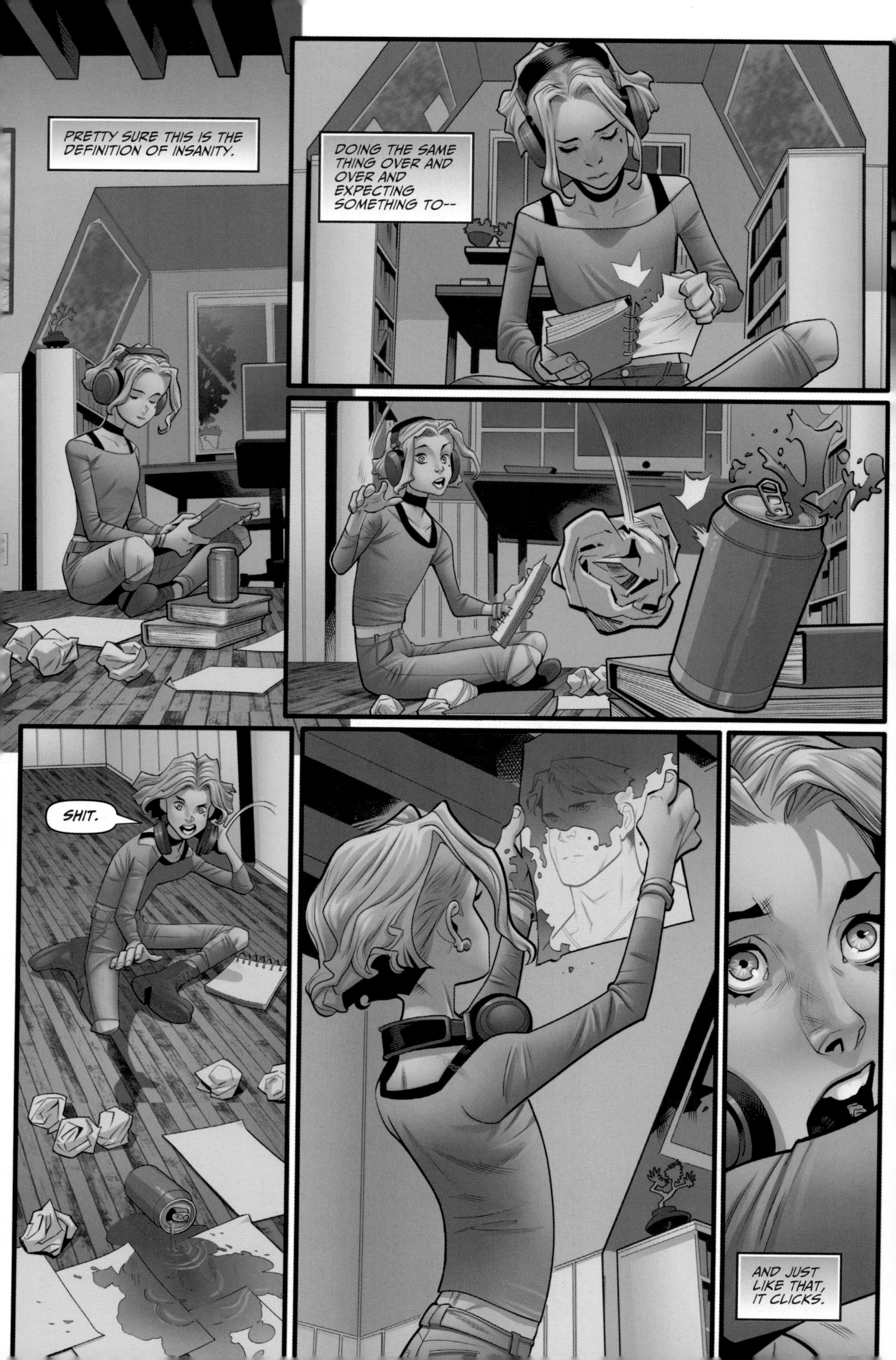
PRETTY SURE THIS IS THE DEFINITION OF INSANITY.
DOING THE SAME THING OVER AND OVER AND EXPECTING SOMETHING TO--
SHIT.
AND JUST LIKE THAT, IT CLICKS.

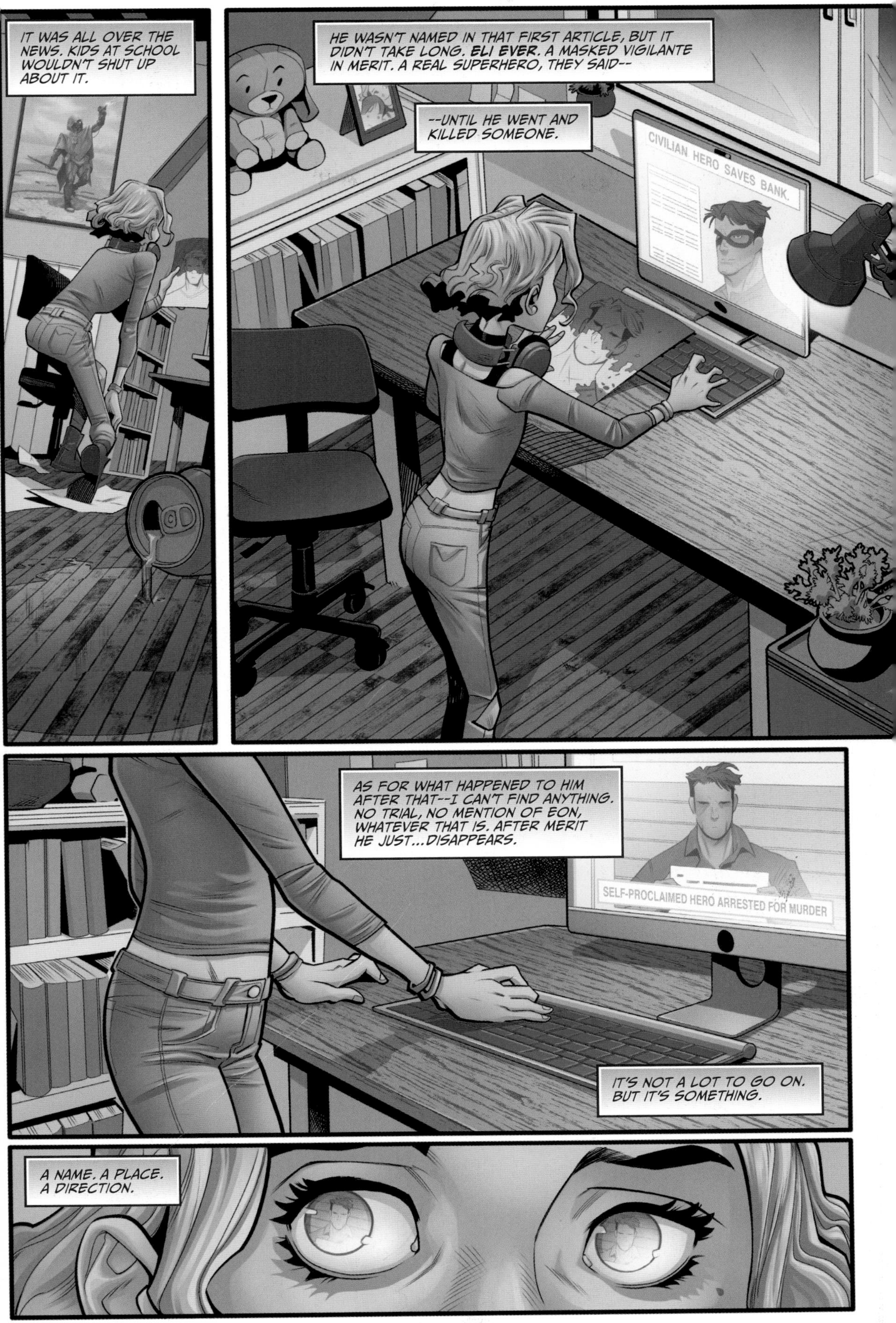
IT WAS ALL OVER THE NEWS. KIDS AT SCHOOL WOULDN'T SHUT UP ABOUT IT.
HE WASN'T NAMED IN THAT FIRST ARTICLE, BUT IT DIDN'T TAKE LONG. ELI EVER. A MASKED VIGILANTE IN MERIT. A REAL SUPERHERO, THEY SAID--
--UNTIL HE WENT AND KILLED SOMEONE.
CIVILIAN HERO SAVES BANK.
AS FOR WHAT HAPPENED TO HIM AFTER THAT--I CAN'T FIND ANYTHING. NO TRIAL, NO MENTION OF EON, WHATEVER THAT IS. AFTER MERIT HE JUST...DISAPPEARS.
SELF-PROCLAIMED HERO ARRESTED FOR MURDER
IT'S NOT A LOT TO GO ON. BUT IT'S SOMETHING.
A NAME. A PLACE. A DIRECTION.

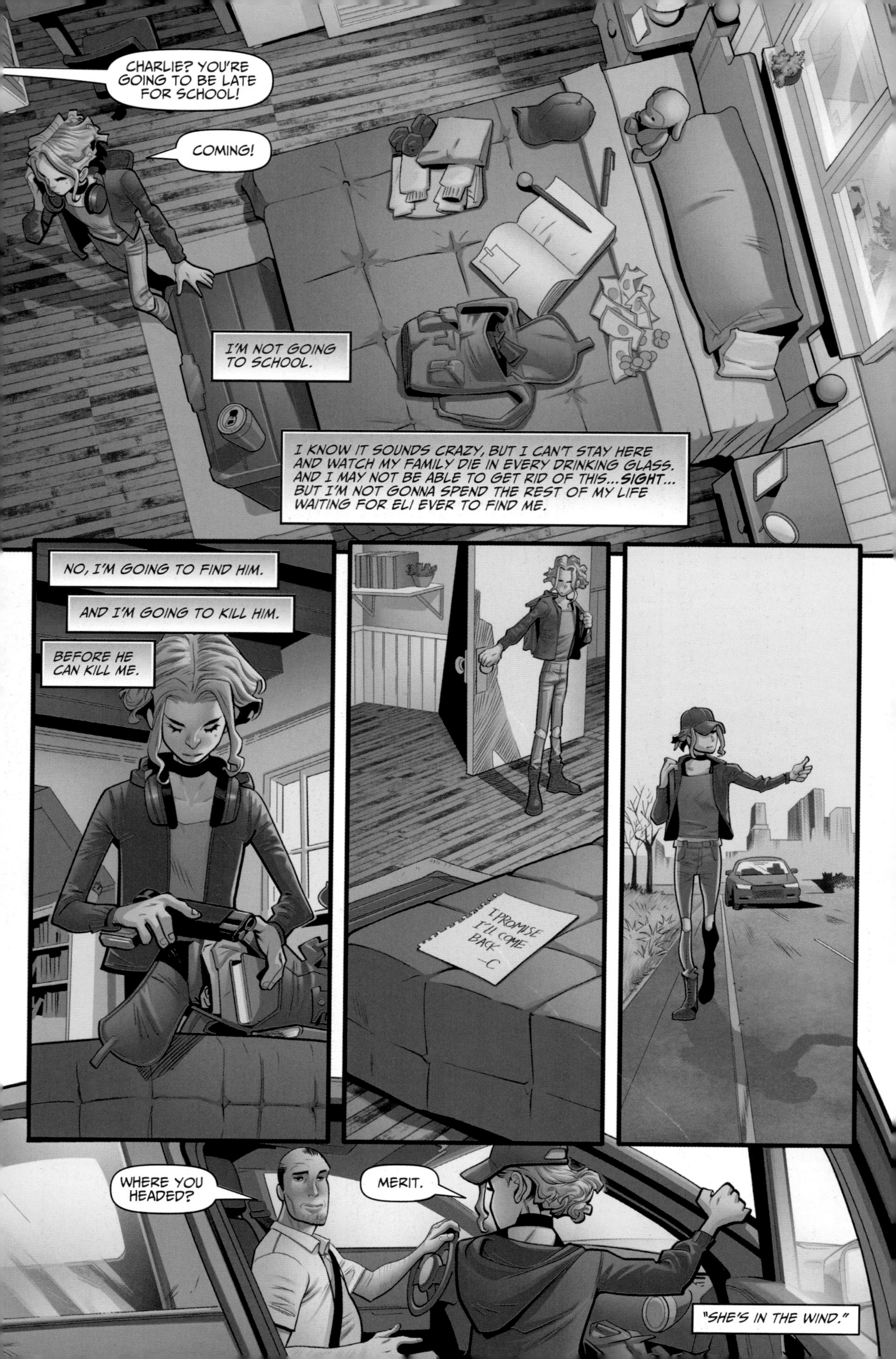
CHARLIE? YOU'RE GOING TO BE LATE FOR SCHOOL!
COMING!
I'M NOT GOING TO SCHOOL.
I KNOW IT SOUNDS CRAZY, BUT I CAN'T STAY HERE AND WATCH MY FAMILY DIE IN EVERY DRINKING GLASS. AND I MAY NOT BE ABLE TO GET RID OF THIS... SIGHT... BUT I'M NOT GONNA SPEND THE REST OF MY LIFE WAITING FOR ELI EVER TO FIND ME.
NO, I'M GOING TO FIND HIM.
AND I'M GOING TO KILL HIM.
BEFORE HE CAN KILL ME.
I PROMISE I'LL COME BACK —C
WHERE YOU HEADED?
MERIT.
"SHE'S IN THE WIND."

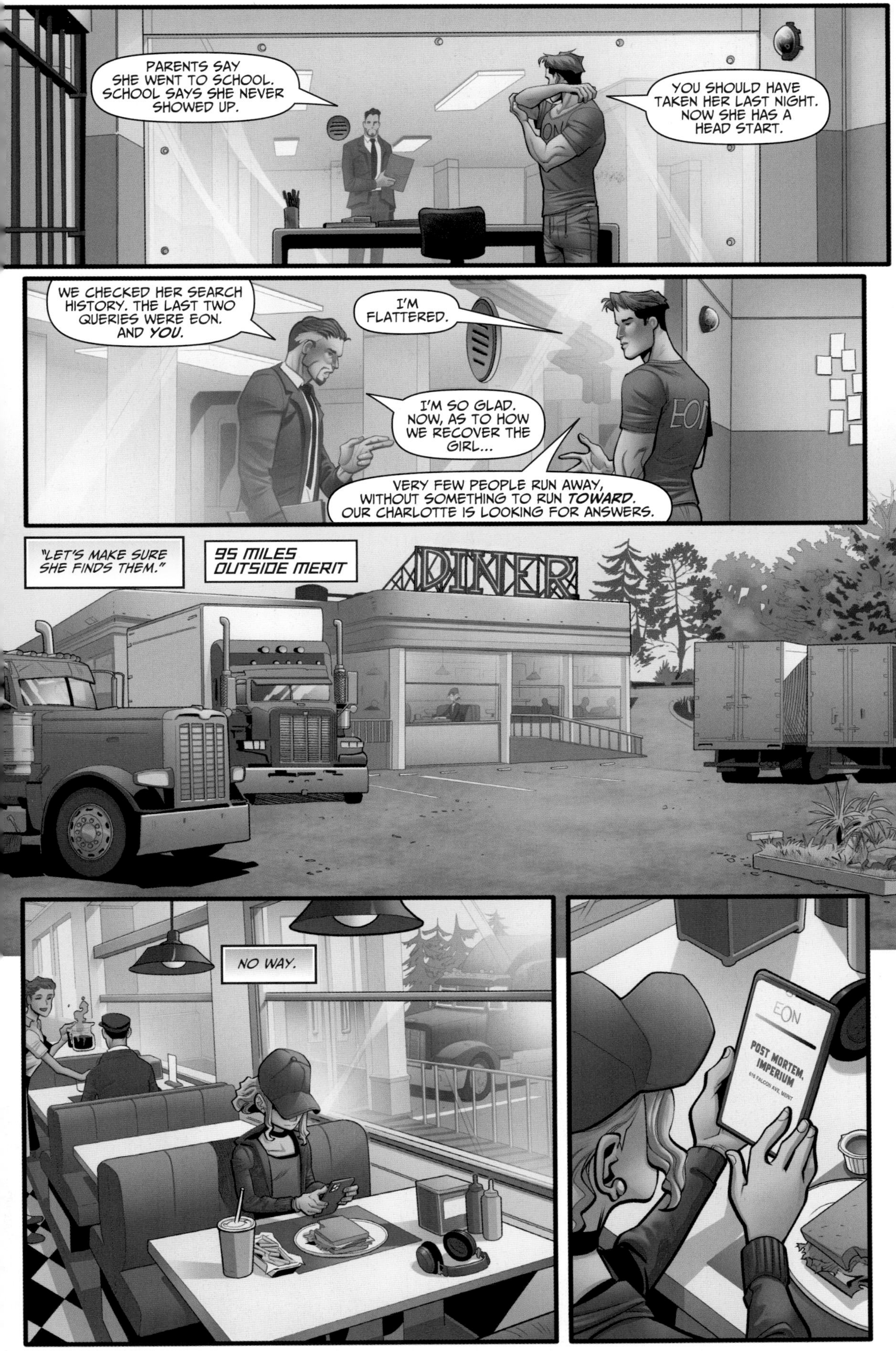
PARENTS SAY SHE WENT TO SCHOOL. SCHOOL SAYS SHE NEVER SHOWED UP.
EON
YOU SHOULD HAVE TAKEN HER LAST NIGHT. NOW SHE HAS A HEAD START.
WE CHECKED HER SEARCH HISTORY. THE LAST TWO QUERIES WERE EON. AND *YOU*.
I'M FLATTERED.
EON
I'M SO GLAD. NOW, AS TO HOW WE RECOVER THE GIRL...
VERY FEW PEOPLE RUN AWAY, WITHOUT SOMETHING TO RUN *TOWARD*. OUR CHARLOTTE IS LOOKING FOR ANSWERS.
"LET'S MAKE SURE SHE FINDS THEM."
95 MILES OUTSIDE MERIT
DINER
NO WAY.
EON
POST MORTEM, IMPERIUM
616 FALCON AVE, MERIT

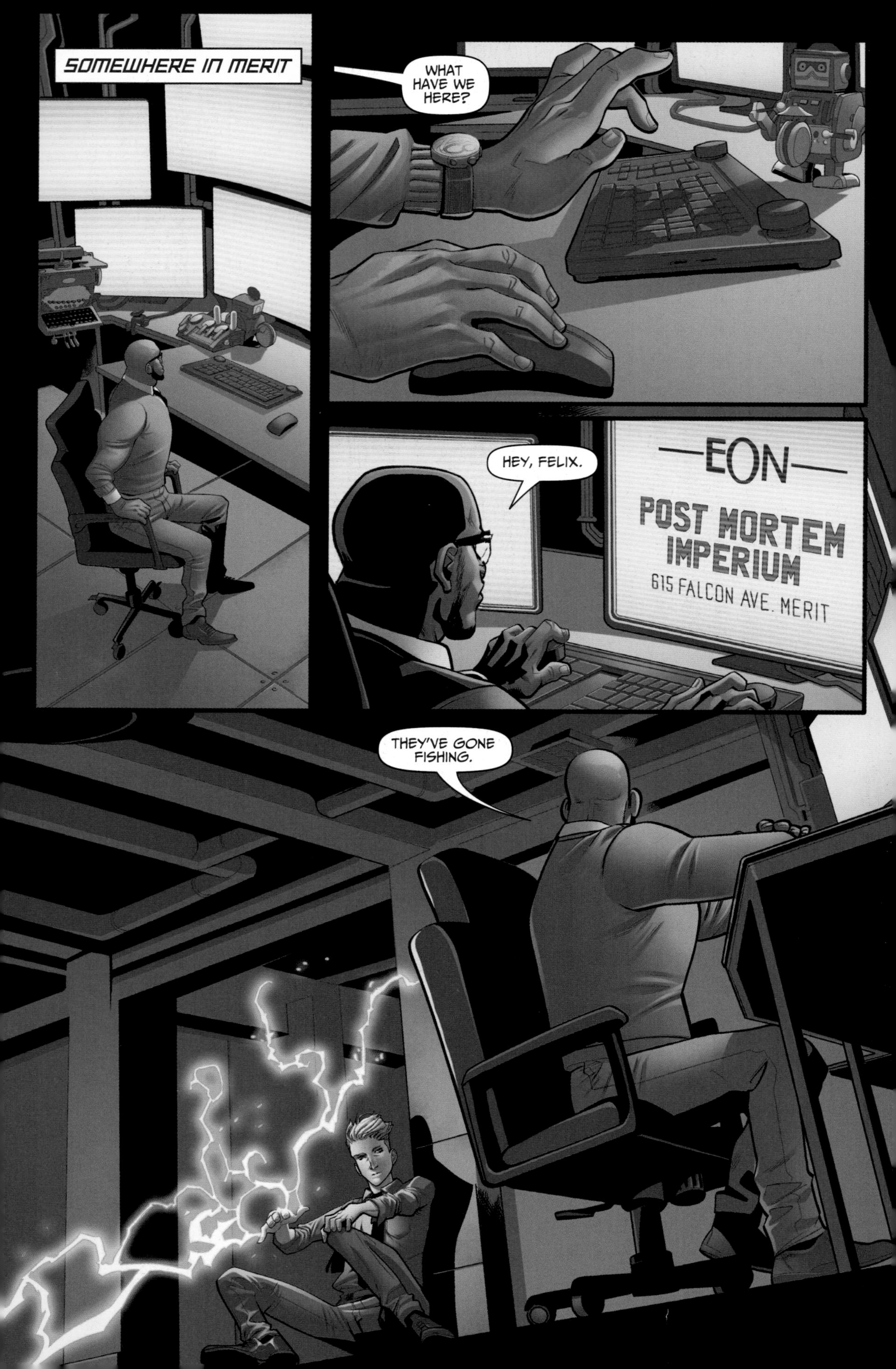
SOMEWHERE IN MERIT
WHAT HAVE WE HERE?
HEY, FELIX.
EON
POST MORTEM IMPERIUM
615 FALCON AVE. MERIT
THEY'VE GONE FISHING.

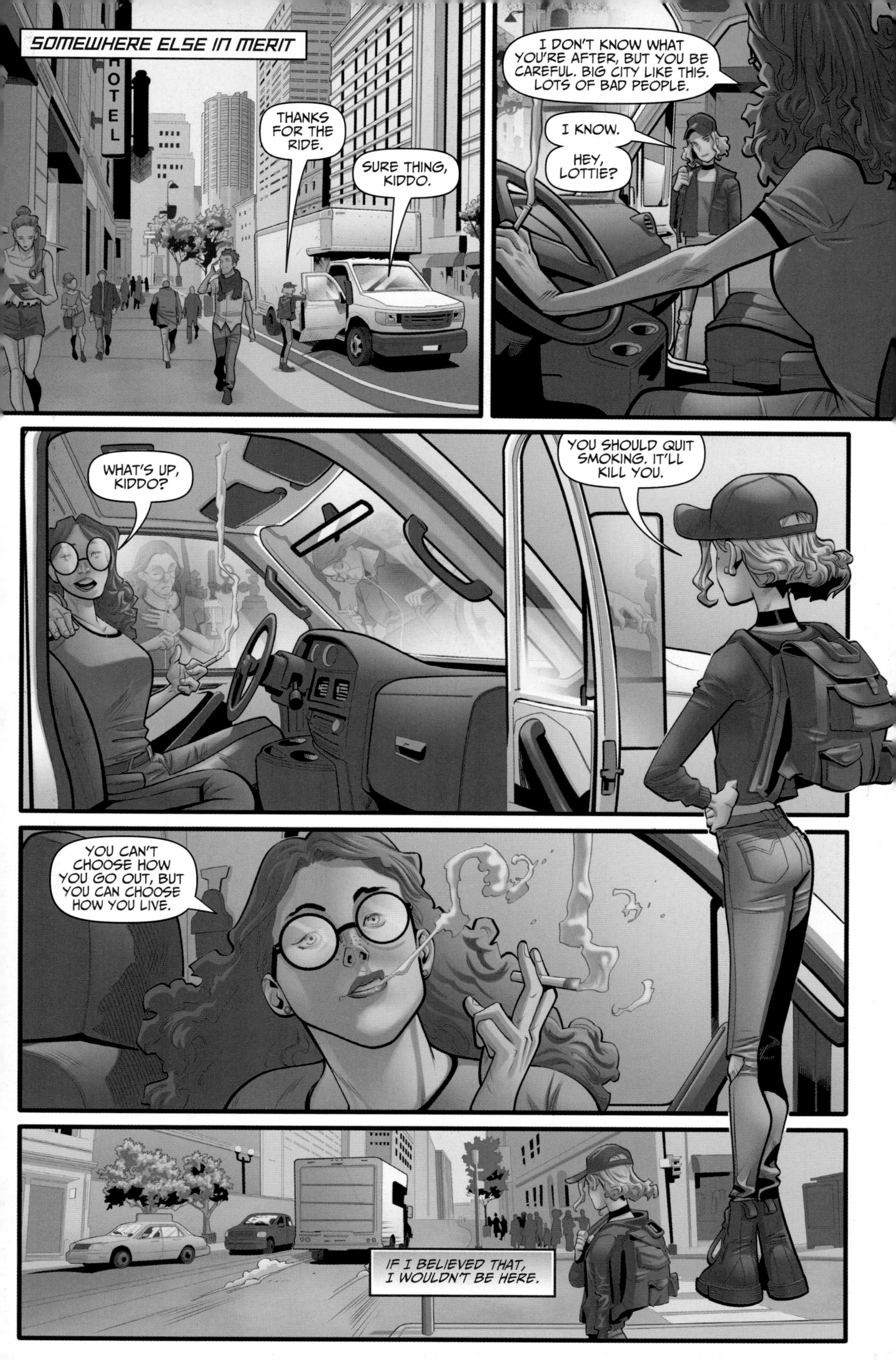
SOMEWHERE ELSE IN MERIT
HOTEL
THANKS FOR THE RIDE.
SURE THING, KIDDO.
I DON'T KNOW WHAT YOU'RE AFTER, BUT YOU BE CAREFUL. BIG CITY LIKE THIS. LOTS OF BAD PEOPLE.
I KNOW.
HEY, LOTTIE?
WHAT'S UP, KIDDO?
YOU SHOULD QUIT SMOKING. IT'LL KILL YOU.
YOU CAN'T CHOOSE HOW YOU GO OUT, BUT YOU CAN CHOOSE HOW YOU LIVE.
IF I BELIEVED THAT, I WOULDN'T BE HERE.

POST MORTEM, IMPERIUM.
AFTER DEATH, POWER
(THANKS, LATIN CLASS).

MY VISION CHANGED AFTER
THE ACCIDENT. AFTER I DIED--

--AND CAME BACK.

FALCON AVE.

615 FALCON AVE

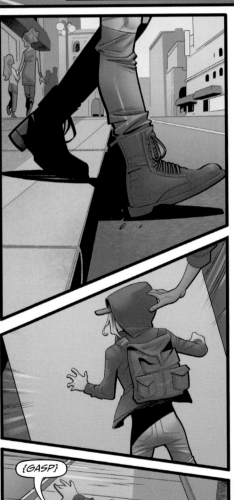

{GASP}

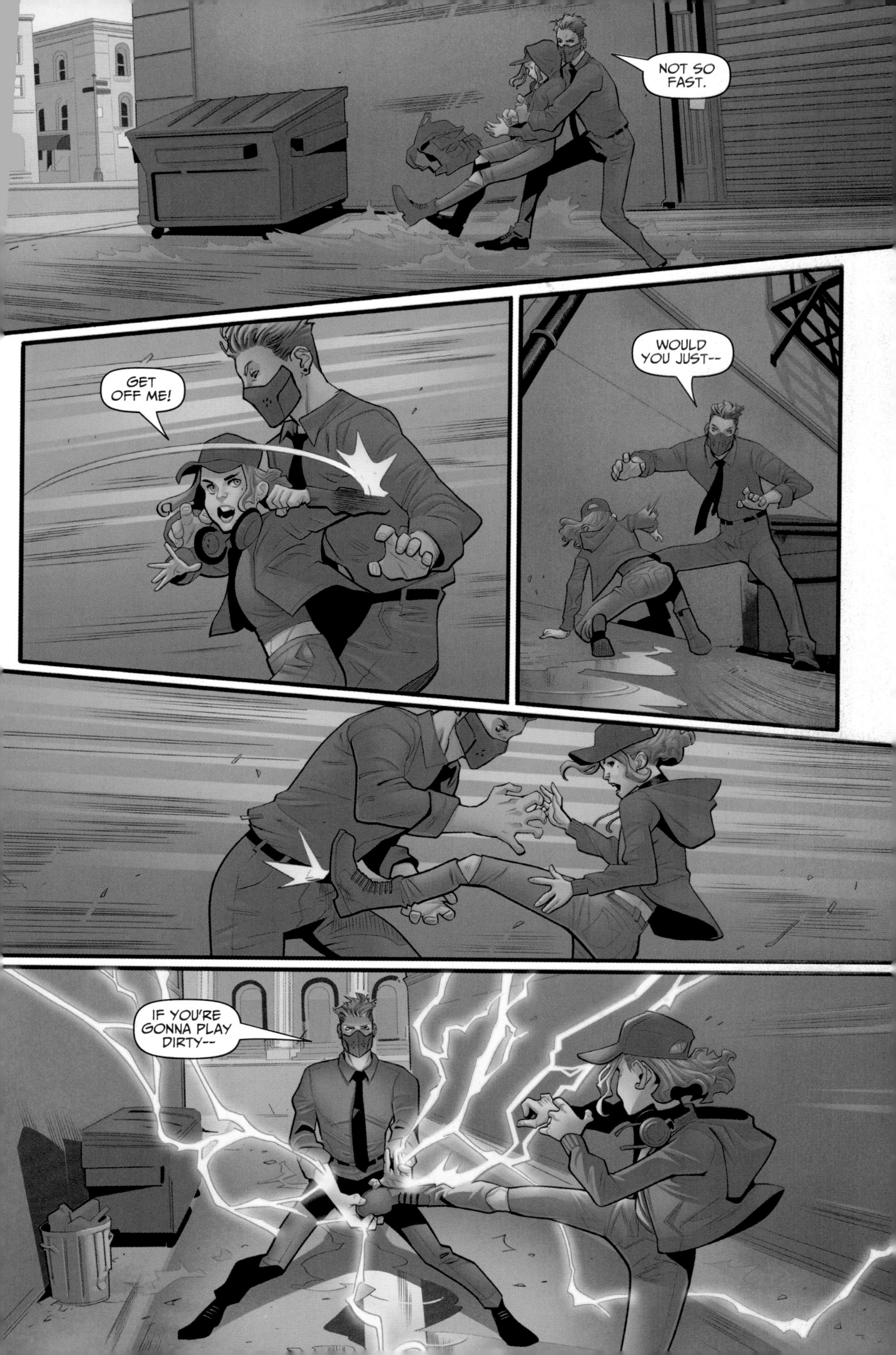
NOT SO FAST.
GET OFF ME!
WOULD YOU JUST--
IF YOU'RE GONNA PLAY DIRTY--

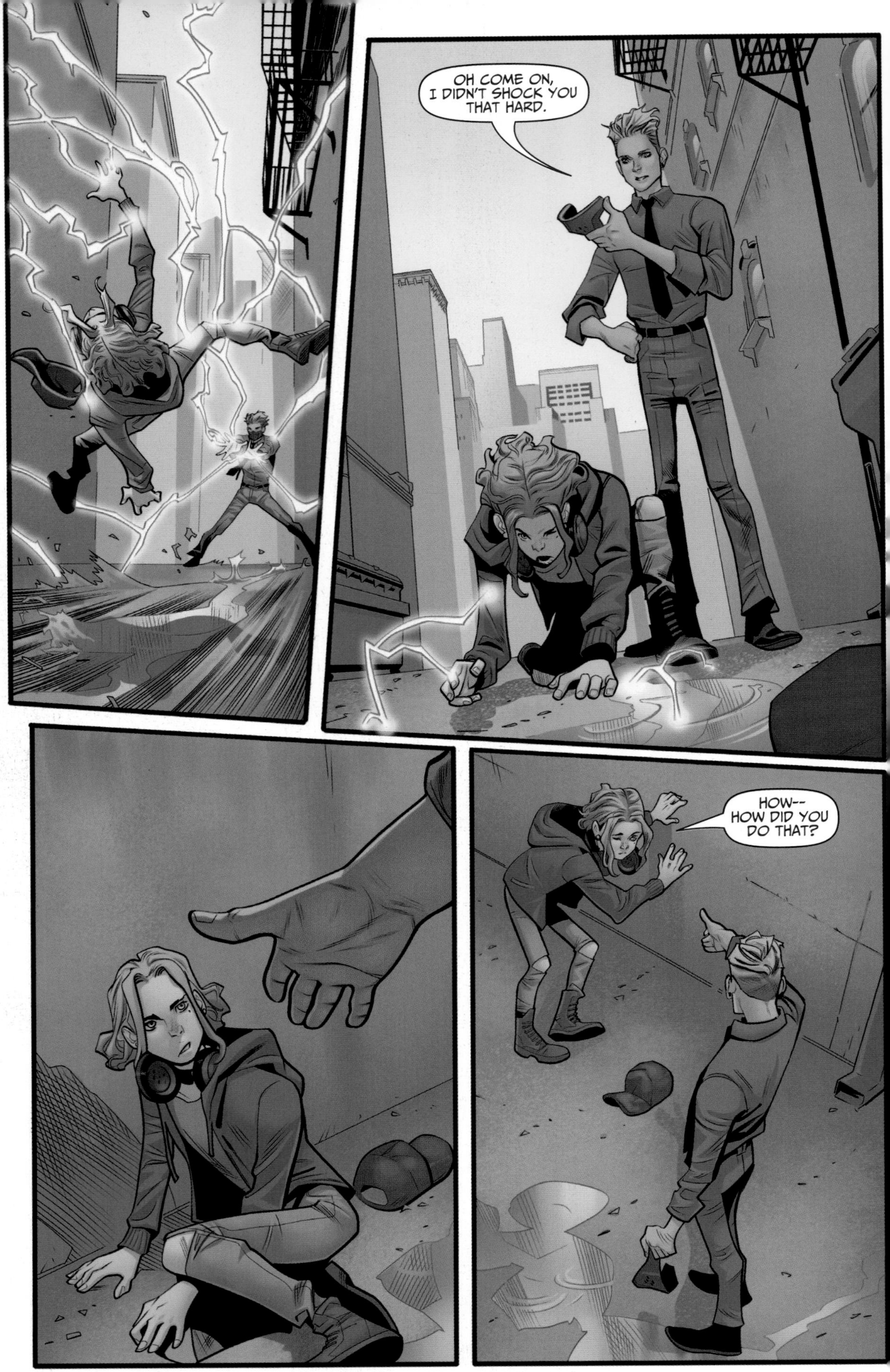
OH COME ON, I DIDN'T SHOCK YOU THAT HARD.
HOW-- HOW DID YOU DO THAT?

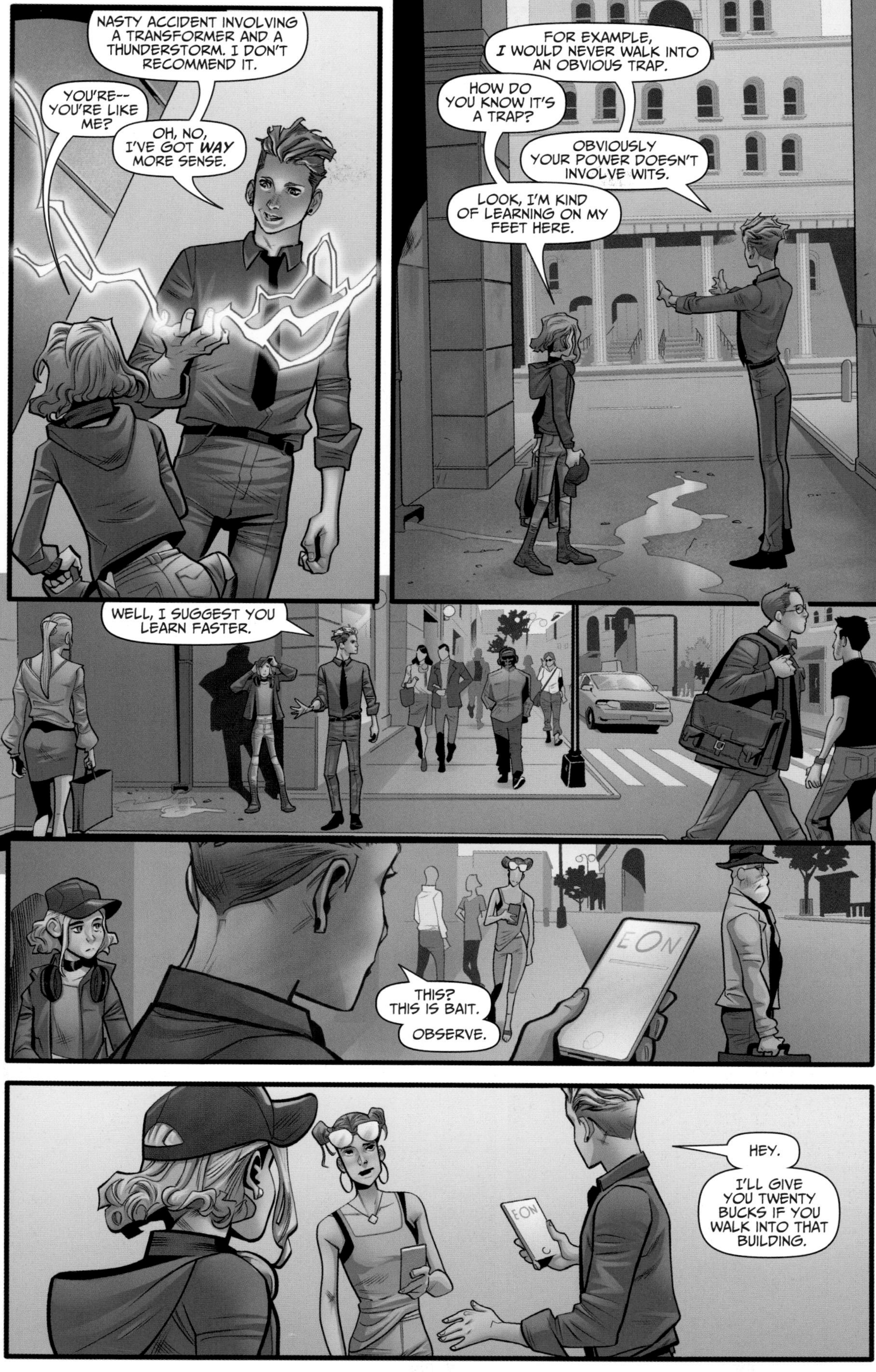
NASTY ACCIDENT INVOLVING A TRANSFORMER AND A THUNDERSTORM. I DON'T RECOMMEND IT.
YOU'RE-- YOU'RE LIKE ME?
OH, NO, I'VE GOT **WAY** MORE SENSE.
FOR EXAMPLE, I WOULD NEVER WALK INTO AN OBVIOUS TRAP.
HOW DO YOU KNOW IT'S A TRAP?
OBVIOUSLY YOUR POWER DOESN'T INVOLVE WITS.
LOOK, I'M KIND OF LEARNING ON MY FEET HERE.
WELL, I SUGGEST YOU LEARN FASTER.
EON
THIS? THIS IS BAIT.
OBSERVE.
HEY.
I'LL GIVE YOU TWENTY BUCKS IF YOU WALK INTO THAT BUILDING.

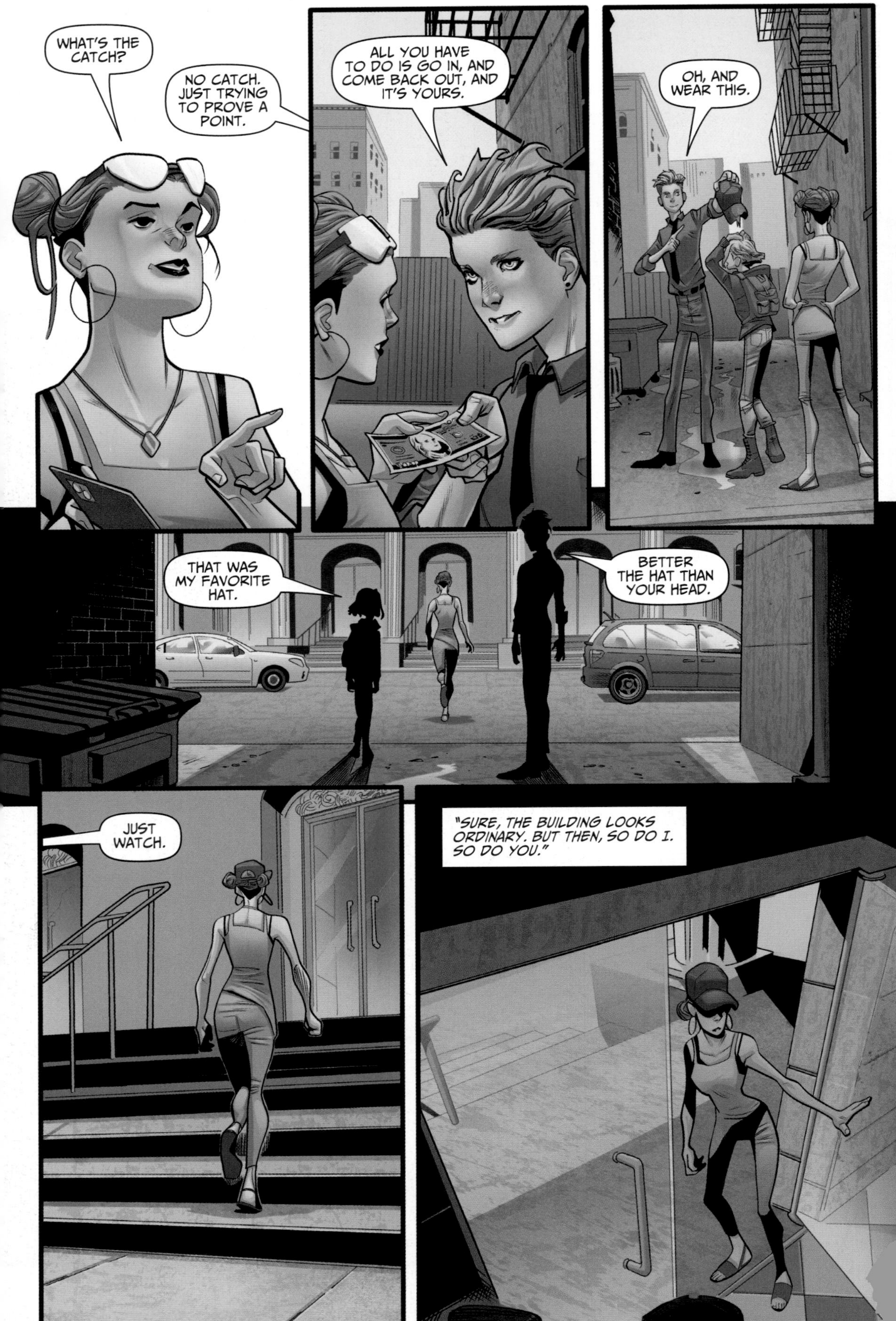
WHAT'S THE CATCH?
NO CATCH. JUST TRYING TO PROVE A POINT.
ALL YOU HAVE TO DO IS GO IN, AND COME BACK OUT, AND IT'S YOURS.
OH, AND WEAR THIS.
THAT WAS MY FAVORITE HAT.
BETTER THE HAT THAN YOUR HEAD.
JUST WATCH.
"SURE, THE BUILDING LOOKS ORDINARY. BUT THEN, SO DO I. SO DO YOU."

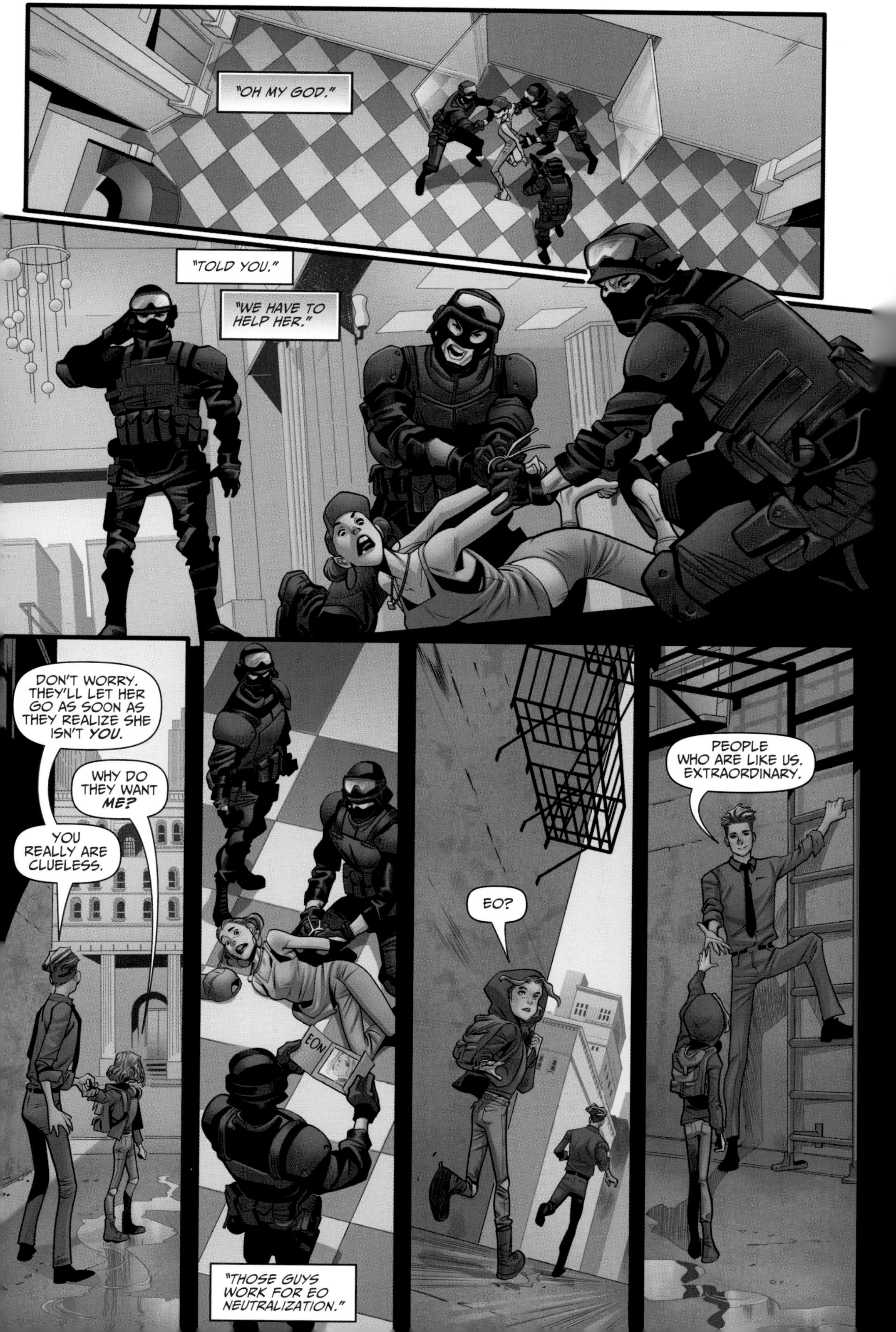
"OH MY GOD."
"TOLD YOU."
"WE HAVE TO HELP HER."
DON'T WORRY. THEY'LL LET HER GO AS SOON AS THEY REALIZE SHE ISN'T YOU.
WHY DO THEY WANT ME?
YOU REALLY ARE CLUELESS.
EON
"THOSE GUYS WORK FOR EO NEUTRALIZATION."
EO?
PEOPLE WHO ARE LIKE US. EXTRAORDINARY.

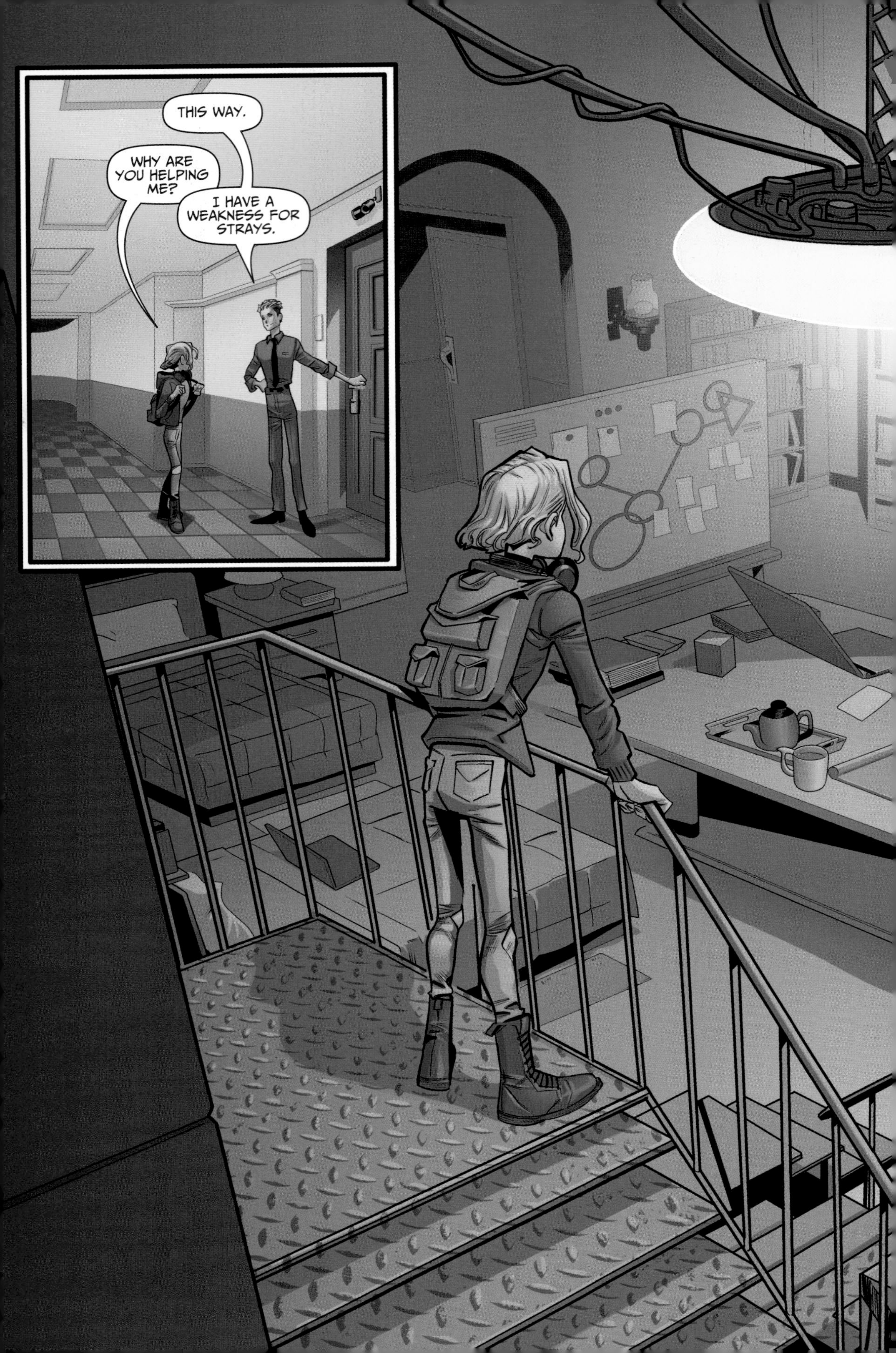
THIS WAY.
WHY ARE YOU HELPING ME?
I HAVE A WEAKNESS FOR STRAYS.

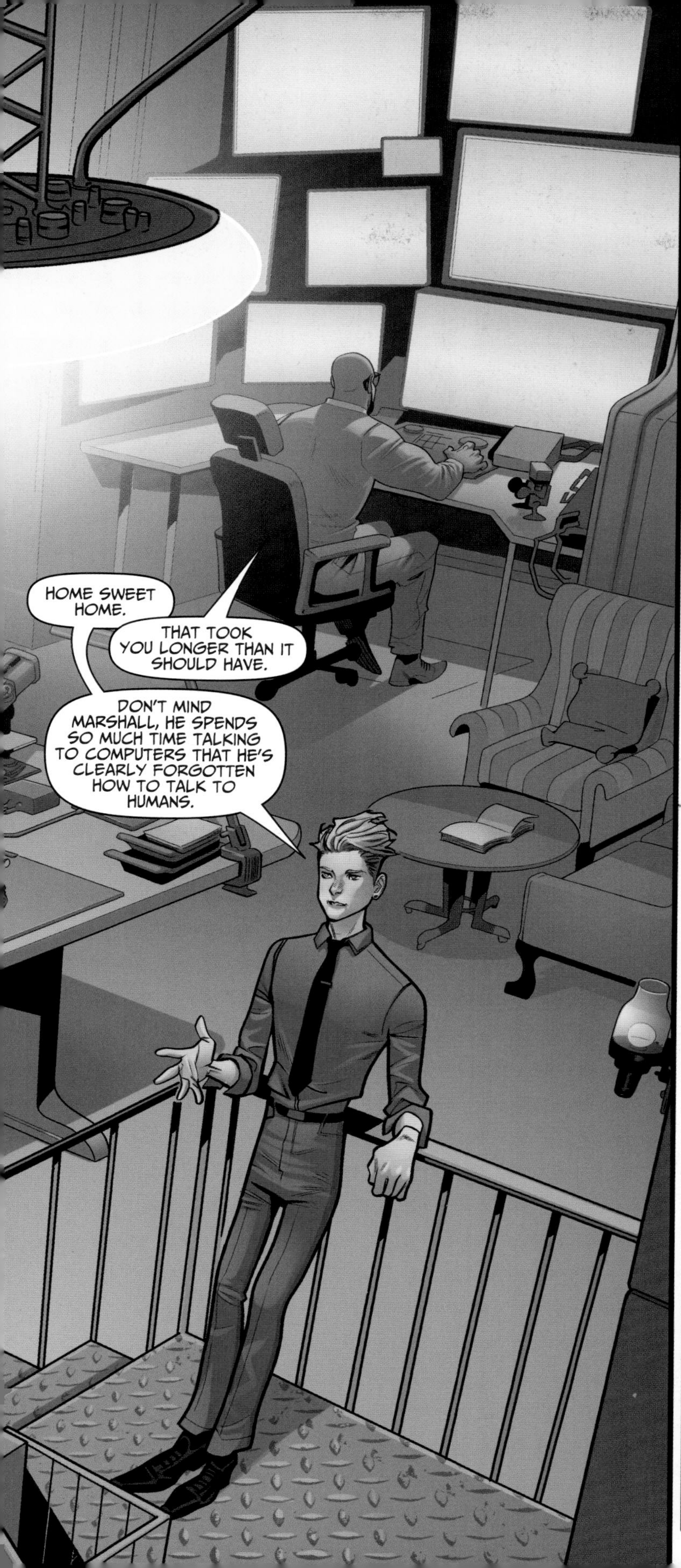
HOME SWEET HOME.
THAT TOOK YOU LONGER THAN IT SHOULD HAVE.
DON'T MIND MARSHALL, HE SPENDS SO MUCH TIME TALKING TO COMPUTERS THAT HE'S CLEARLY FORGOTTEN HOW TO TALK TO HUMANS.
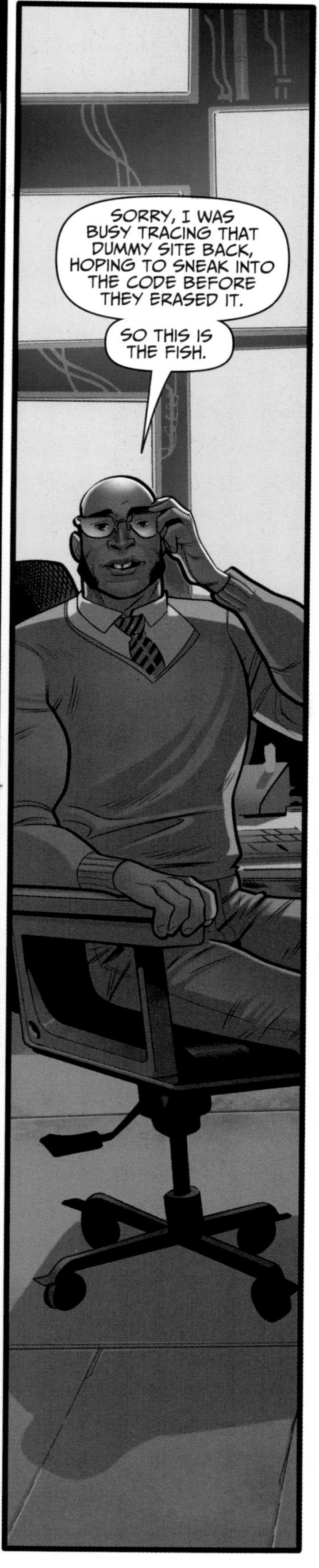
SORRY, I WAS BUSY TRACING THAT DUMMY SITE BACK, HOPING TO SNEAK INTO THE CODE BEFORE THEY ERASED IT.
SO THIS IS THE FISH.

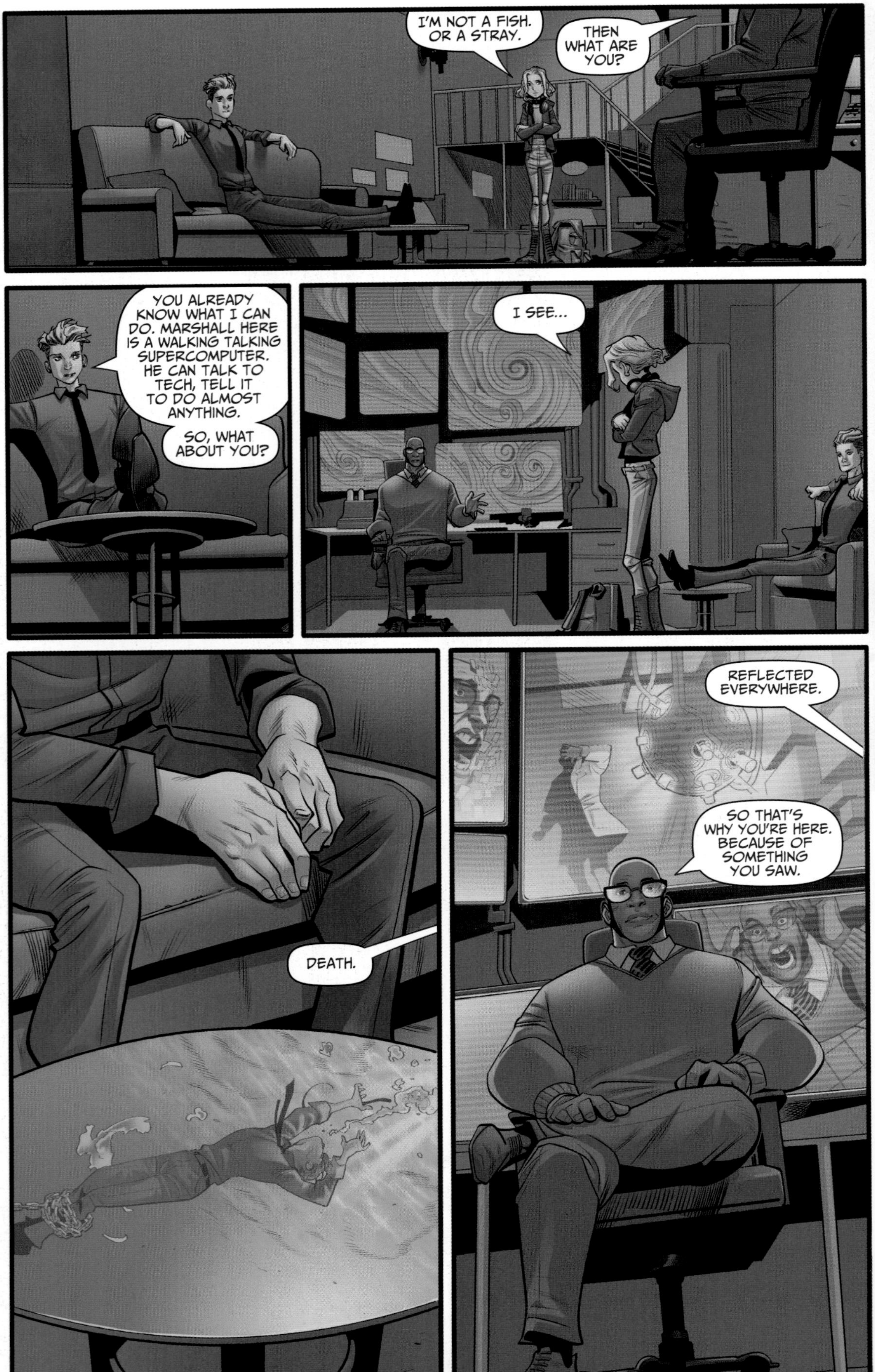
I'M NOT A FISH. OR A STRAY.
THEN WHAT ARE YOU?
YOU ALREADY KNOW WHAT I CAN DO. MARSHALL HERE IS A WALKING TALKING SUPERCOMPUTER. HE CAN TALK TO TECH, TELL IT TO DO ALMOST ANYTHING.
SO, WHAT ABOUT YOU?
I SEE...
DEATH.
REFLECTED EVERYWHERE.
SO THAT'S WHY YOU'RE HERE. BECAUSE OF SOMETHING YOU SAW.

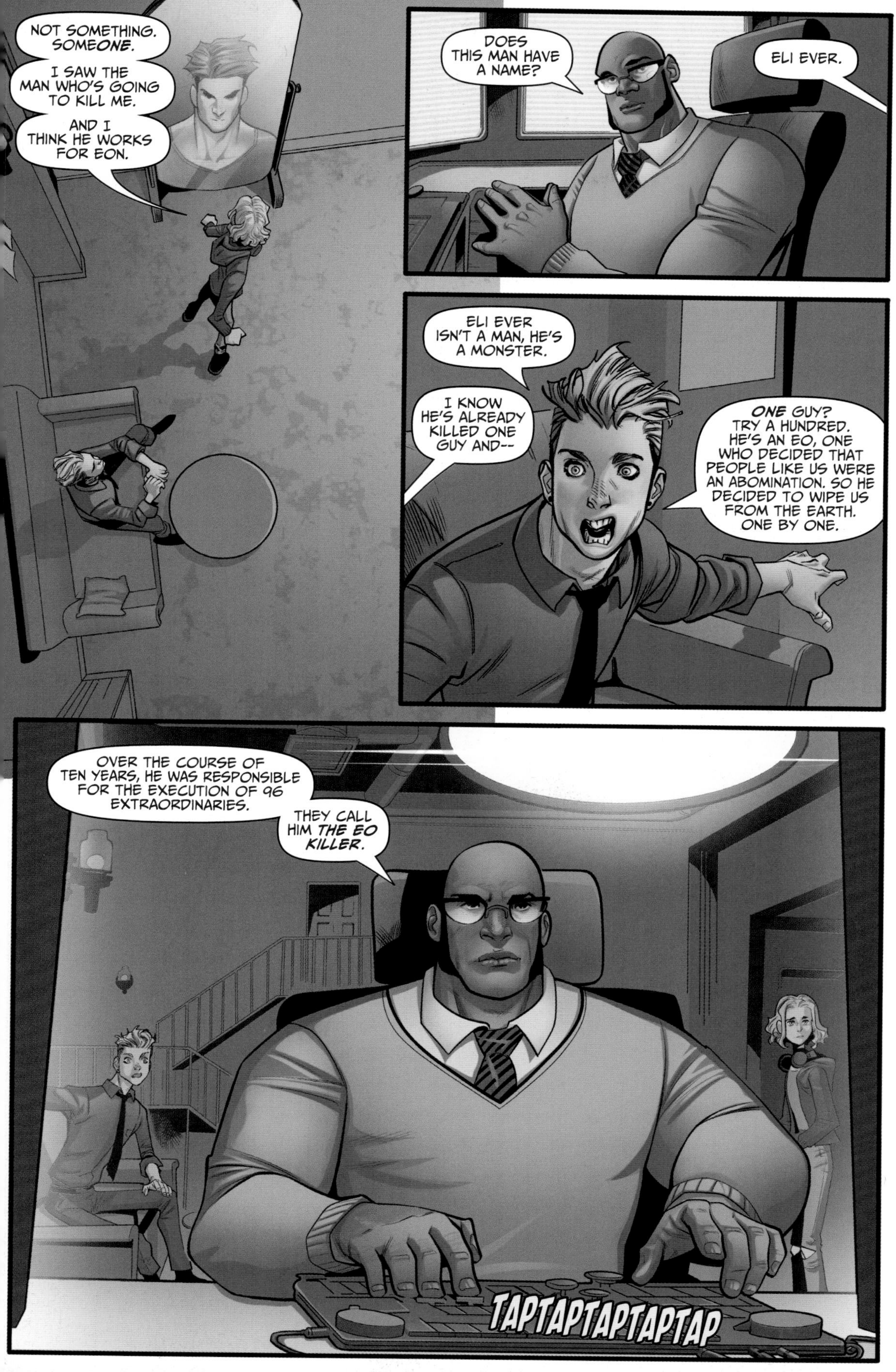
NOT SOMETHING. SOMEONE.
I SAW THE MAN WHO'S GOING TO KILL ME.
AND I THINK HE WORKS FOR EON.
DOES THIS MAN HAVE A NAME?
ELI EVER.
ELI EVER ISN'T A MAN, HE'S A MONSTER.
I KNOW HE'S ALREADY KILLED ONE GUY AND--
ONE GUY? TRY A HUNDRED. HE'S AN EO, ONE WHO DECIDED THAT PEOPLE LIKE US WERE AN ABOMINATION. SO HE DECIDED TO WIPE US FROM THE EARTH. ONE BY ONE.
OVER THE COURSE OF TEN YEARS, HE WAS RESPONSIBLE FOR THE EXECUTION OF 96 EXTRAORDINARIES.
THEY CALL HIM THE EO KILLER.
TAPTAPTAPTAPTAP

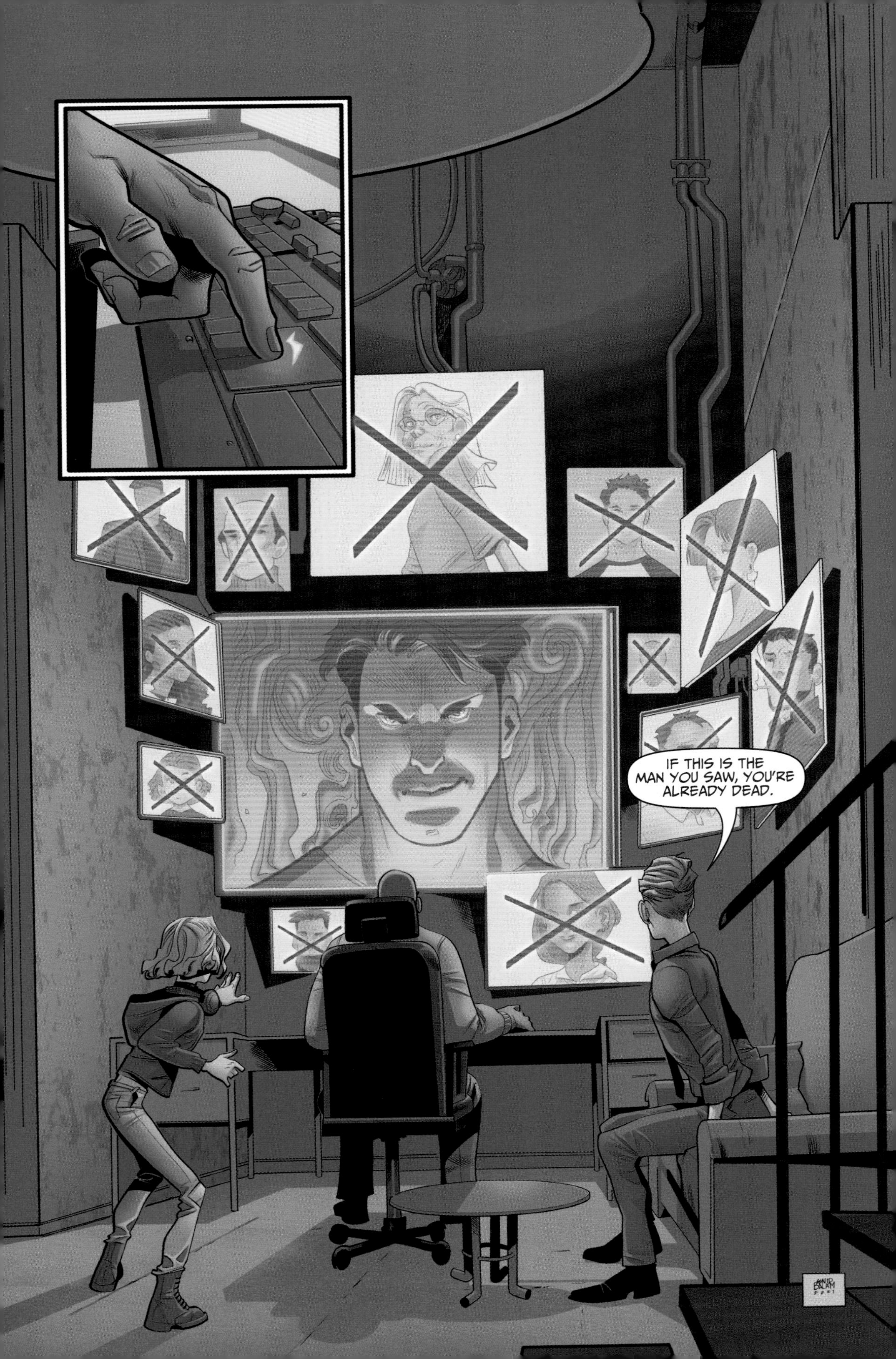
IF THIS IS THE MAN YOU SAW, YOU'RE ALREADY DEAD.

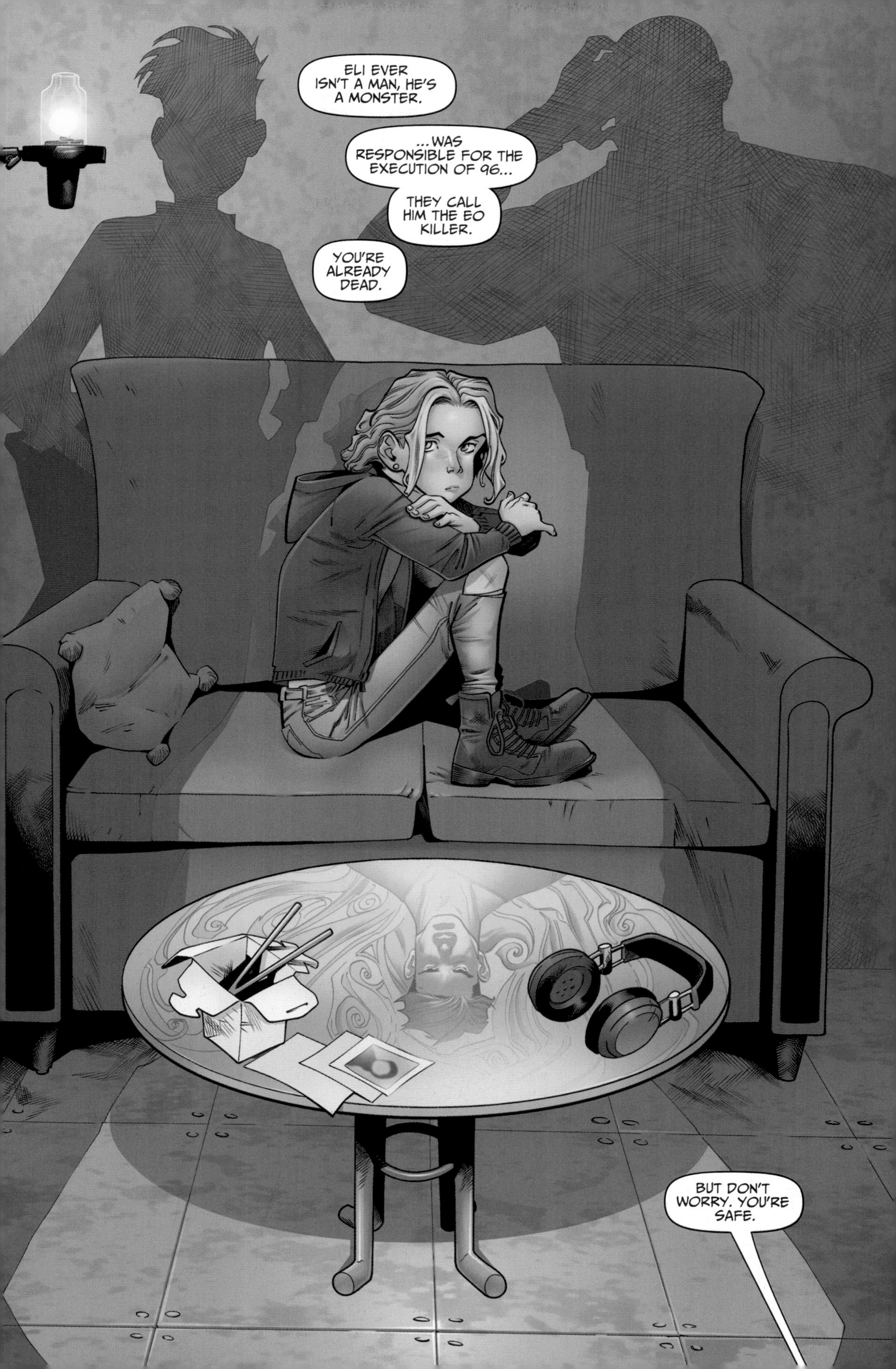
ELI EVER ISN'T A MAN, HE'S A MONSTER.
...WAS RESPONSIBLE FOR THE EXECUTION OF 96...
THEY CALL HIM THE EO KILLER.
YOU'RE ALREADY DEAD.
BUT DON'T WORRY. YOU'RE SAFE.

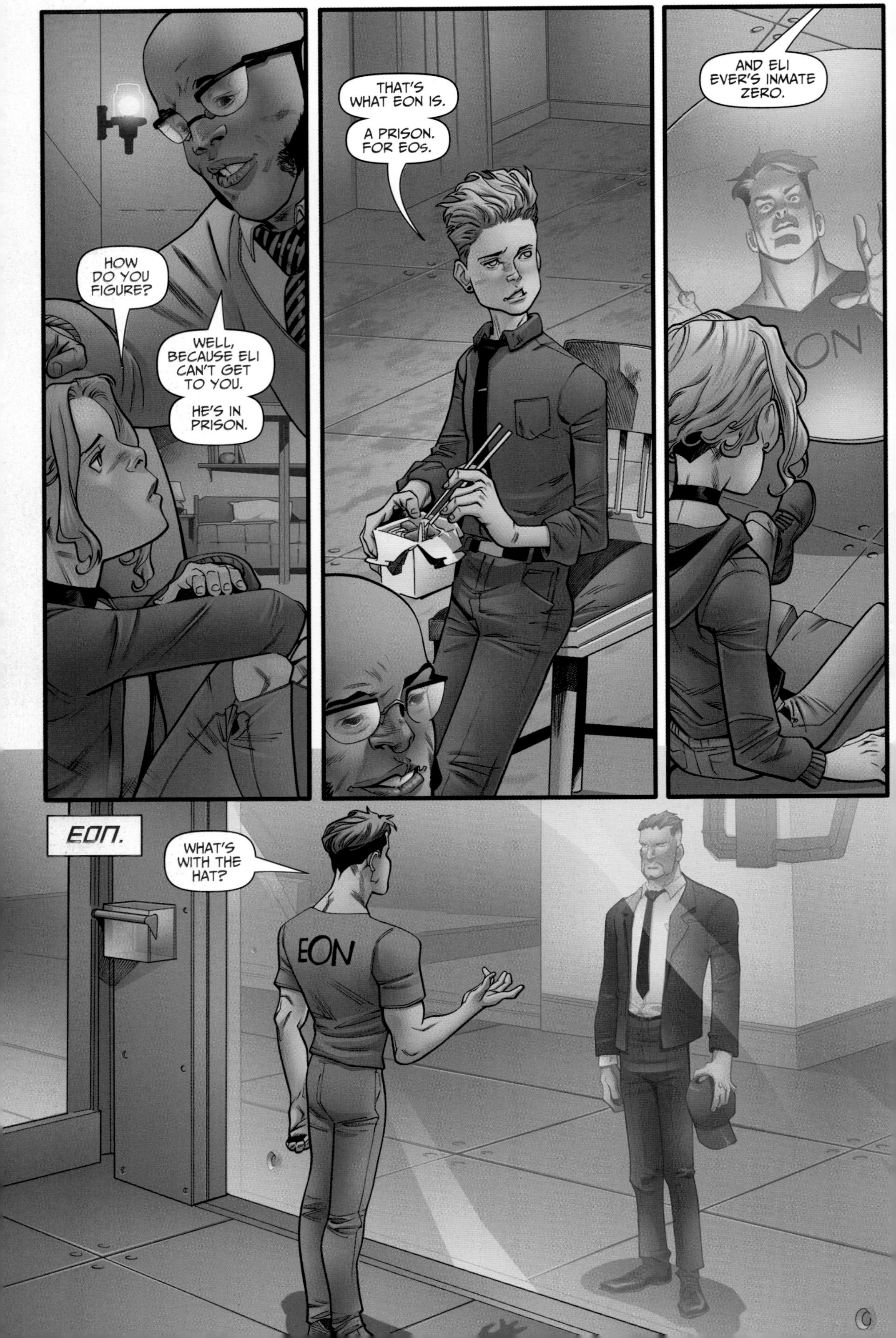
HOW DO YOU FIGURE?
WELL, BECAUSE ELI CAN'T GET TO YOU.
HE'S IN PRISON.
THAT'S WHAT EON IS.
A PRISON. FOR EOs.
AND ELI EVER'S INMATE ZERO.
EON
EON.
WHAT'S WITH THE HAT?
EON

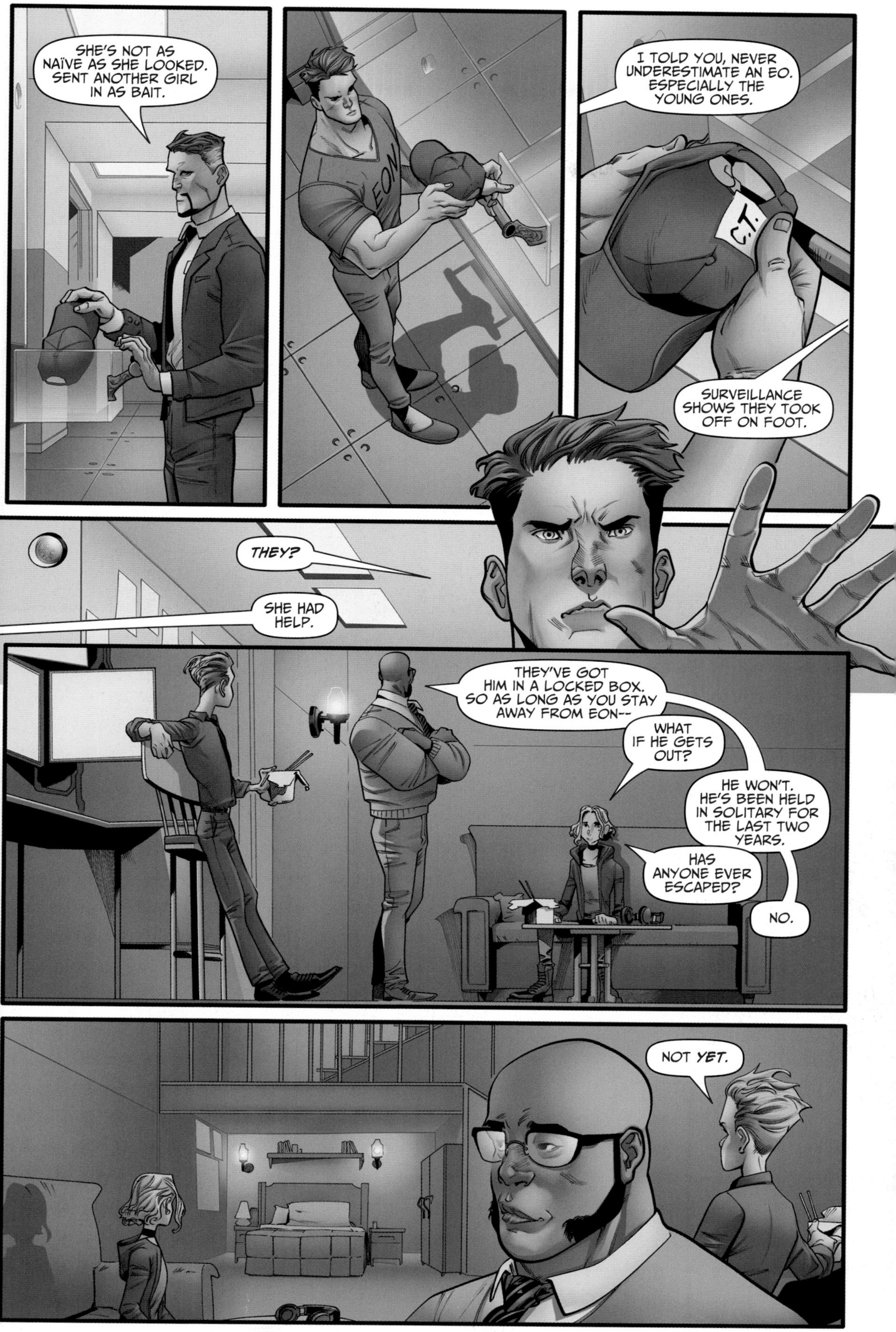
SHE'S NOT AS NAÏVE AS SHE LOOKED. SENT ANOTHER GIRL IN AS BAIT.
I TOLD YOU, NEVER UNDERESTIMATE AN EO. ESPECIALLY THE YOUNG ONES.
C.T.
SURVEILLANCE SHOWS THEY TOOK OFF ON FOOT.
THEY?
SHE HAD HELP.
THEY'VE GOT HIM IN A LOCKED BOX. SO AS LONG AS YOU STAY AWAY FROM EON--
WHAT IF HE GETS OUT?
HE WON'T. HE'S BEEN HELD IN SOLITARY FOR THE LAST TWO YEARS.
HAS ANYONE EVER ESCAPED?
NO.
NOT YET.

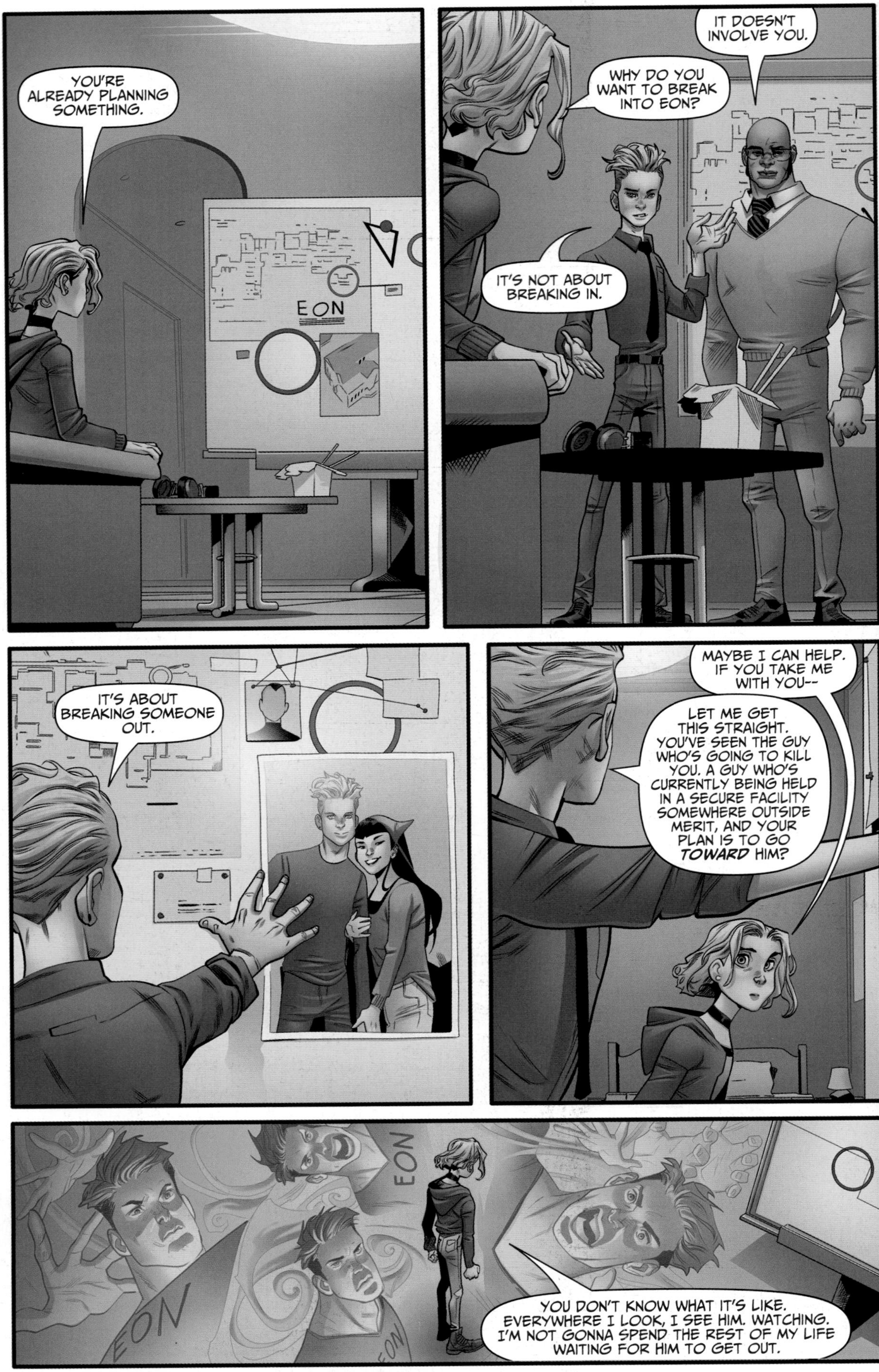
YOU'RE ALREADY PLANNING SOMETHING.
EON
WHY DO YOU WANT TO BREAK INTO EON?
IT DOESN'T INVOLVE YOU.
IT'S NOT ABOUT BREAKING IN.
IT'S ABOUT BREAKING SOMEONE OUT.
MAYBE I CAN HELP. IF YOU TAKE ME WITH YOU--
LET ME GET THIS STRAIGHT. YOU'VE SEEN THE GUY WHO'S GOING TO KILL YOU. A GUY WHO'S CURRENTLY BEING HELD IN A SECURE FACILITY SOMEWHERE OUTSIDE MERIT, AND YOUR PLAN IS TO GO *TOWARD* HIM?
EON
EON
EON
YOU DON'T KNOW WHAT IT'S LIKE. EVERYWHERE I LOOK, I SEE HIM. WATCHING. I'M NOT GONNA SPEND THE REST OF MY LIFE WAITING FOR HIM TO GET OUT.

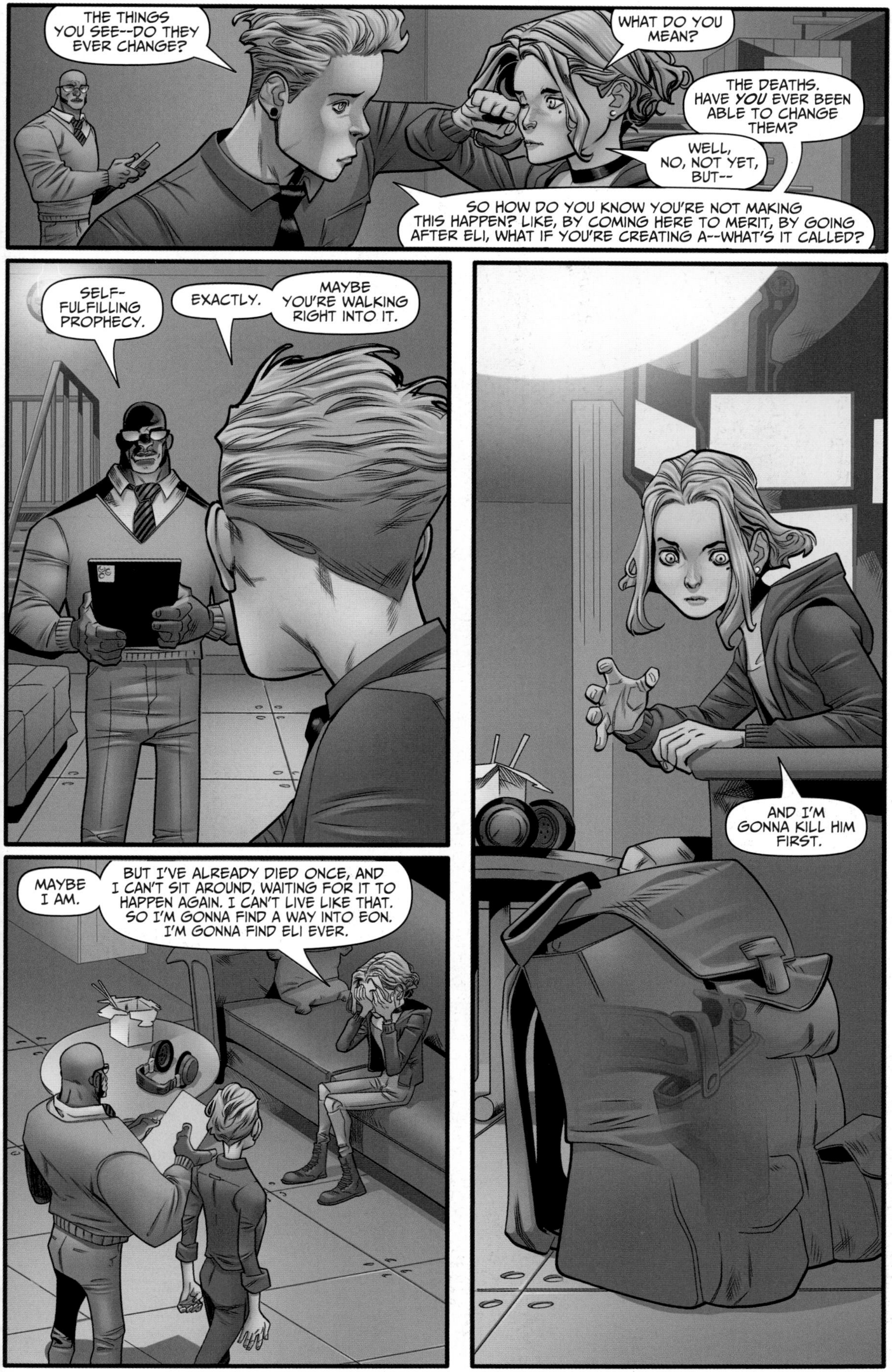
THE THINGS YOU SEE--DO THEY EVER CHANGE?
WHAT DO YOU MEAN?
THE DEATHS. HAVE YOU EVER BEEN ABLE TO CHANGE THEM?
WELL, NO, NOT YET, BUT--
SO HOW DO YOU KNOW YOU'RE NOT MAKING THIS HAPPEN? LIKE, BY COMING HERE TO MERIT, BY GOING AFTER ELI, WHAT IF YOU'RE CREATING A--WHAT'S IT CALLED?
SELF-FULFILLING PROPHECY.
EXACTLY.
MAYBE YOU'RE WALKING RIGHT INTO IT.
MAYBE I AM.
BUT I'VE ALREADY DIED ONCE, AND I CAN'T SIT AROUND, WAITING FOR IT TO HAPPEN AGAIN. I CAN'T LIVE LIKE THAT. SO I'M GONNA FIND A WAY INTO EON. I'M GONNA FIND ELI EVER.
AND I'M GONNA KILL HIM FIRST.

CONGRATULATIONS ON YOUR DEATH WISH.

FELIX. WITH HER HELP, OUR CHANCES WOULD IMPROVE BY A FACTOR OF--

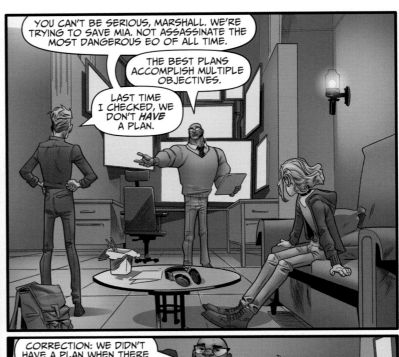

YOU CAN'T BE SERIOUS, MARSHALL. WE'RE TRYING TO SAVE MIA. NOT ASSASSINATE THE MOST DANGEROUS EO OF ALL TIME.

THE BEST PLANS ACCOMPLISH MULTIPLE OBJECTIVES.

LAST TIME I CHECKED, WE DON'T *HAVE* A PLAN.

CORRECTION: WE DIDN'T HAVE A PLAN WHEN THERE WERE TWO OF US.

BUT I MIGHT HAVE ONE FOR THREE.

HEY, IS THERE A BATHROOM?

BLUE DOOR.

I NEED YOUR PHONE.

MAKE SURE YOU KEEP IT OFF. IF IT'S ON, THEY CAN TRACK IT.

YEAH, I'VE WATCHED ENOUGH TV TO KNOW THAT.

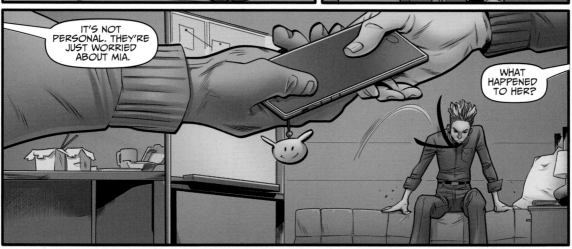

IT'S NOT PERSONAL. THEY'RE JUST WORRIED ABOUT MIA.

WHAT HAPPENED TO HER?

THE SAME THING THAT ALMOST HAPPENED TO YOU.

SHE GOT CAUGHT.

"COME ON... COME ON..."

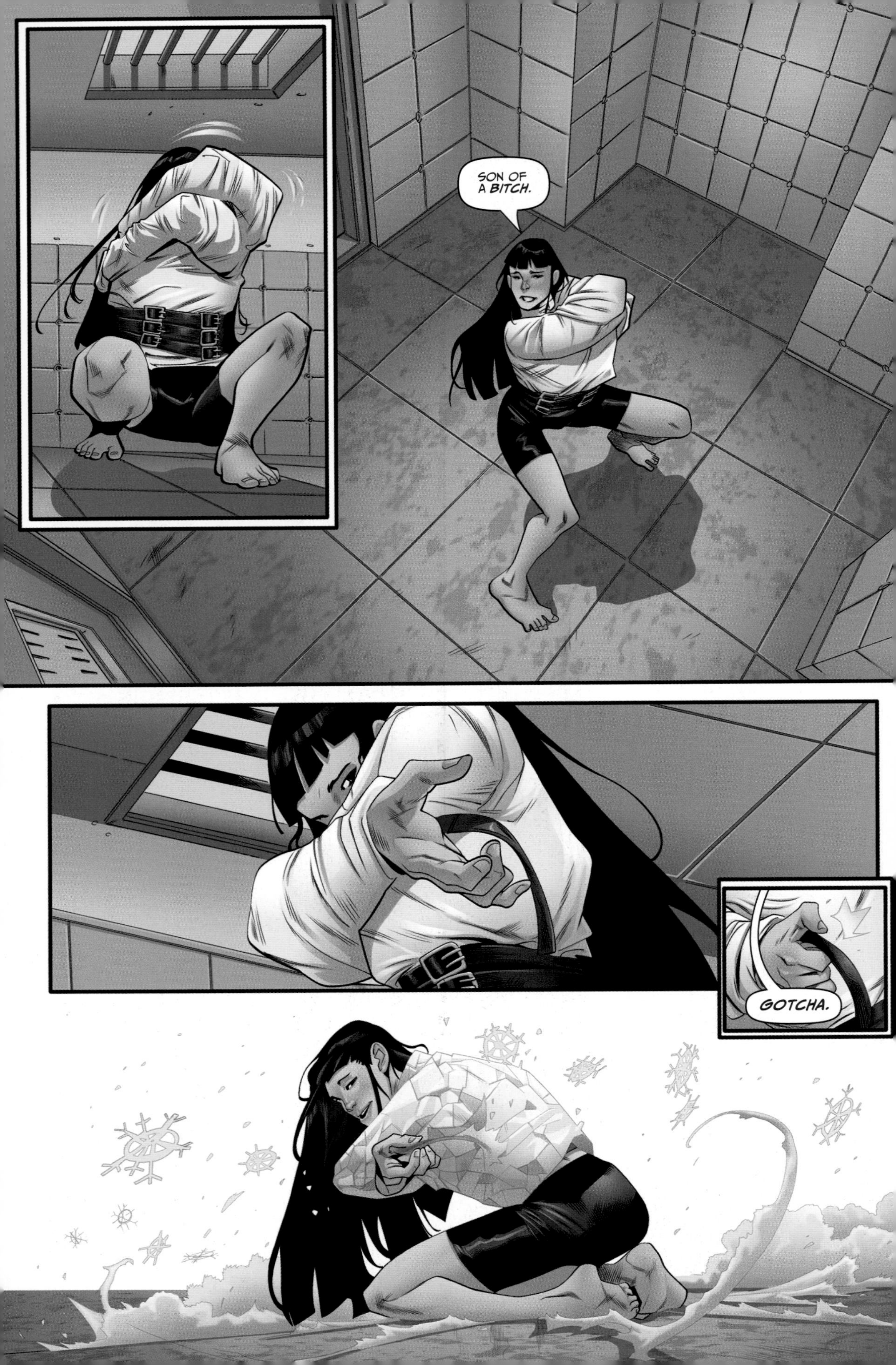
SON OF A BITCH.
GOTCHA.

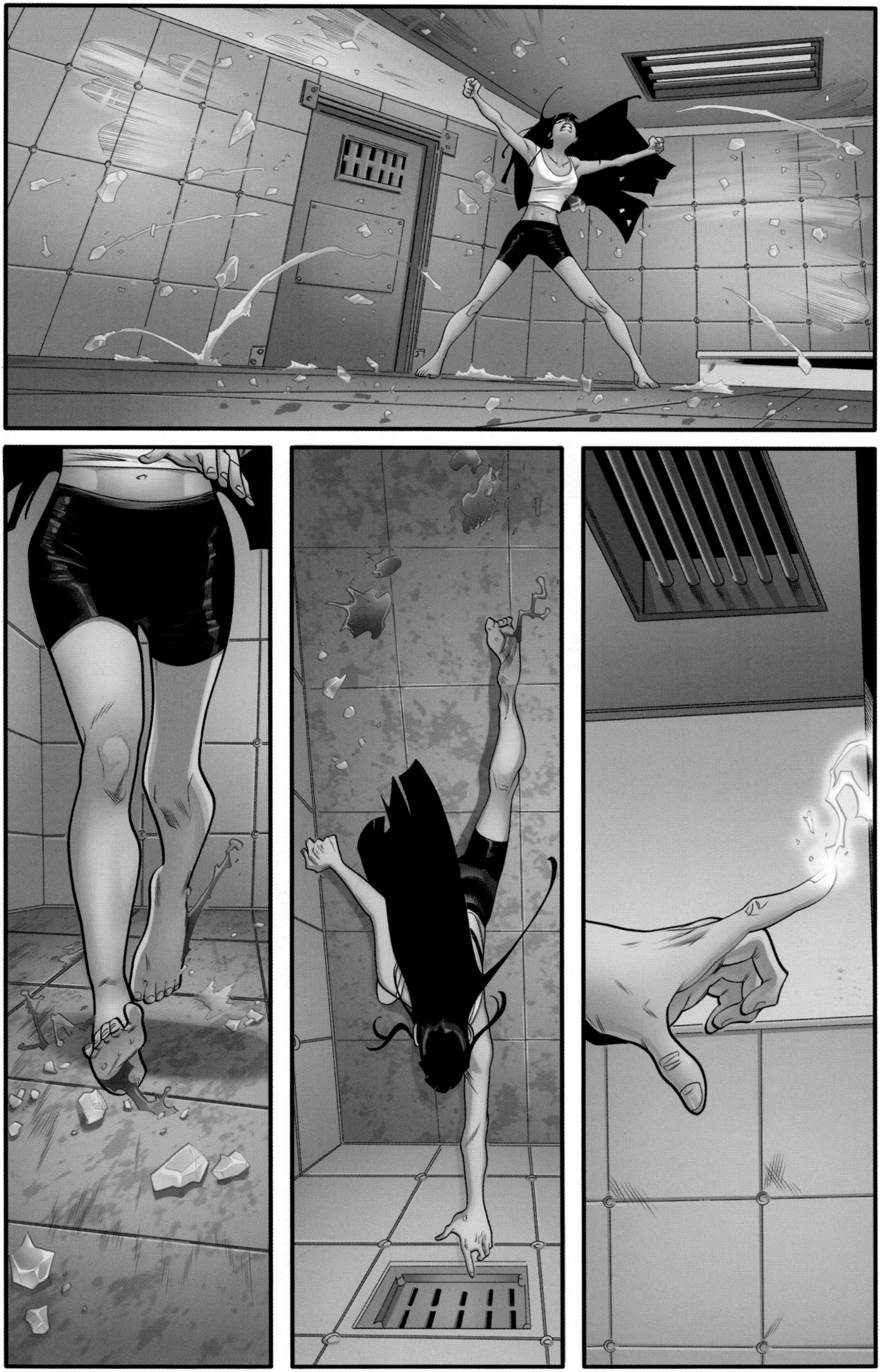

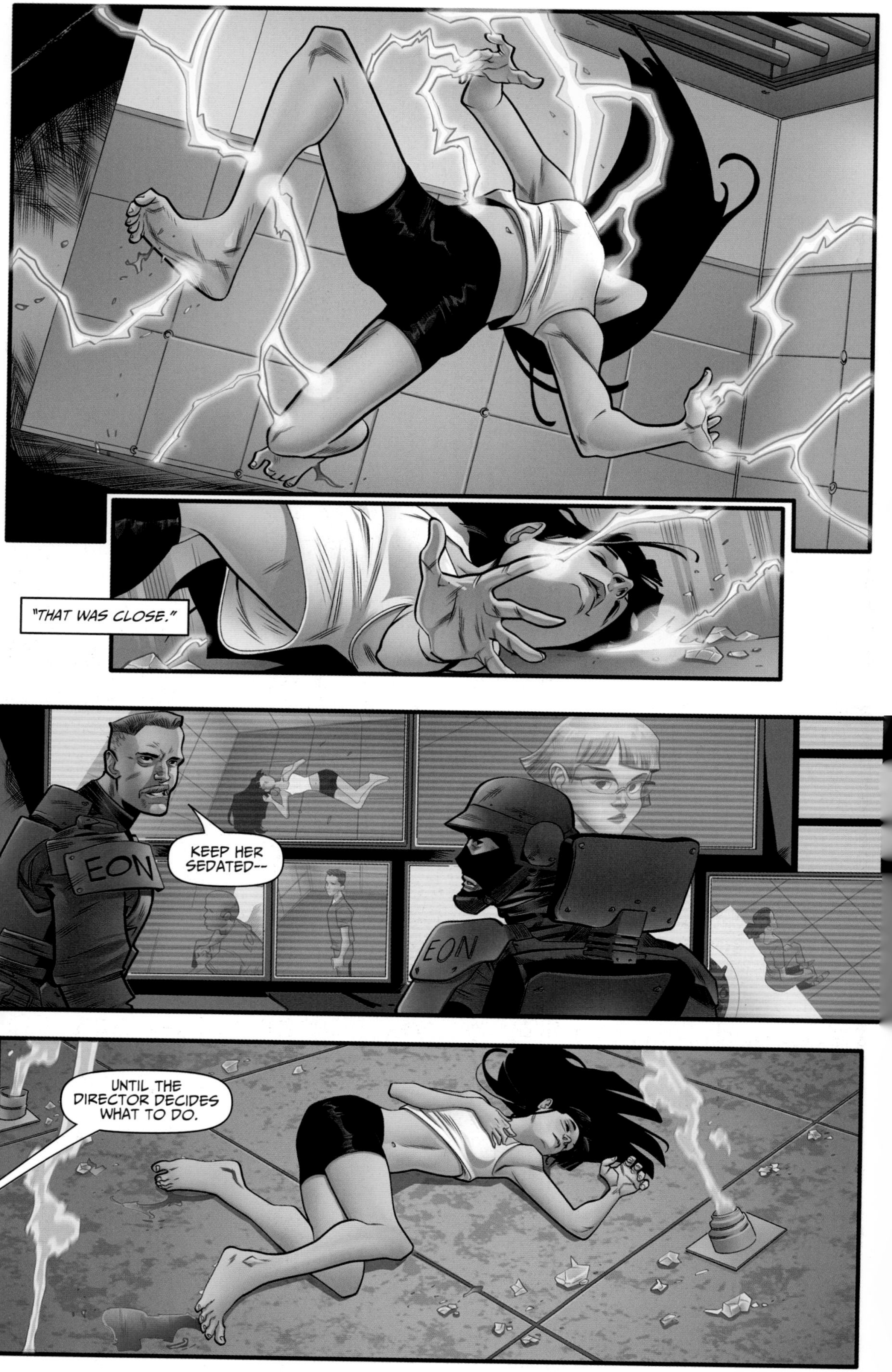
"THAT WAS CLOSE."
KEEP HER SEDATED--
EON
EON
UNTIL THE DIRECTOR DECIDES WHAT TO DO.

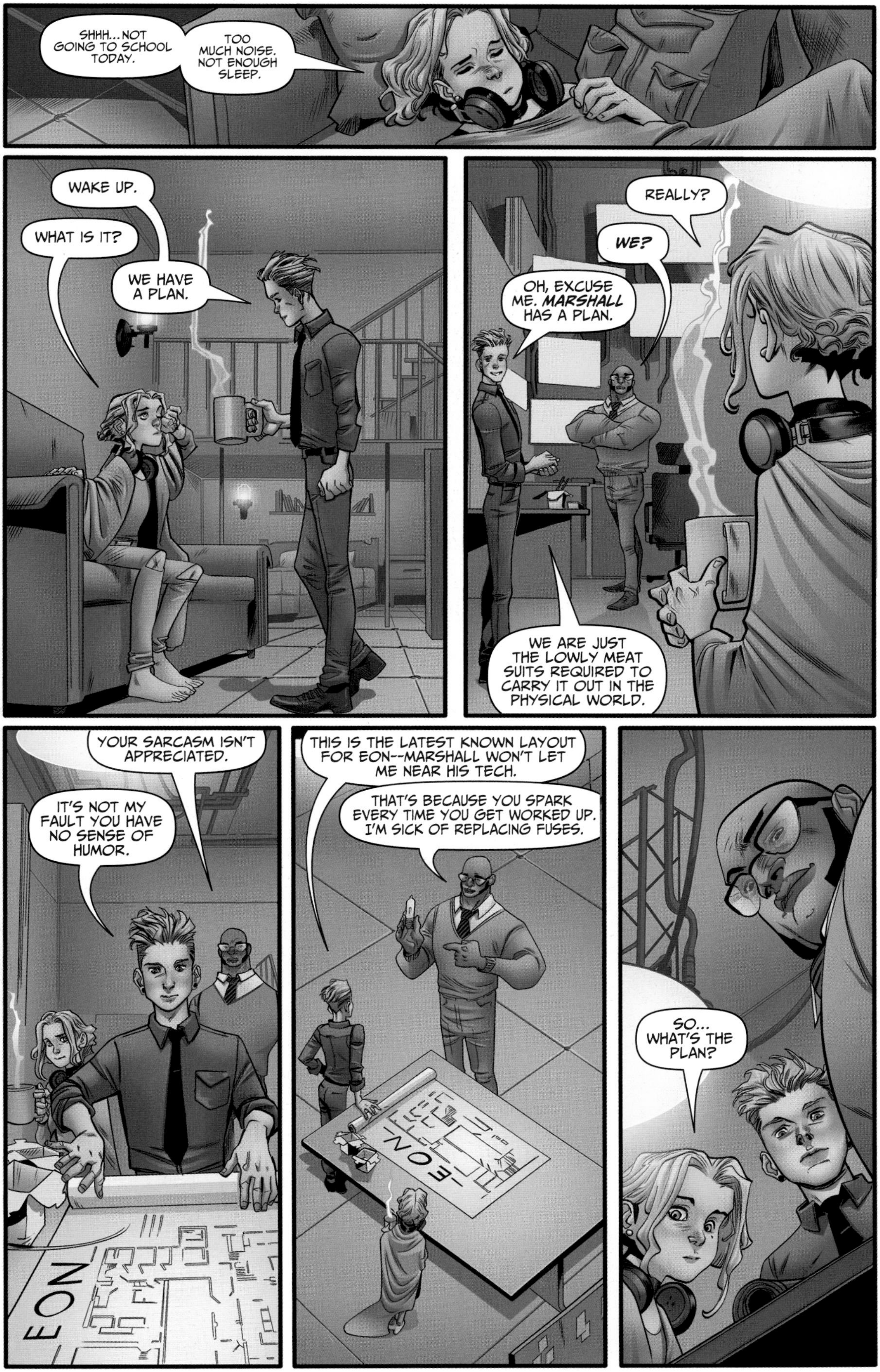
SHHH...NOT GOING TO SCHOOL TODAY.
TOO MUCH NOISE. NOT ENOUGH SLEEP.
WAKE UP.
WHAT IS IT?
WE HAVE A PLAN.
REALLY?
WE?
OH, EXCUSE ME. MARSHALL HAS A PLAN.
WE ARE JUST THE LOWLY MEAT SUITS REQUIRED TO CARRY IT OUT IN THE PHYSICAL WORLD.
YOUR SARCASM ISN'T APPRECIATED.
IT'S NOT MY FAULT YOU HAVE NO SENSE OF HUMOR.
EON
THIS IS THE LATEST KNOWN LAYOUT FOR EON--MARSHALL WON'T LET ME NEAR HIS TECH.
THAT'S BECAUSE YOU SPARK EVERY TIME YOU GET WORKED UP. I'M SICK OF REPLACING FUSES.
EON
SO... WHAT'S THE PLAN?

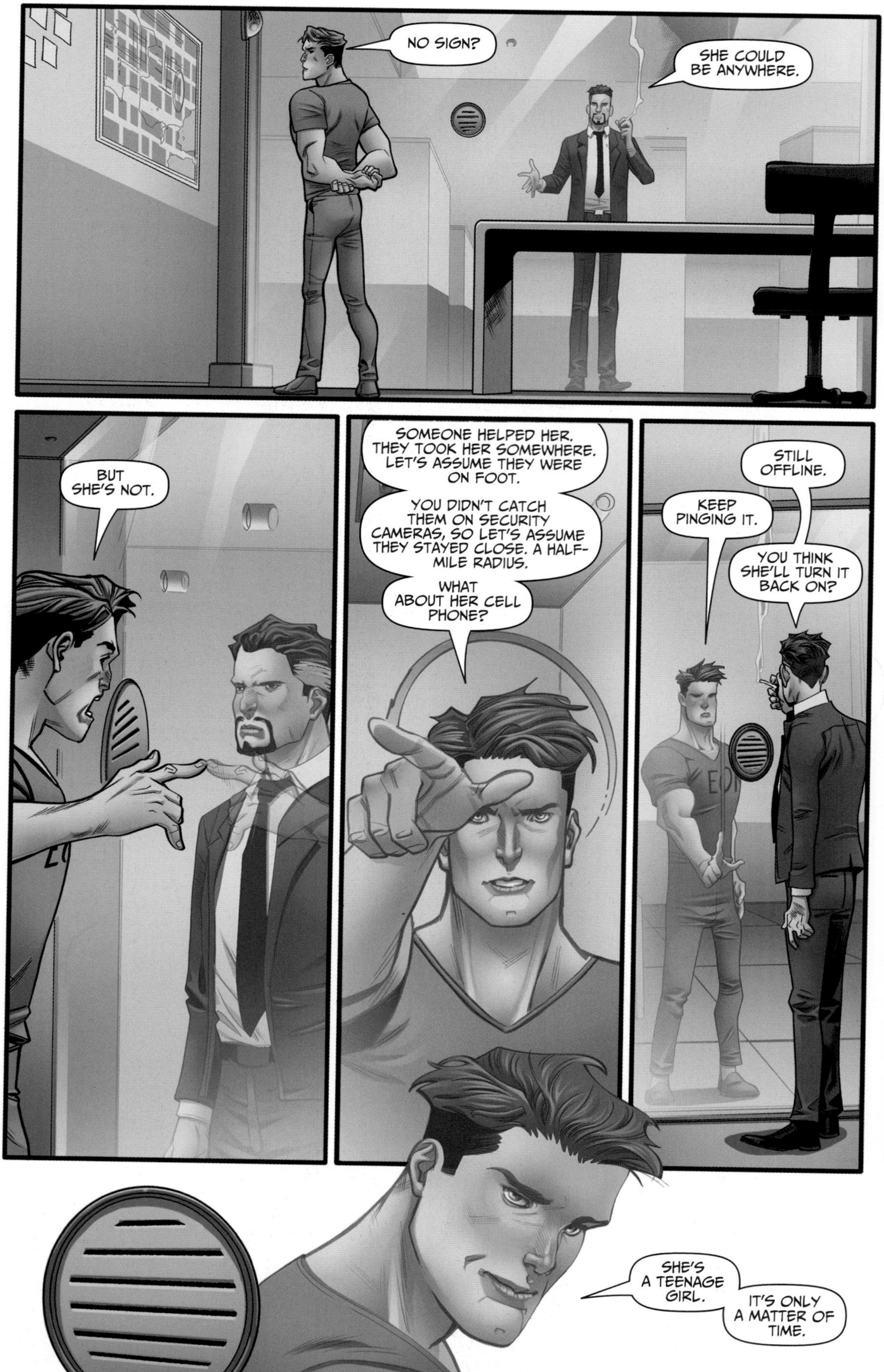
NO SIGN?
SHE COULD BE ANYWHERE.
BUT SHE'S NOT.
SOMEONE HELPED HER. THEY TOOK HER SOMEWHERE. LET'S ASSUME THEY WERE ON FOOT.
YOU DIDN'T CATCH THEM ON SECURITY CAMERAS, SO LET'S ASSUME THEY STAYED CLOSE. A HALF-MILE RADIUS.
WHAT ABOUT HER CELL PHONE?
STILL OFFLINE.
KEEP PINGING IT.
YOU THINK SHE'LL TURN IT BACK ON?
SHE'S A TEENAGE GIRL.
IT'S ONLY A MATTER OF TIME.

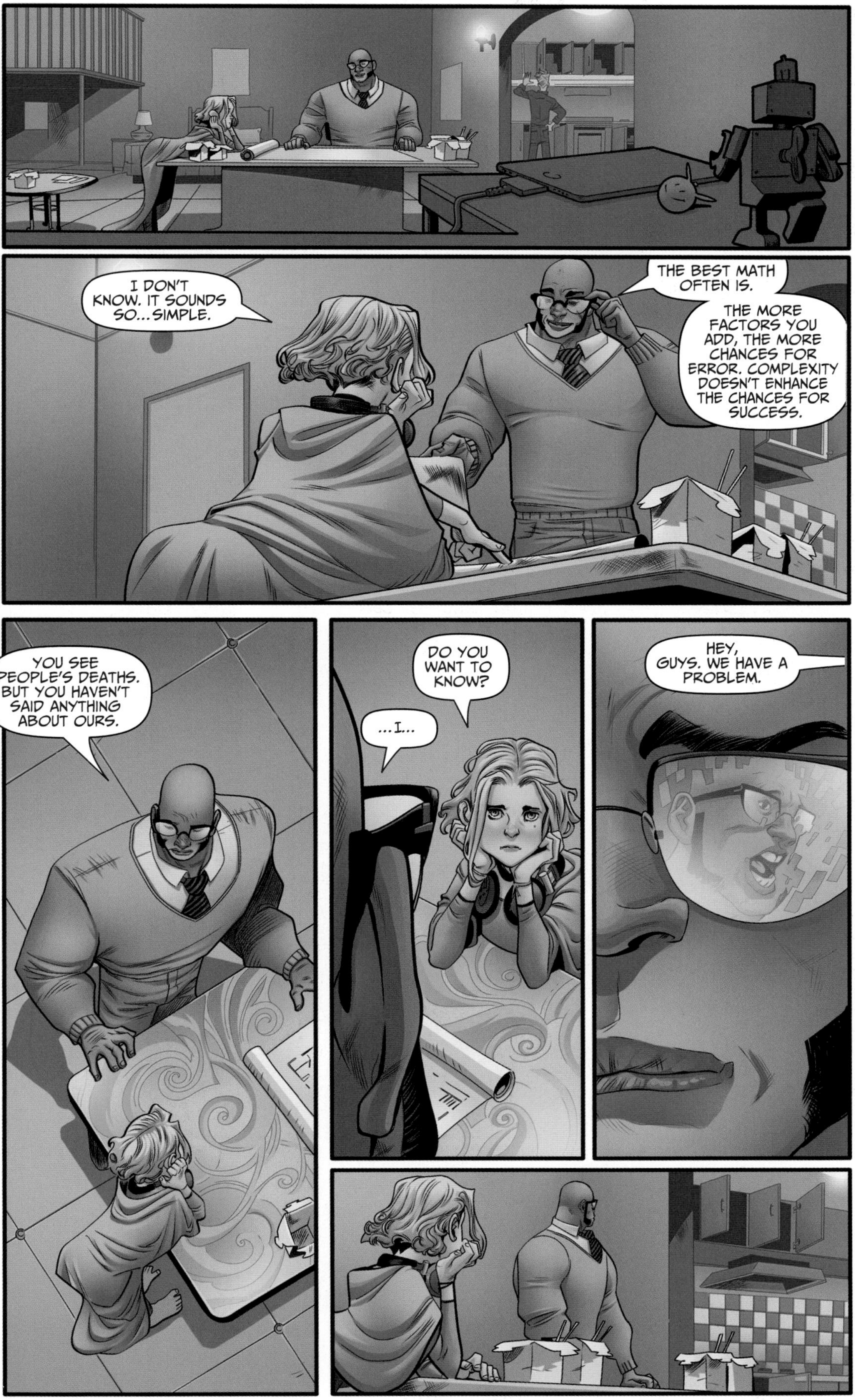
I DON'T KNOW. IT SOUNDS SO... SIMPLE.
THE BEST MATH OFTEN IS.
THE MORE FACTORS YOU ADD, THE MORE CHANCES FOR ERROR. COMPLEXITY DOESN'T ENHANCE THE CHANCES FOR SUCCESS.
YOU SEE PEOPLE'S DEATHS. BUT YOU HAVEN'T SAID ANYTHING ABOUT OURS.
DO YOU WANT TO KNOW?
...I...
HEY, GUYS. WE HAVE A PROBLEM.

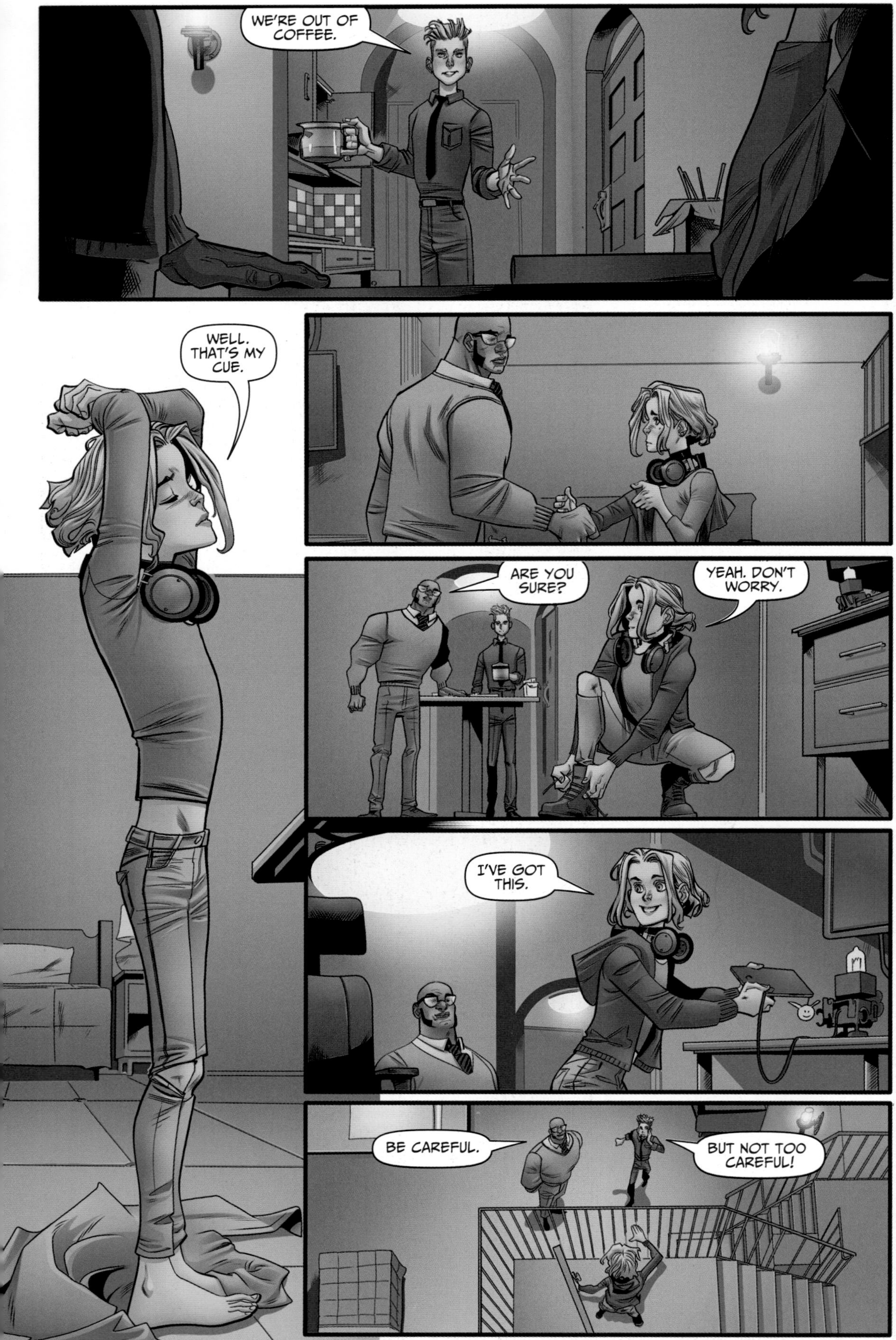
WE'RE OUT OF COFFEE.
WELL. THAT'S MY CUE.
ARE YOU SURE?
YEAH. DON'T WORRY.
I'VE GOT THIS.
BE CAREFUL.
BUT NOT TOO CAREFUL!

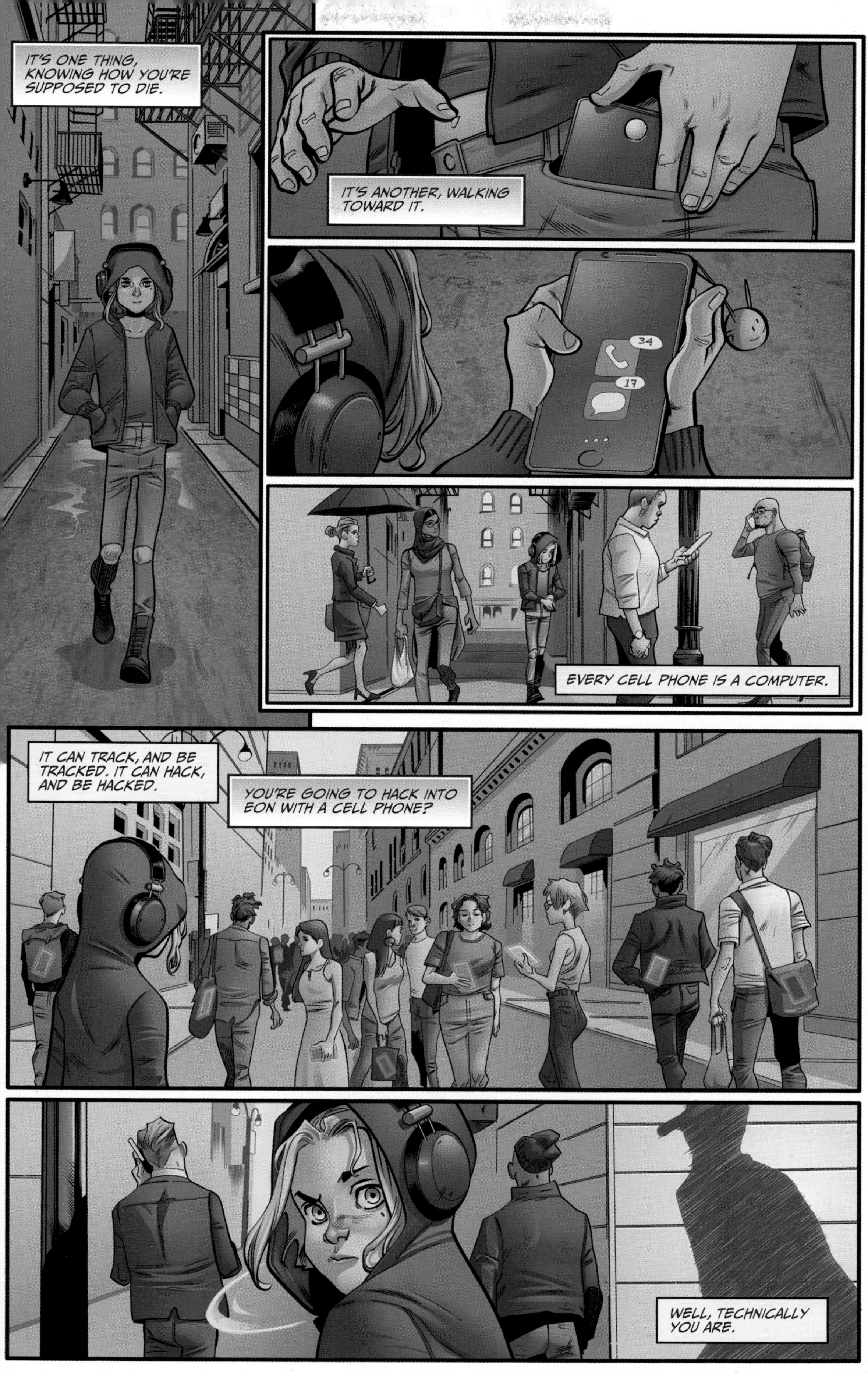
IT'S ONE THING, KNOWING HOW YOU'RE SUPPOSED TO DIE.
IT'S ANOTHER, WALKING TOWARD IT.
34
17
EVERY CELL PHONE IS A COMPUTER.
IT CAN TRACK, AND BE TRACKED. IT CAN HACK, AND BE HACKED.
YOU'RE GOING TO HACK INTO EON WITH A CELL PHONE?
WELL, TECHNICALLY YOU ARE.

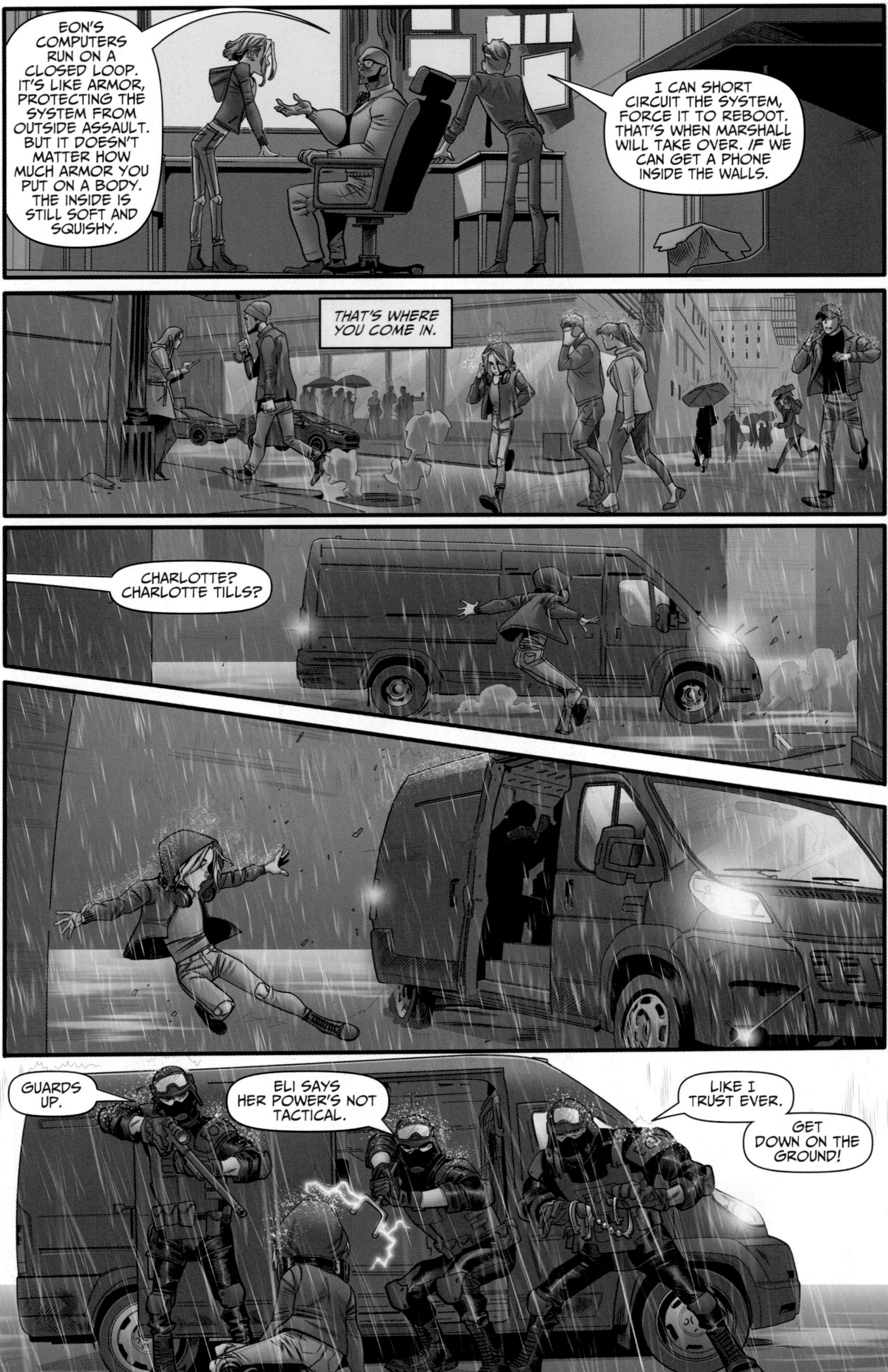
EON'S COMPUTERS RUN ON A CLOSED LOOP. IT'S LIKE ARMOR, PROTECTING THE SYSTEM FROM OUTSIDE ASSAULT. BUT IT DOESN'T MATTER HOW MUCH ARMOR YOU PUT ON A BODY. THE INSIDE IS STILL SOFT AND SQUISHY.
I CAN SHORT CIRCUIT THE SYSTEM, FORCE IT TO REBOOT. THAT'S WHEN MARSHALL WILL TAKE OVER. *IF* WE CAN GET A PHONE INSIDE THE WALLS.
THAT'S WHERE YOU COME IN.
CHARLOTTE? CHARLOTTE TILLS?
GUARDS UP.
ELI SAYS HER POWER'S NOT TACTICAL.
LIKE I TRUST EVER.
GET DOWN ON THE GROUND!

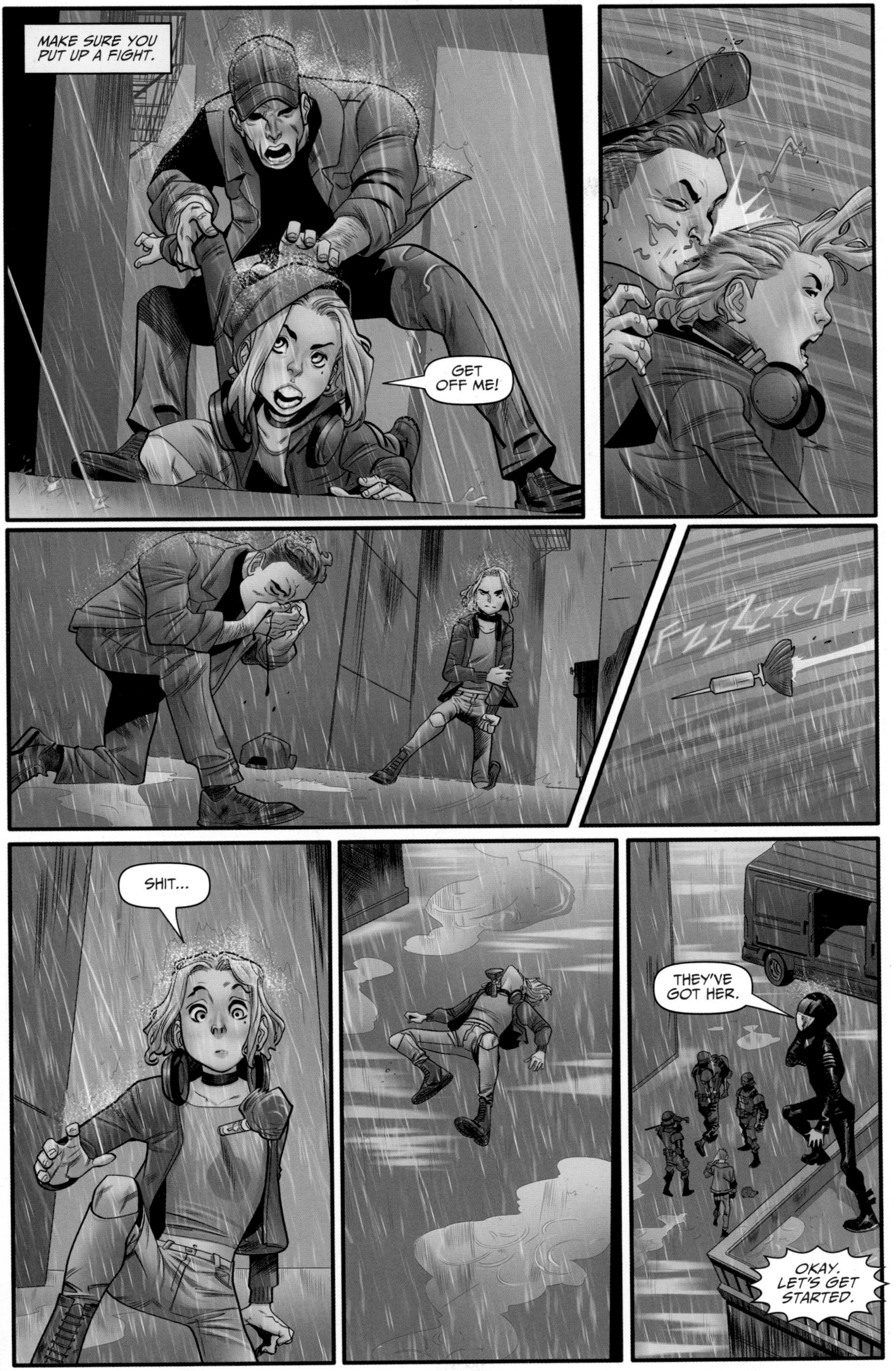
MAKE SURE YOU PUT UP A FIGHT.
GET OFF ME!
FZZZZZCHT
SHIT...
THEY'VE GOT HER.
OKAY. LET'S GET STARTED.

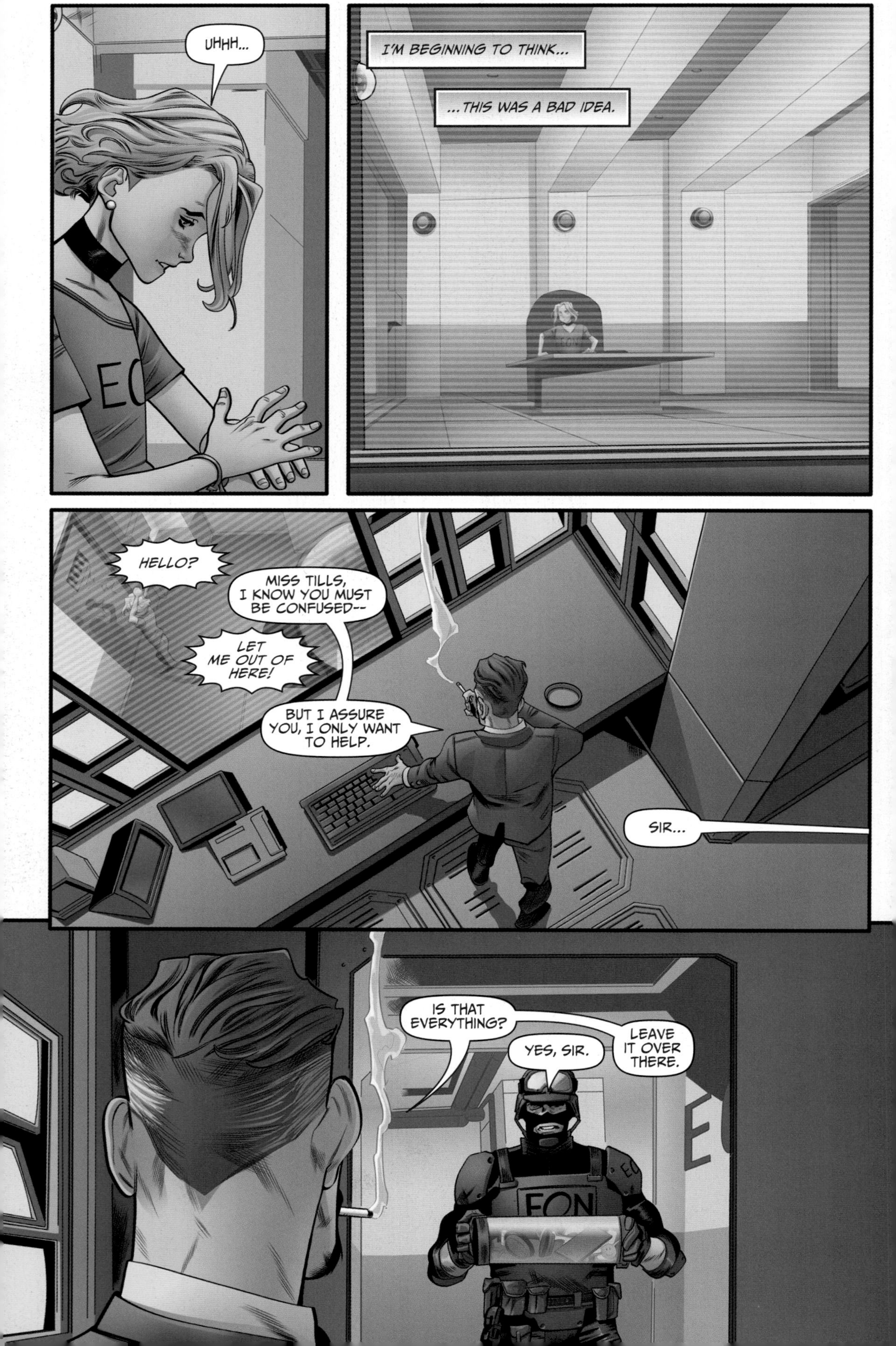
UHHH...
I'M BEGINNING TO THINK...
...THIS WAS A BAD IDEA.
HELLO?
MISS TILLS, I KNOW YOU MUST BE CONFUSED--
LET ME OUT OF HERE!
BUT I ASSURE YOU, I ONLY WANT TO HELP.
SIR...
IS THAT EVERYTHING?
YES, SIR.
LEAVE IT OVER THERE.
FON

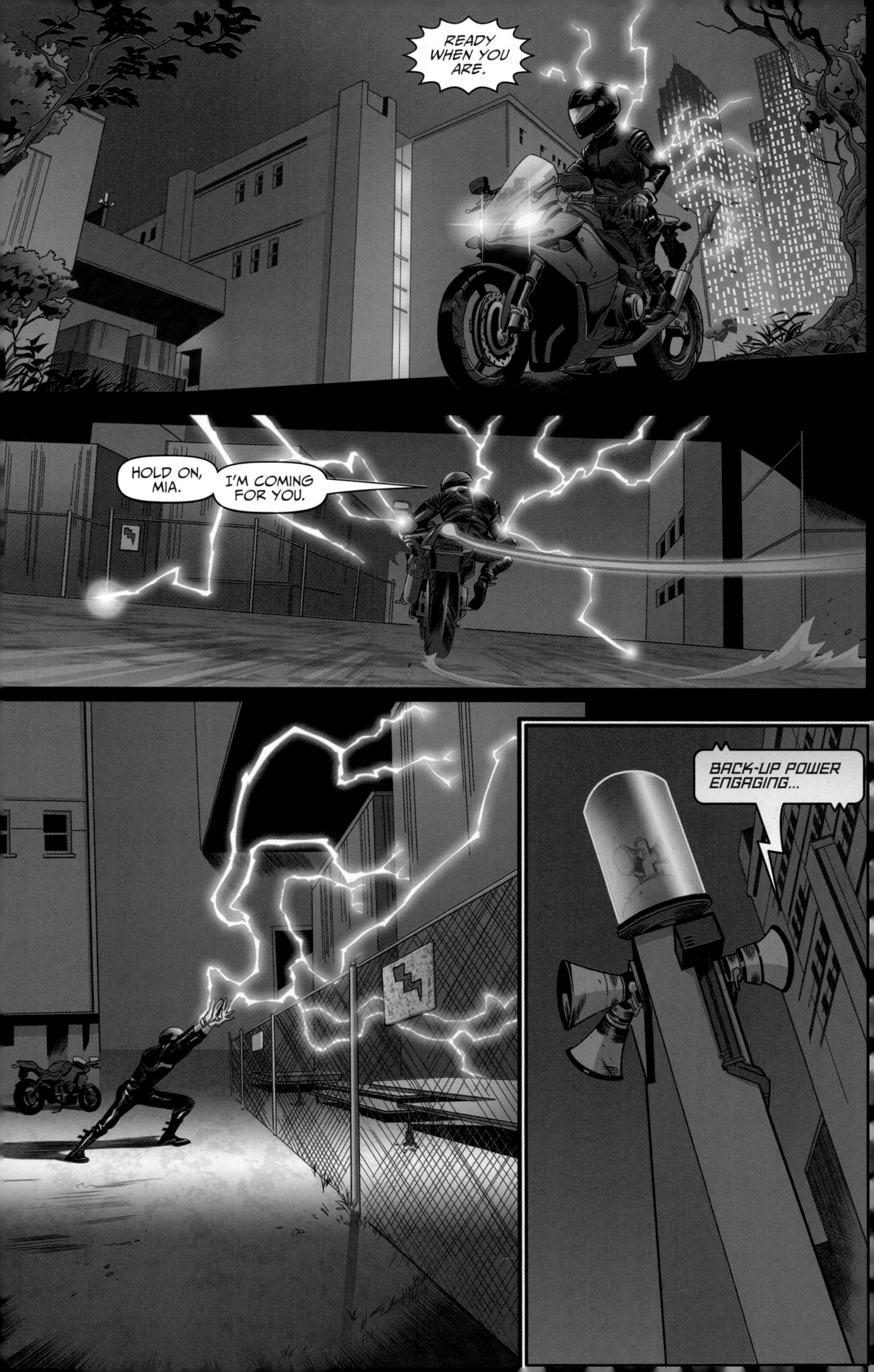
READY WHEN YOU ARE.
HOLD ON, MIA.
I'M COMING FOR YOU.
BACK-UP POWER ENGAGING...

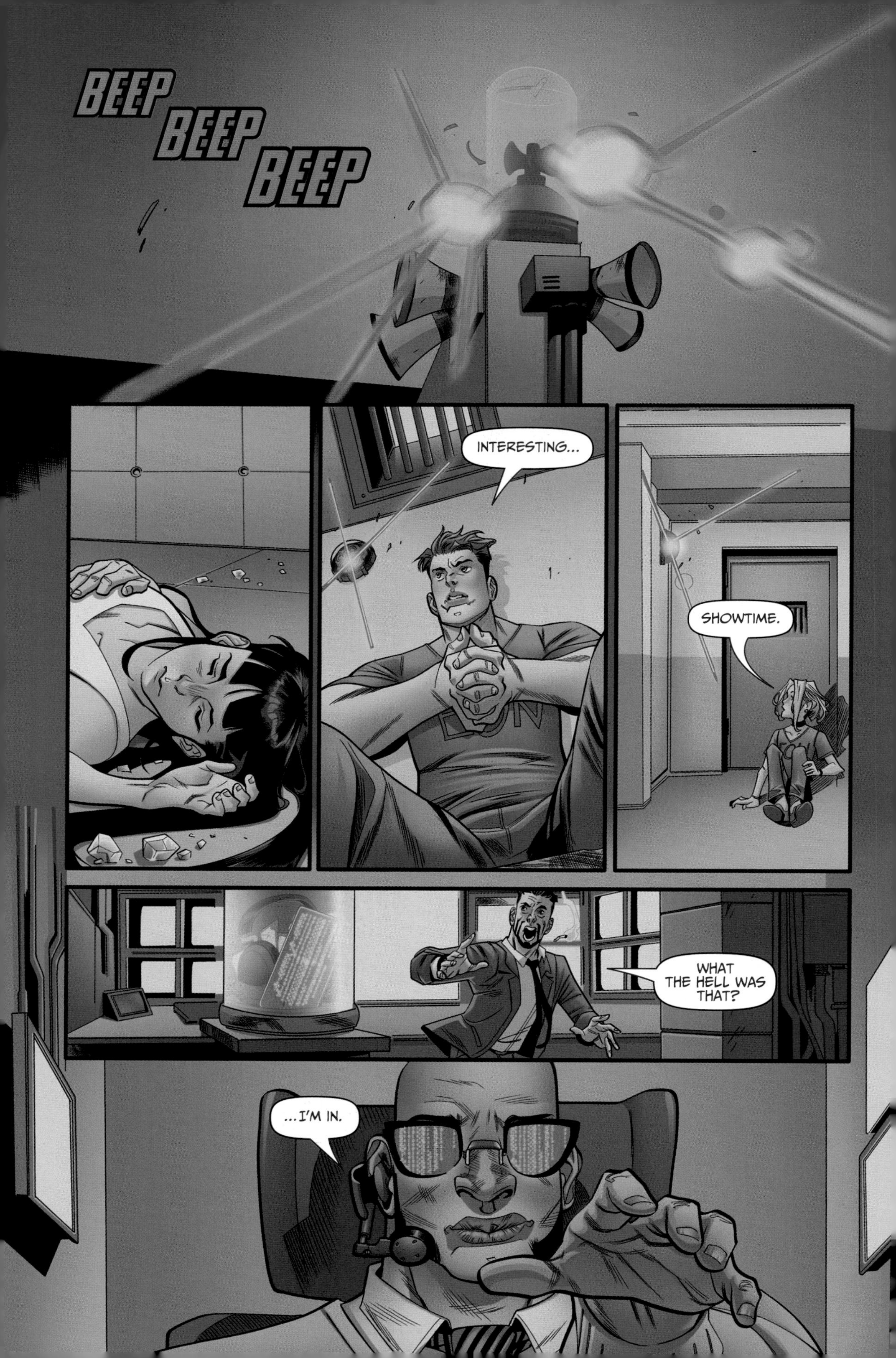
BEEP
BEEP
BEEP
INTERESTING...
SHOWTIME.
WHAT THE HELL WAS THAT?
...I'M IN.

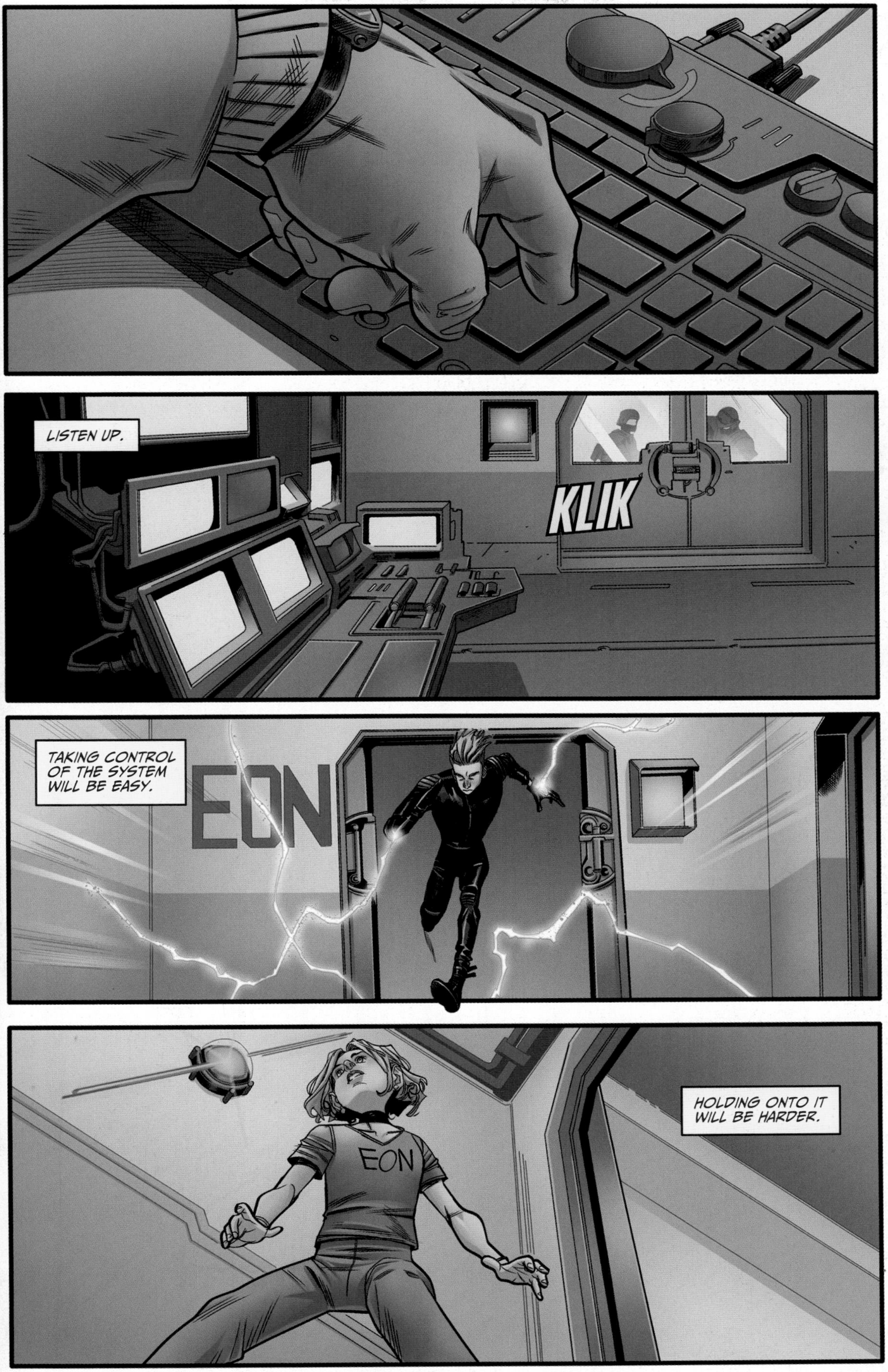
LISTEN UP.
KLIK
TAKING CONTROL OF THE SYSTEM WILL BE EASY.
EON
EON
HOLDING ONTO IT WILL BE HARDER.

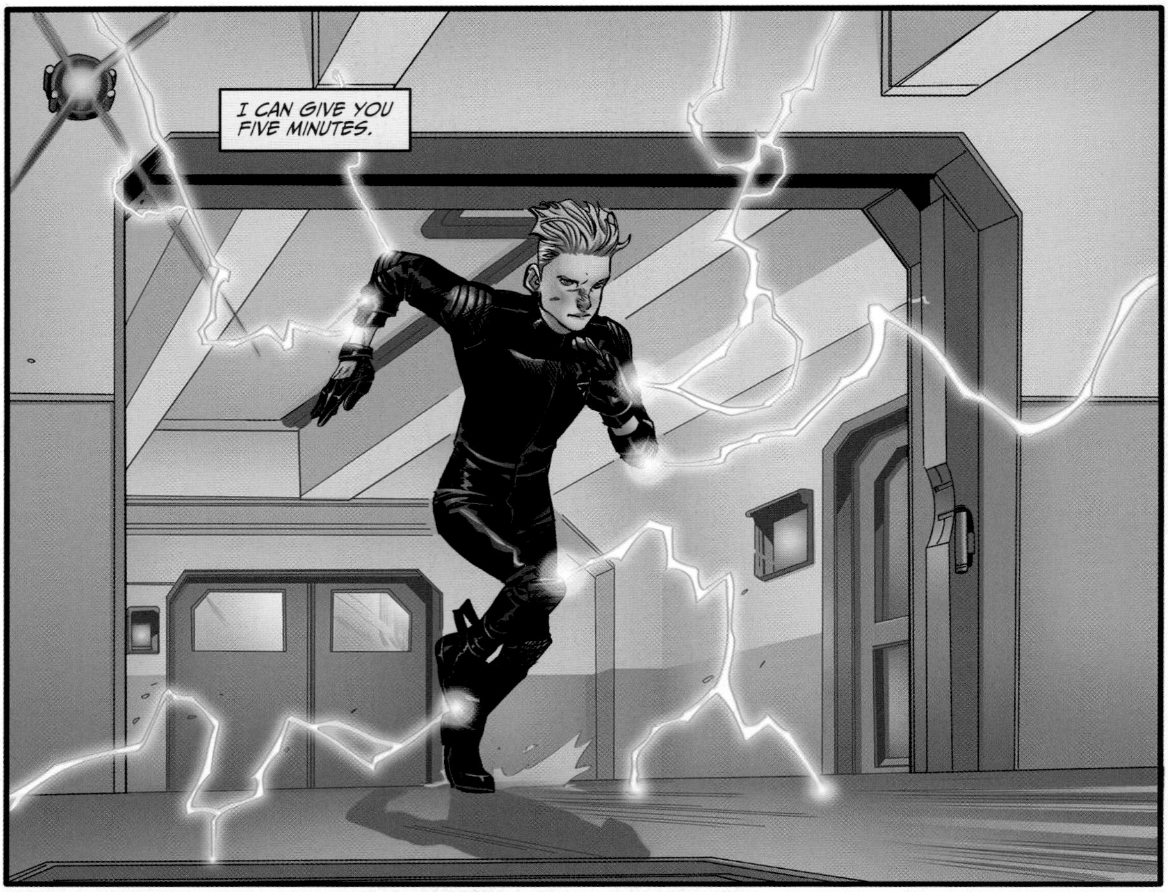
I CAN GIVE YOU FIVE MINUTES.
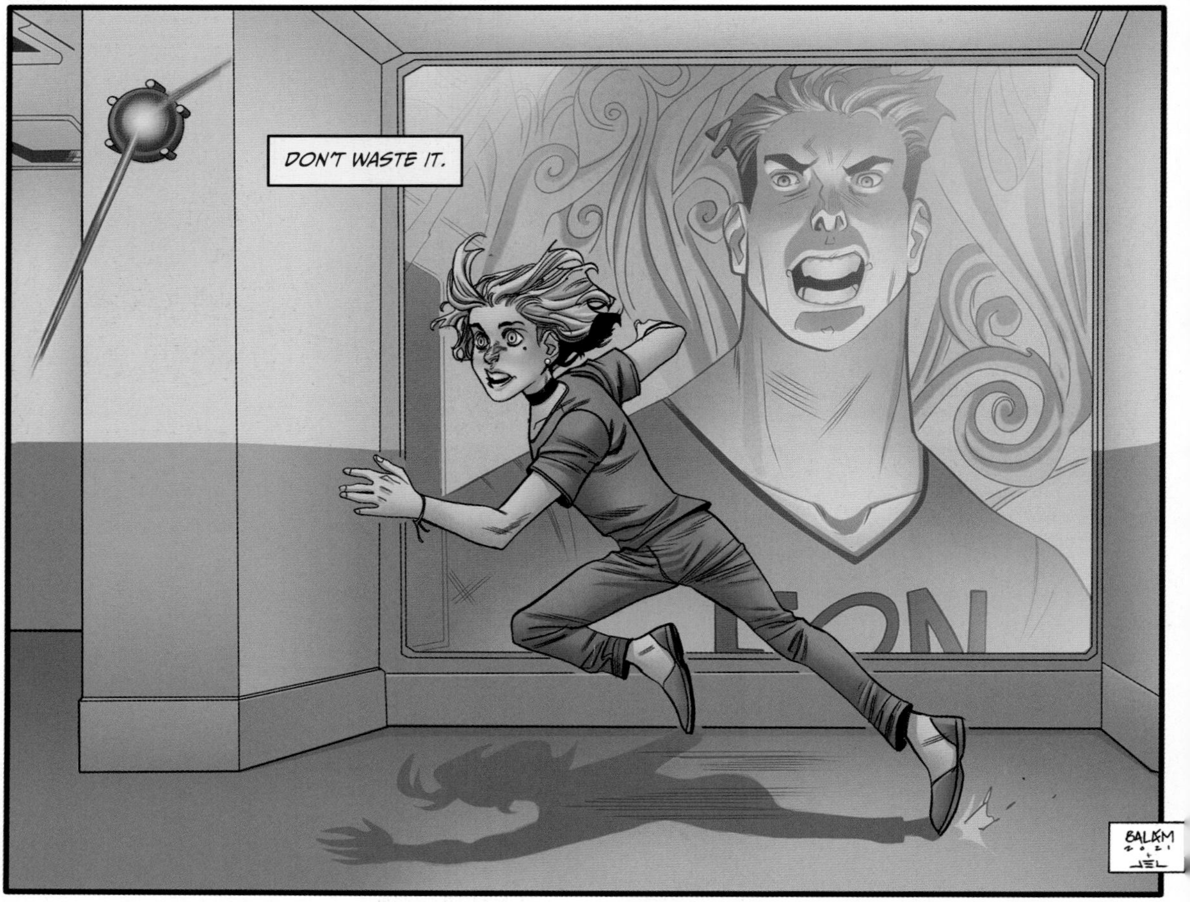
DON'T WASTE IT.

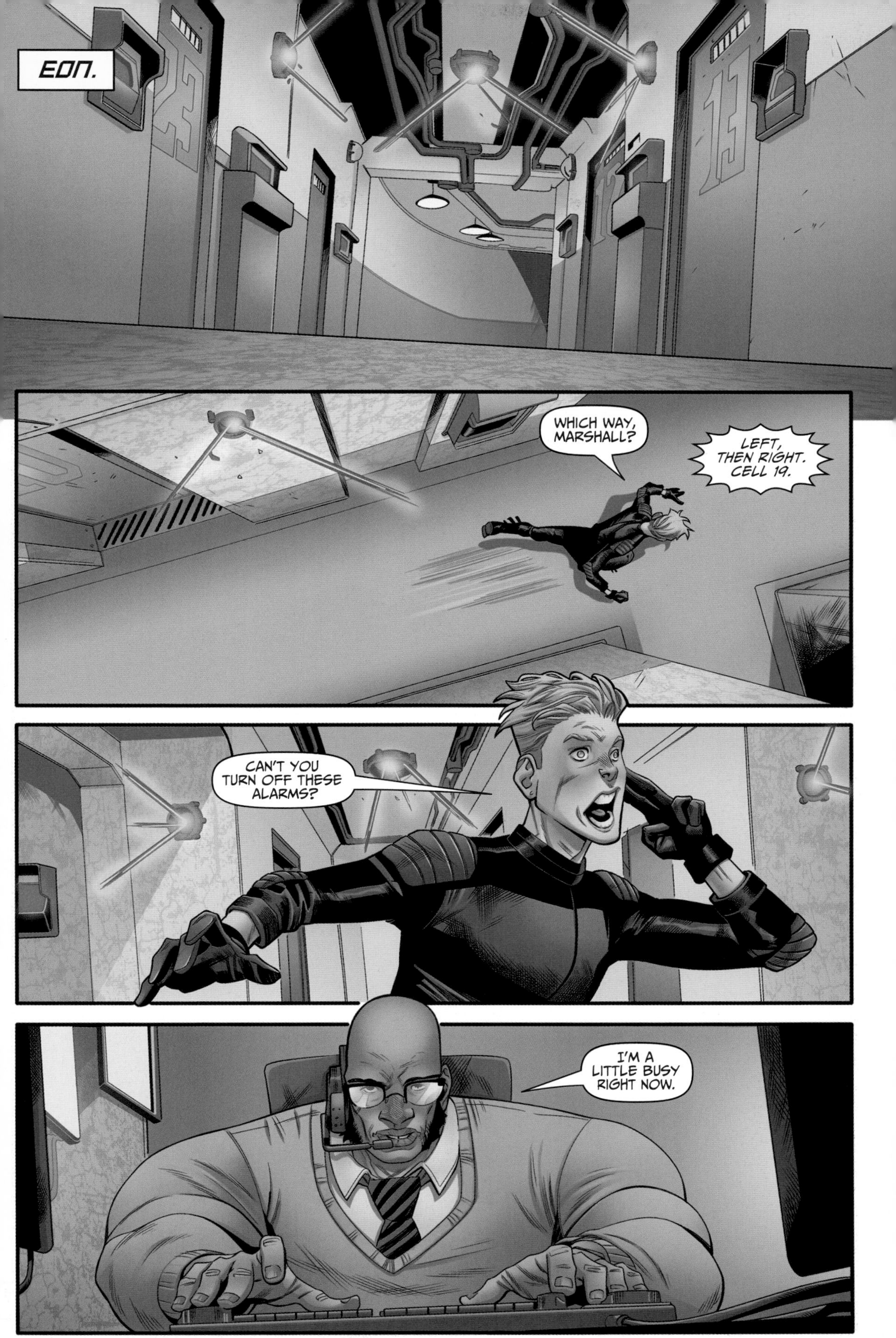
EON.
WHICH WAY, MARSHALL?
LEFT, THEN RIGHT. CELL 19.
CAN'T YOU TURN OFF THESE ALARMS?
I'M A LITTLE BUSY RIGHT NOW.

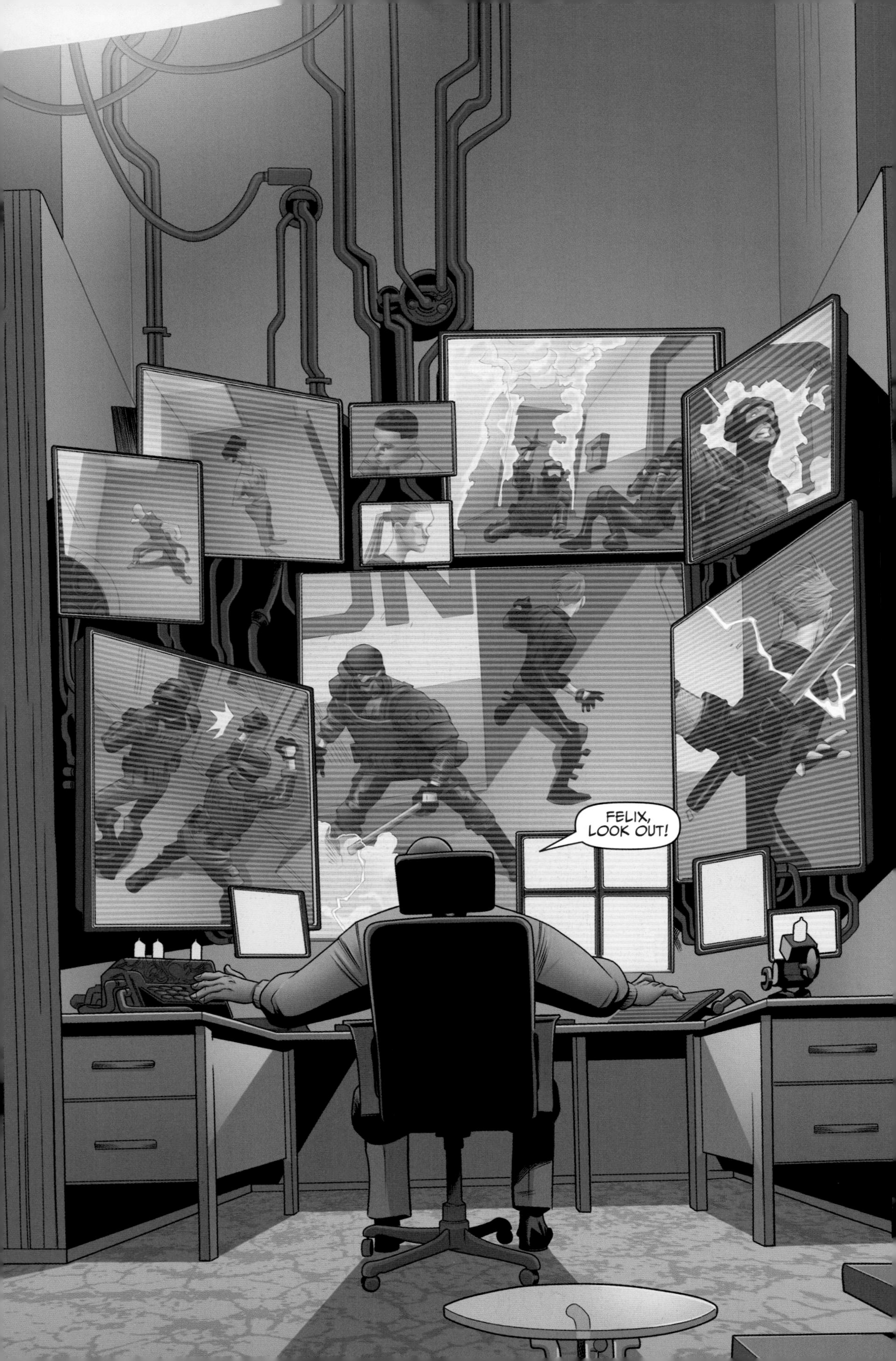
FELIX, LOOK OUT!

IS THAT THE BEST YOU GOT?

ZZZZZZZ

"WHAT THE HELL IS GOING ON?"

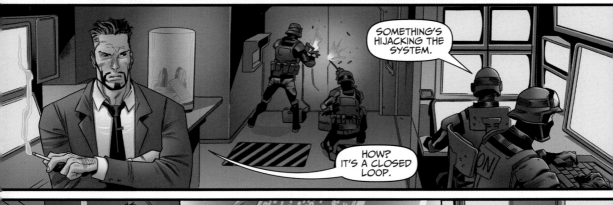

SOMETHING'S HIJACKING THE SYSTEM.

HOW? IT'S A CLOSED LOOP.

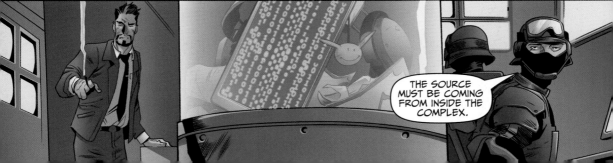

THE SOURCE MUST BE COMING FROM INSIDE THE COMPLEX.

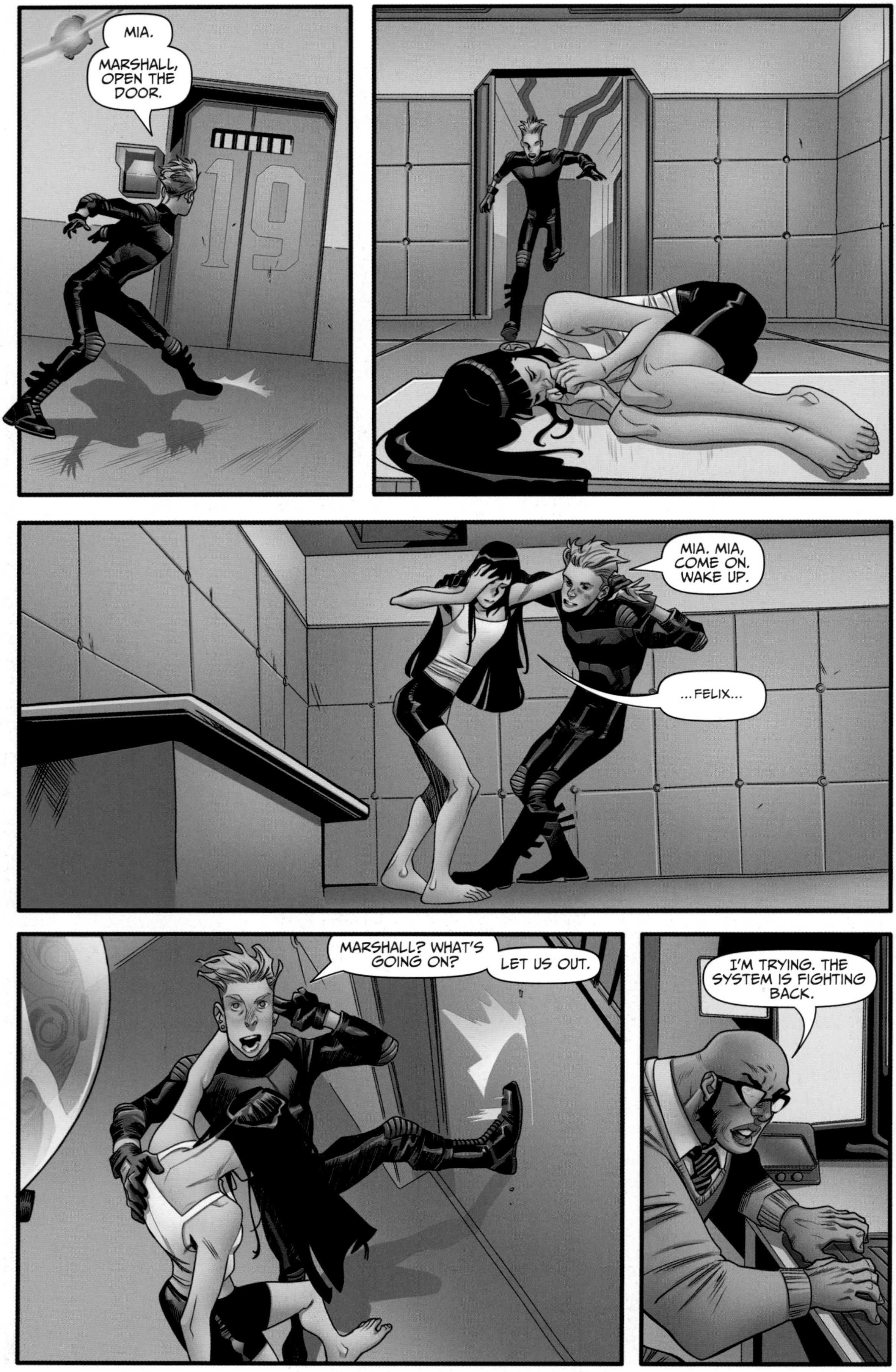
MIA.
MARSHALL, OPEN THE DOOR.
MIA. MIA, COME ON. WAKE UP.
...FELIX...
MARSHALL? WHAT'S GOING ON?
LET US OUT.
I'M TRYING. THE SYSTEM IS FIGHTING BACK.

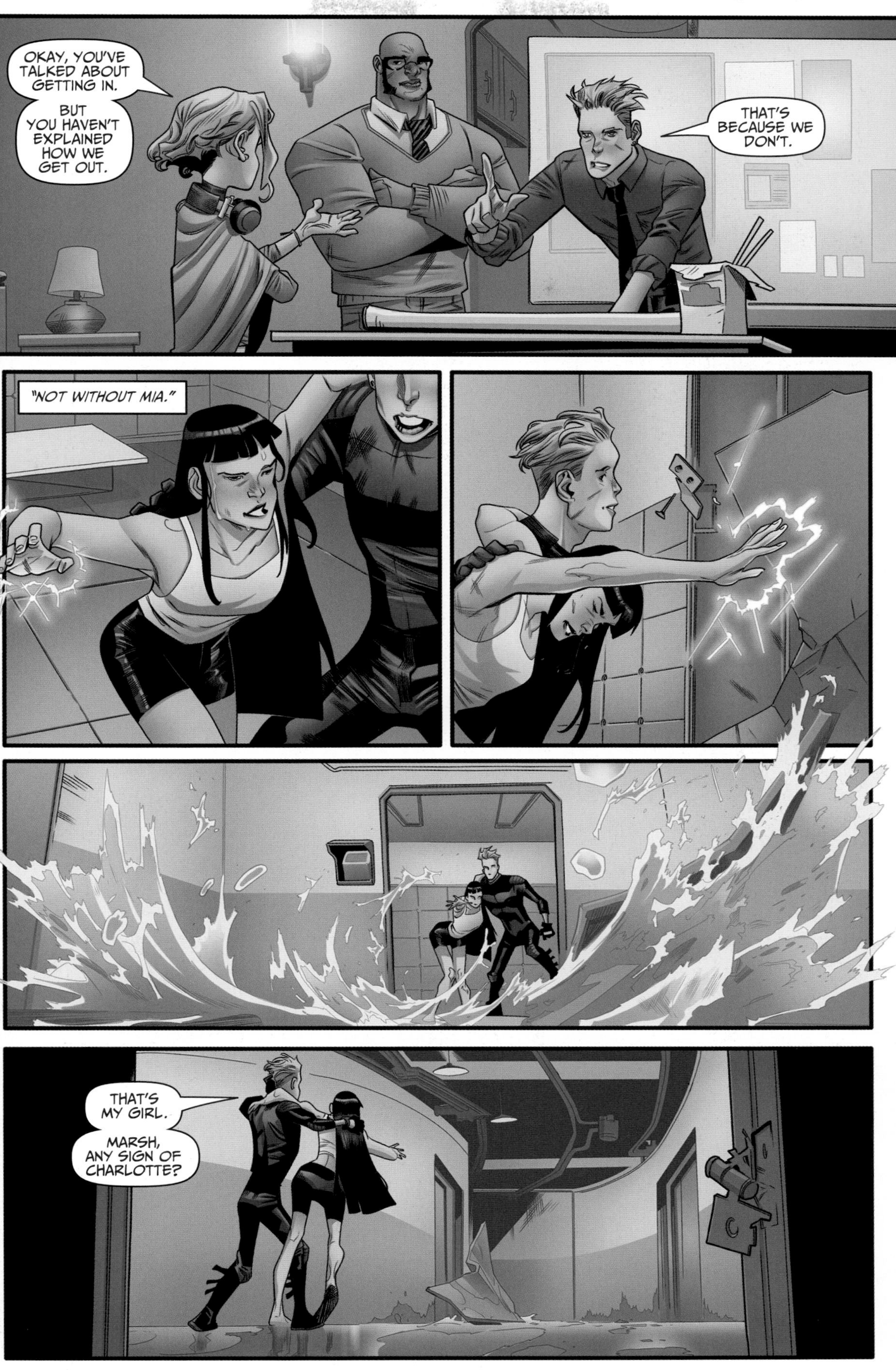
OKAY, YOU'VE TALKED ABOUT GETTING IN.
BUT YOU HAVEN'T EXPLAINED HOW WE GET OUT.
THAT'S BECAUSE WE DON'T.
"NOT WITHOUT MIA."
THAT'S MY GIRL.
MARSH, ANY SIGN OF CHARLOTTE?

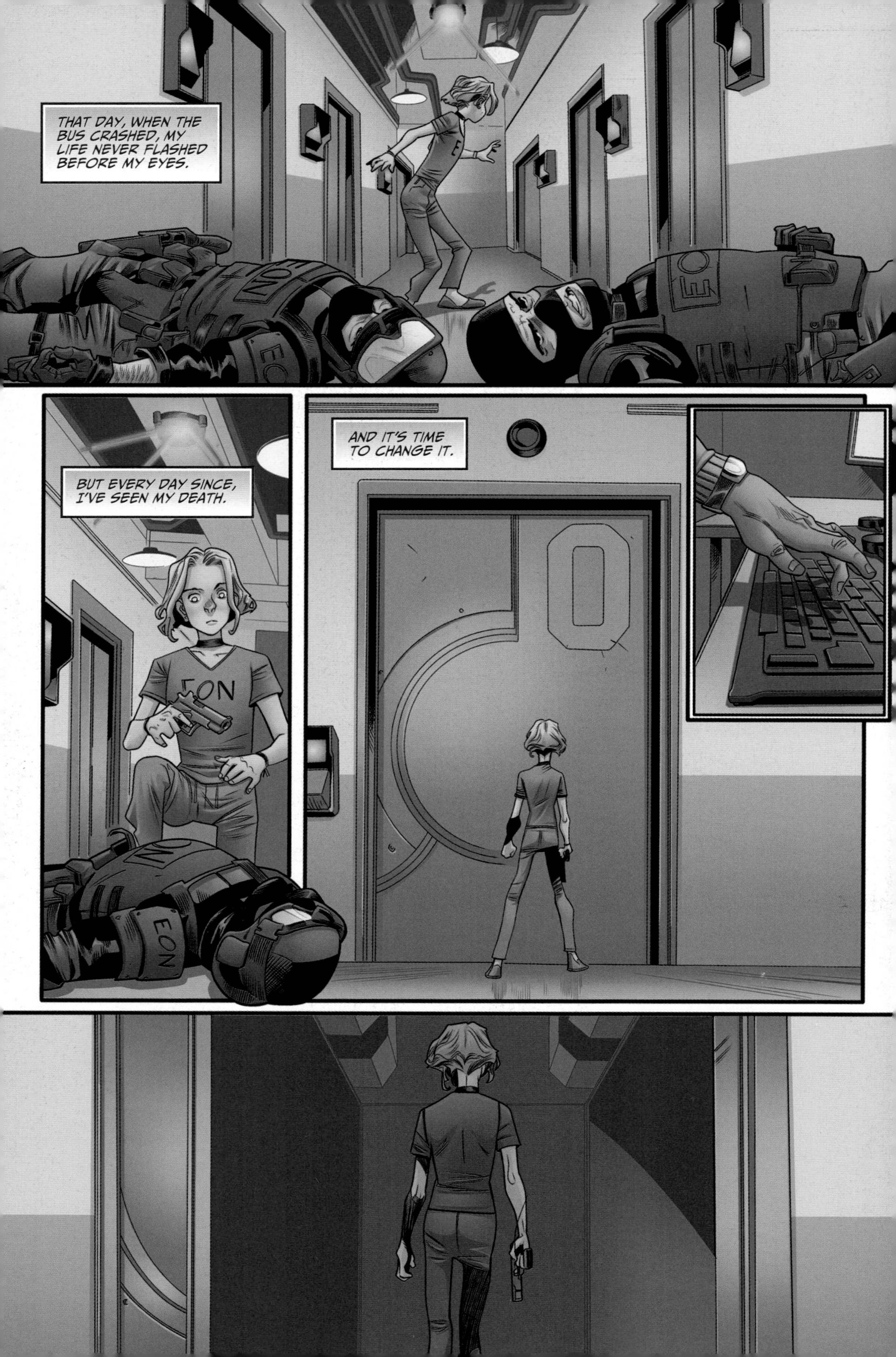
THAT DAY, WHEN THE BUS CRASHED, MY LIFE NEVER FLASHED BEFORE MY EYES.
EON
EON
BUT EVERY DAY SINCE, I'VE SEEN MY DEATH.
EON
EON
AND IT'S TIME TO CHANGE IT.

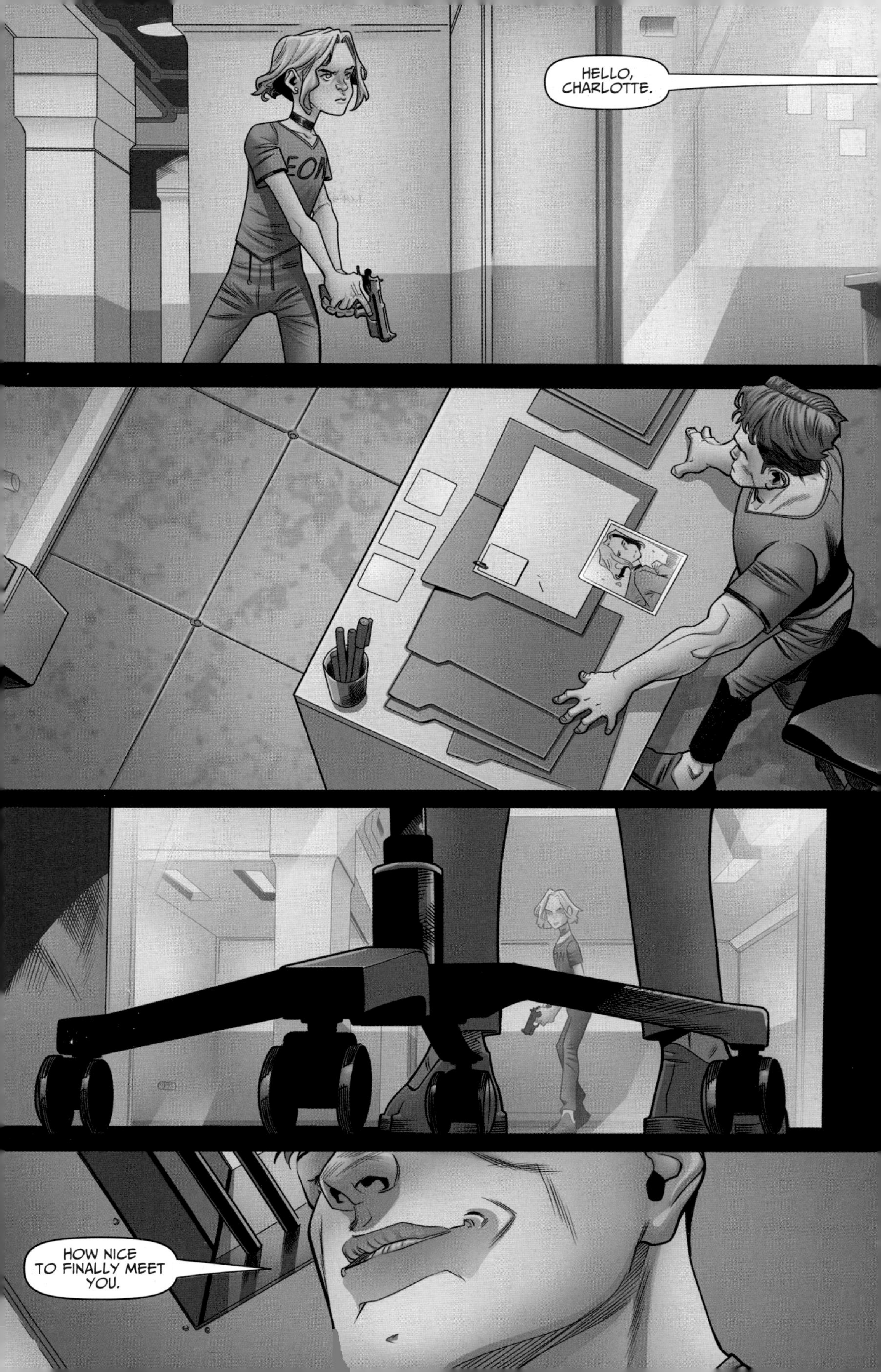
HELLO, CHARLOTTE.
HOW NICE TO FINALLY MEET YOU.

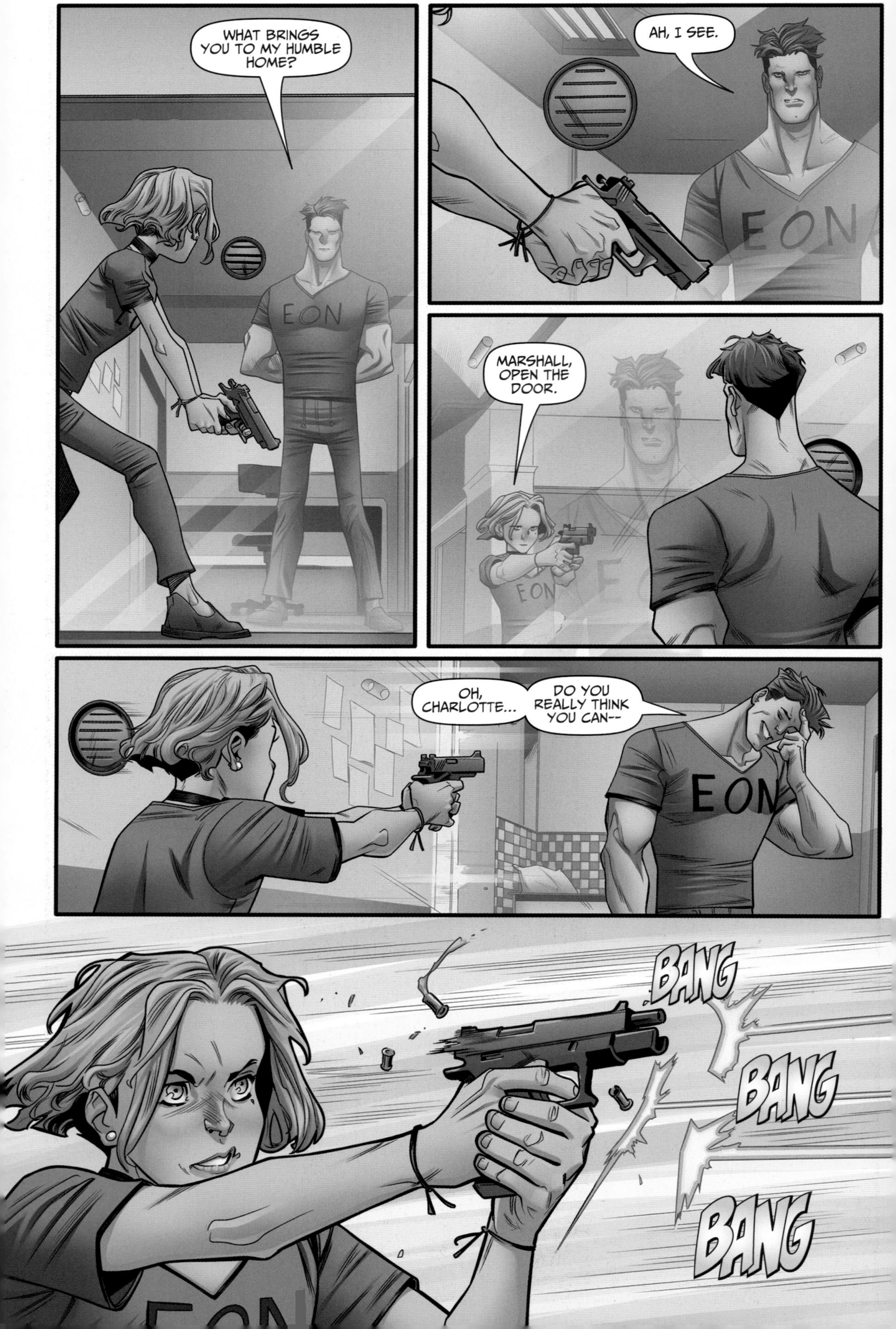
WHAT BRINGS YOU TO MY HUMBLE HOME?
EON
AH, I SEE.
EON
MARSHALL, OPEN THE DOOR.
EON
OH, CHARLOTTE...
DO YOU REALLY THINK YOU CAN--
EON
BANG
BANG
BANG

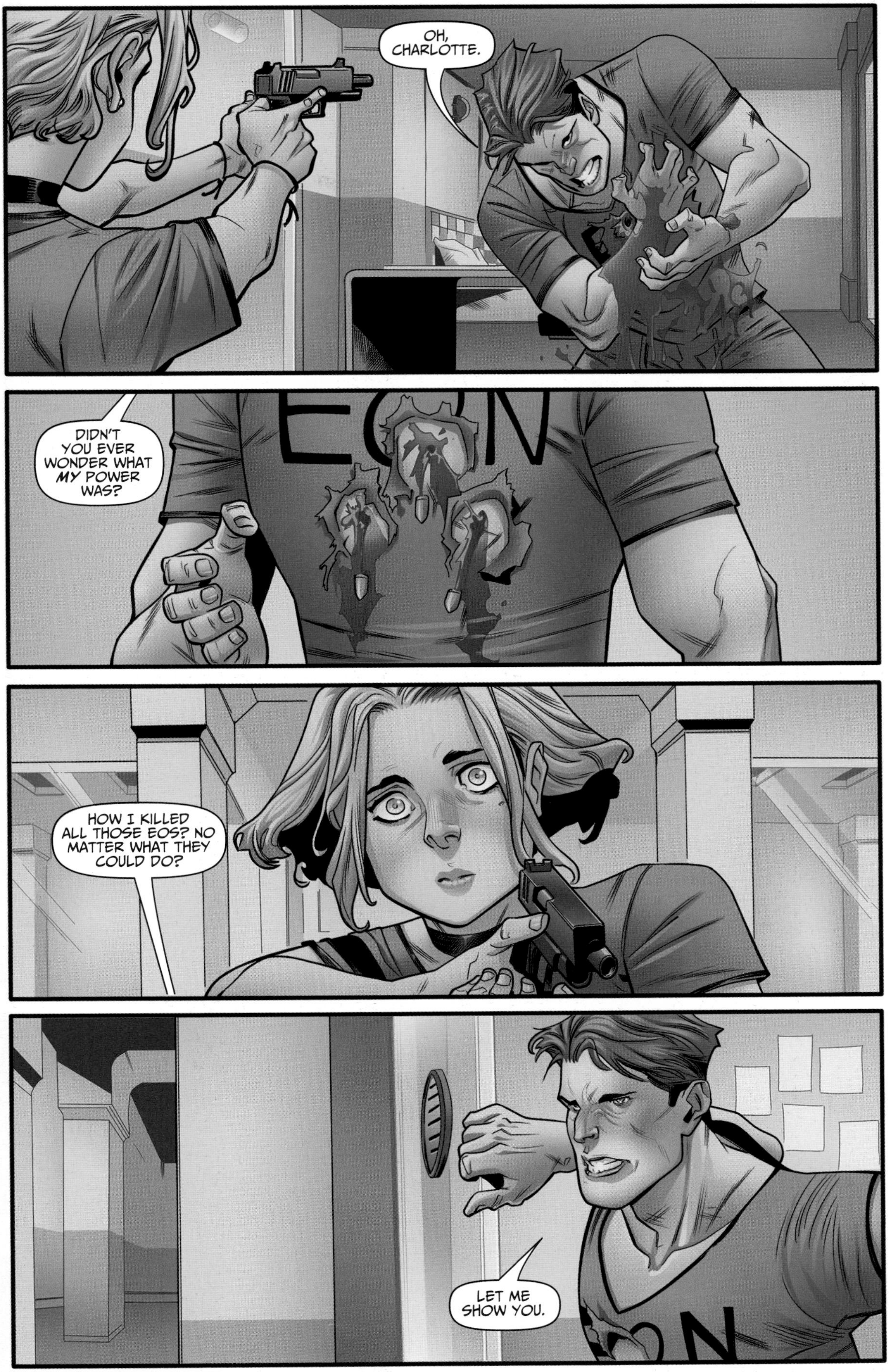
OH, CHARLOTTE.
DIDN'T YOU EVER WONDER WHAT MY POWER WAS?
EON
HOW I KILLED ALL THOSE EOS? NO MATTER WHAT THEY COULD DO?
LET ME SHOW YOU.

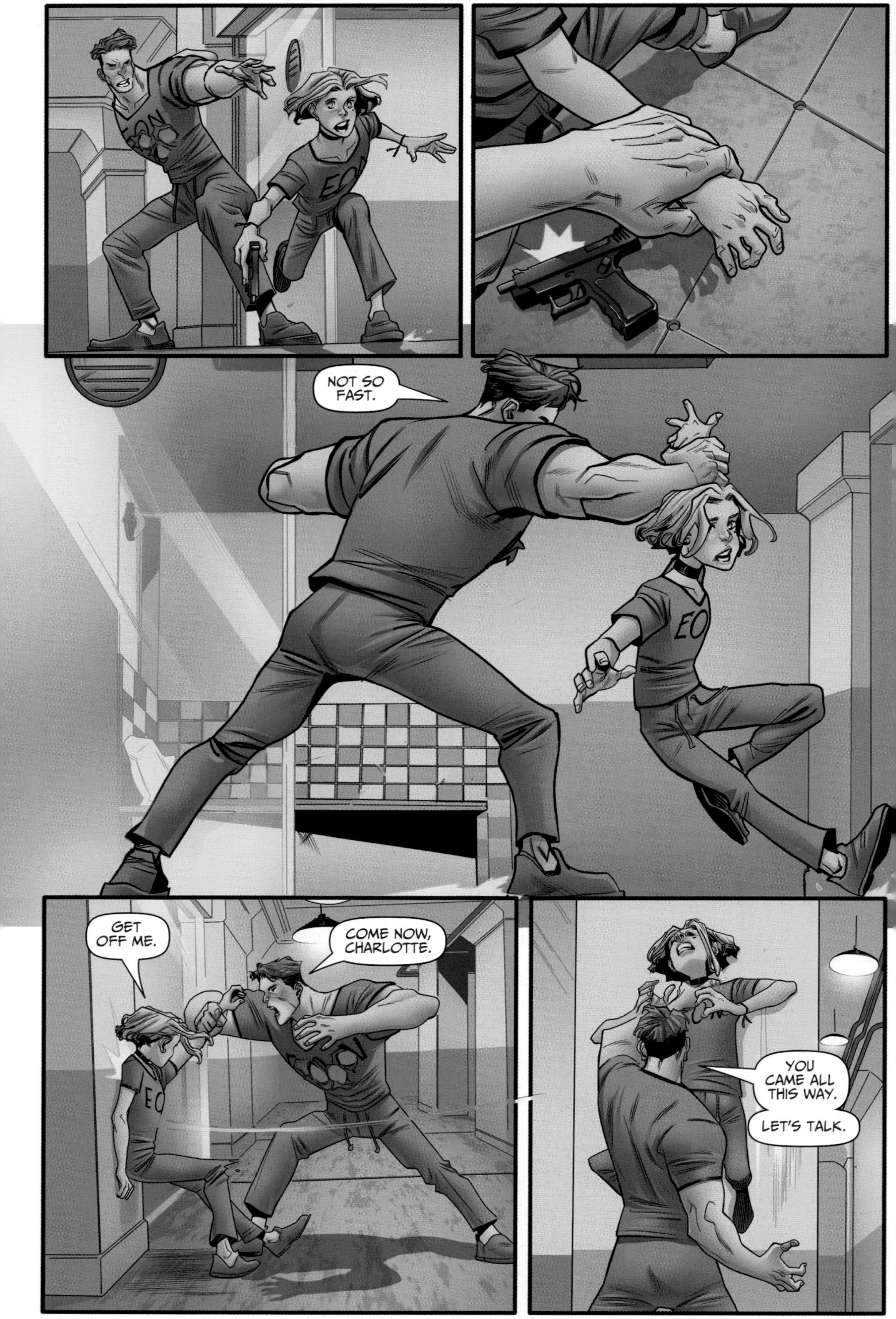
NOT SO FAST.
GET OFF ME.
COME NOW, CHARLOTTE.
YOU CAME ALL THIS WAY.
LET'S TALK.

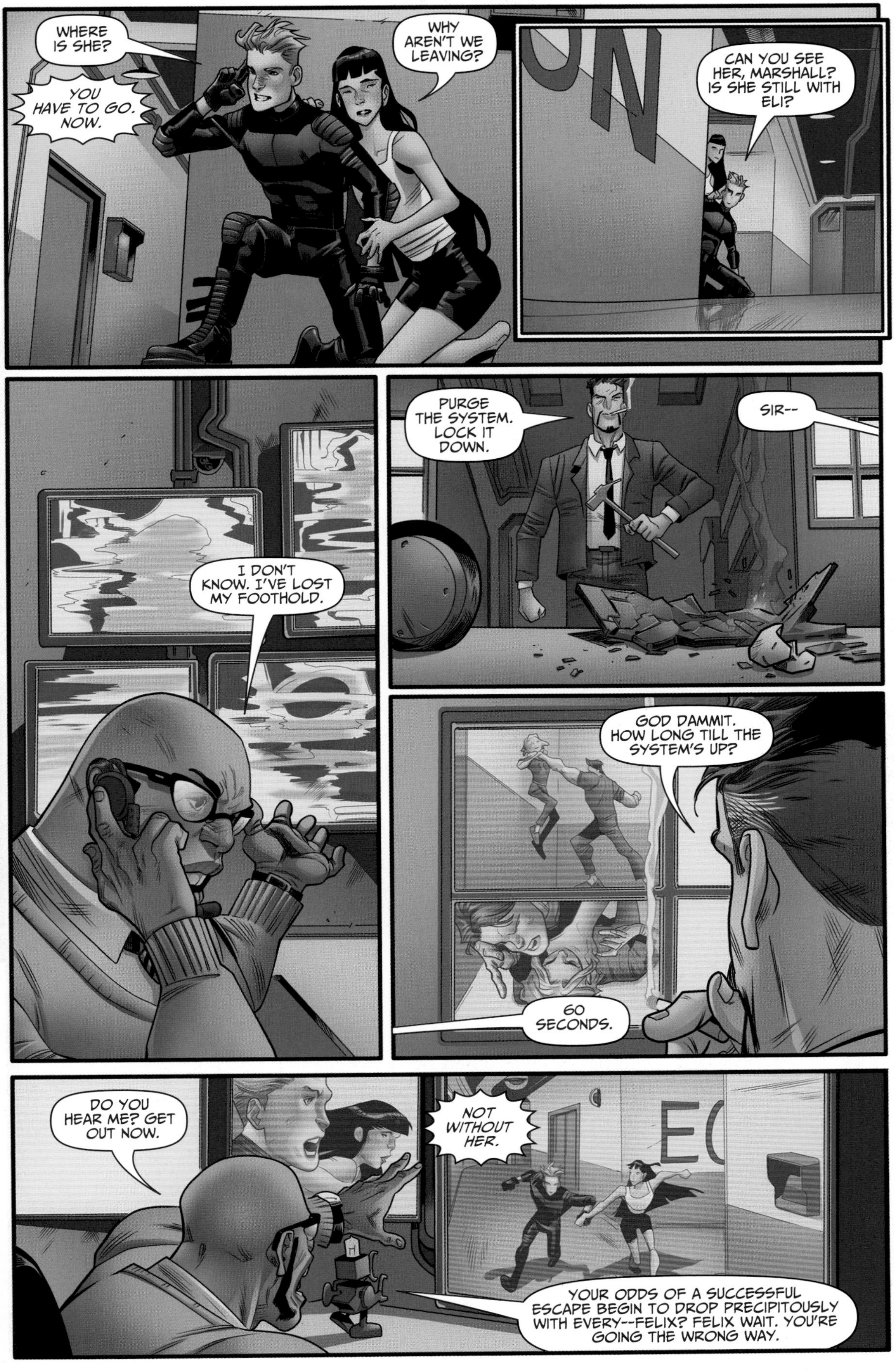
WHERE IS SHE?
YOU HAVE TO GO. NOW.
WHY AREN'T WE LEAVING?
CAN YOU SEE HER, MARSHALL? IS SHE STILL WITH ELI?
I DON'T KNOW. I'VE LOST MY FOOTHOLD.
PURGE THE SYSTEM. LOCK IT DOWN.
SIR--
GOD DAMMIT. HOW LONG TILL THE SYSTEM'S UP?
60 SECONDS.
DO YOU HEAR ME? GET OUT NOW.
NOT WITHOUT HER.
YOUR ODDS OF A SUCCESSFUL ESCAPE BEGIN TO DROP PRECIPITOUSLY WITH EVERY--FELIX? FELIX WAIT. YOU'RE GOING THE WRONG WAY.

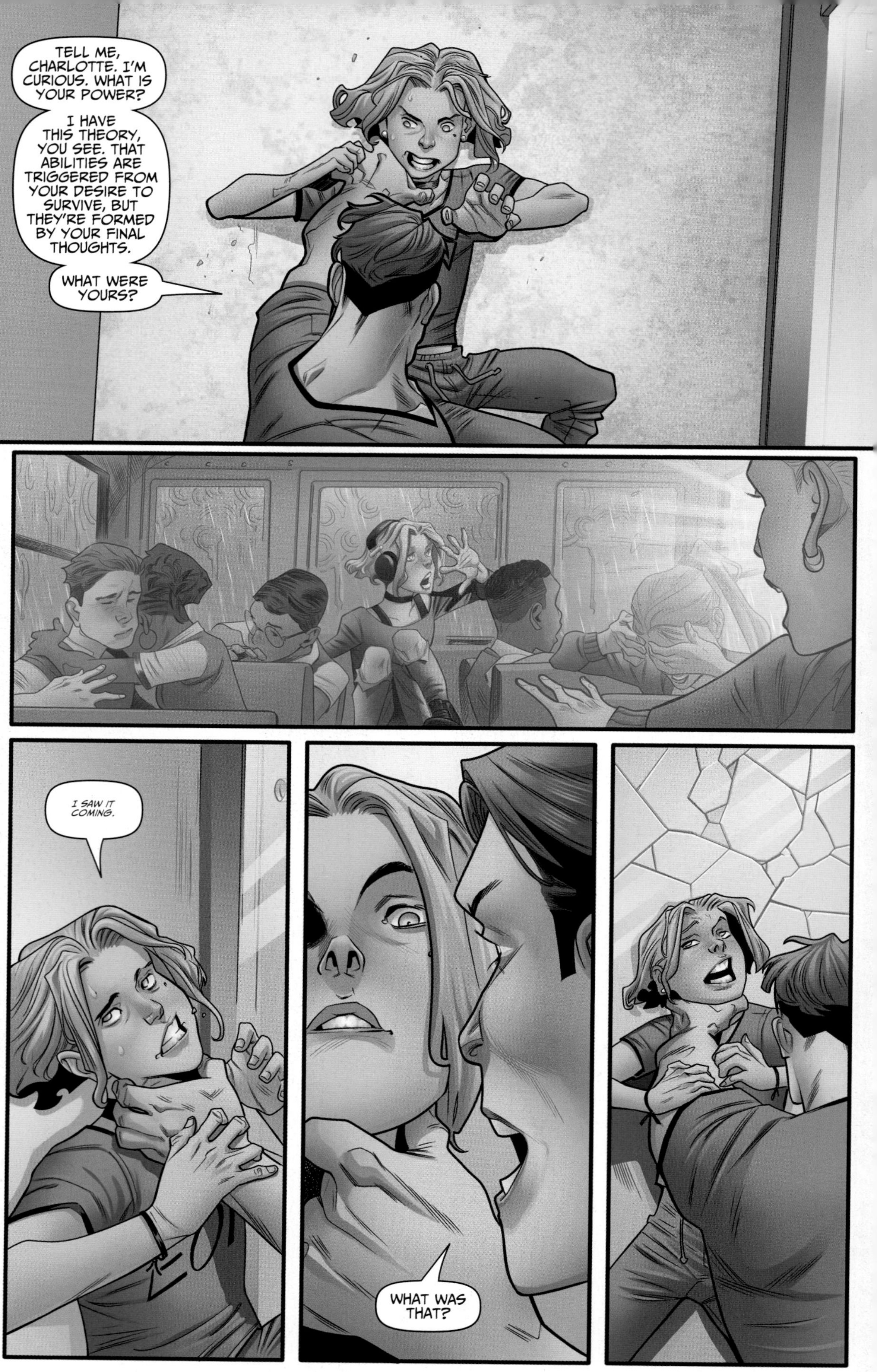
TELL ME, CHARLOTTE. I'M CURIOUS. WHAT IS YOUR POWER?
I HAVE THIS THEORY, YOU SEE. THAT ABILITIES ARE TRIGGERED FROM YOUR DESIRE TO SURVIVE, BUT THEY'RE FORMED BY YOUR FINAL THOUGHTS.
WHAT WERE YOURS?
I SAW IT COMING.
WHAT WAS THAT?

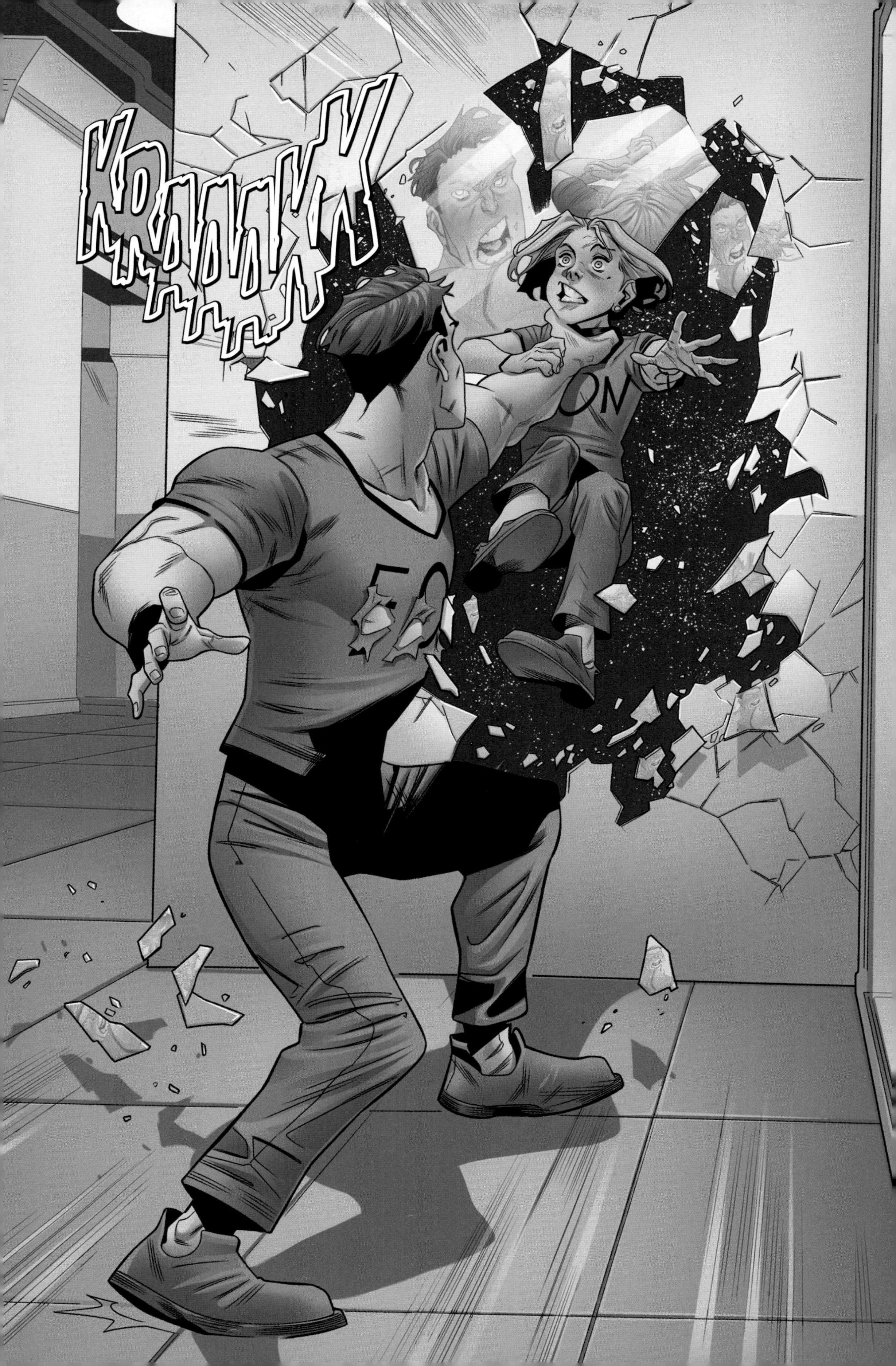
KRAAAAKKK

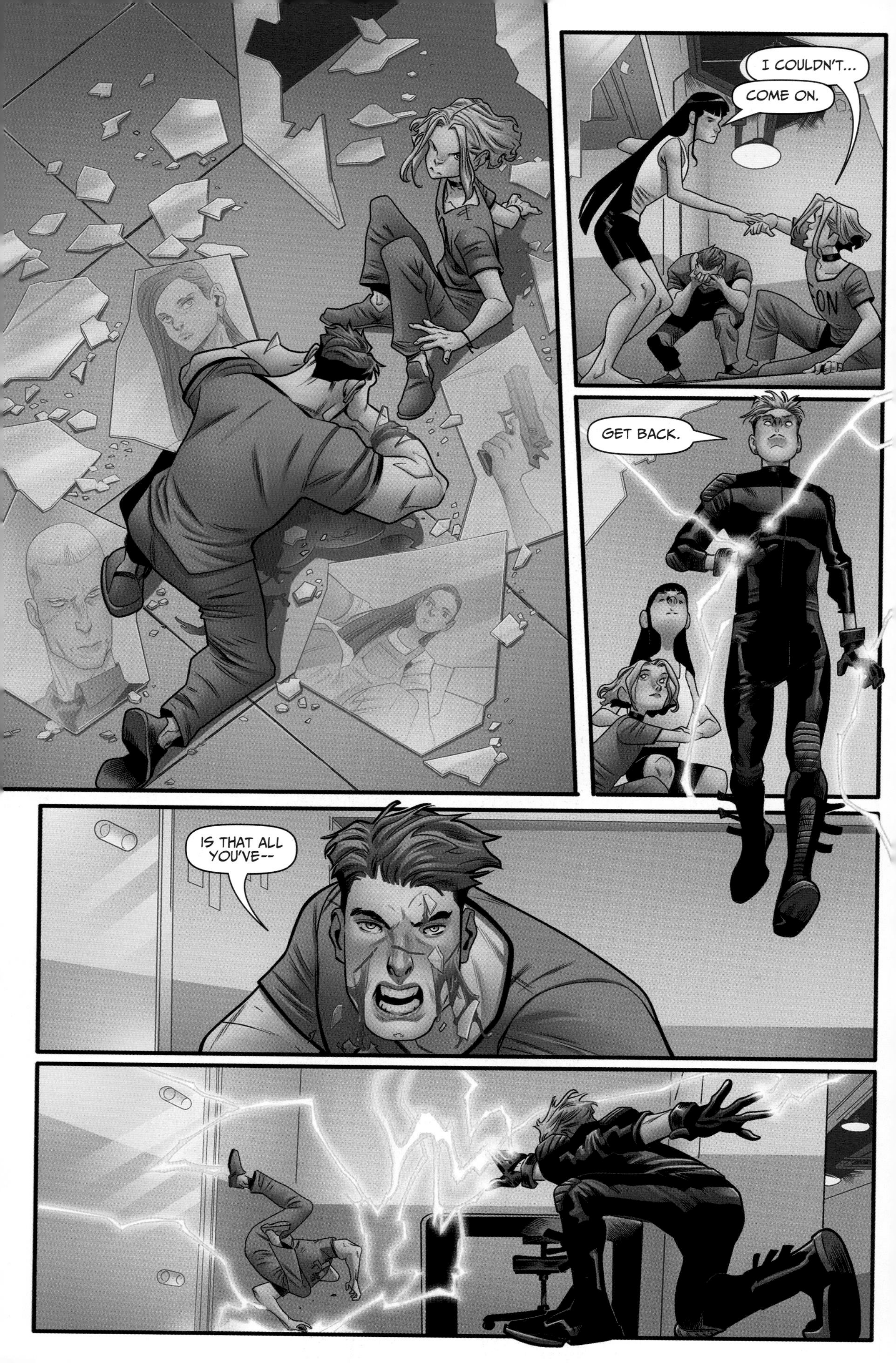

I COULDN'T...
COME ON.
GET BACK.
IS THAT ALL YOU'VE--

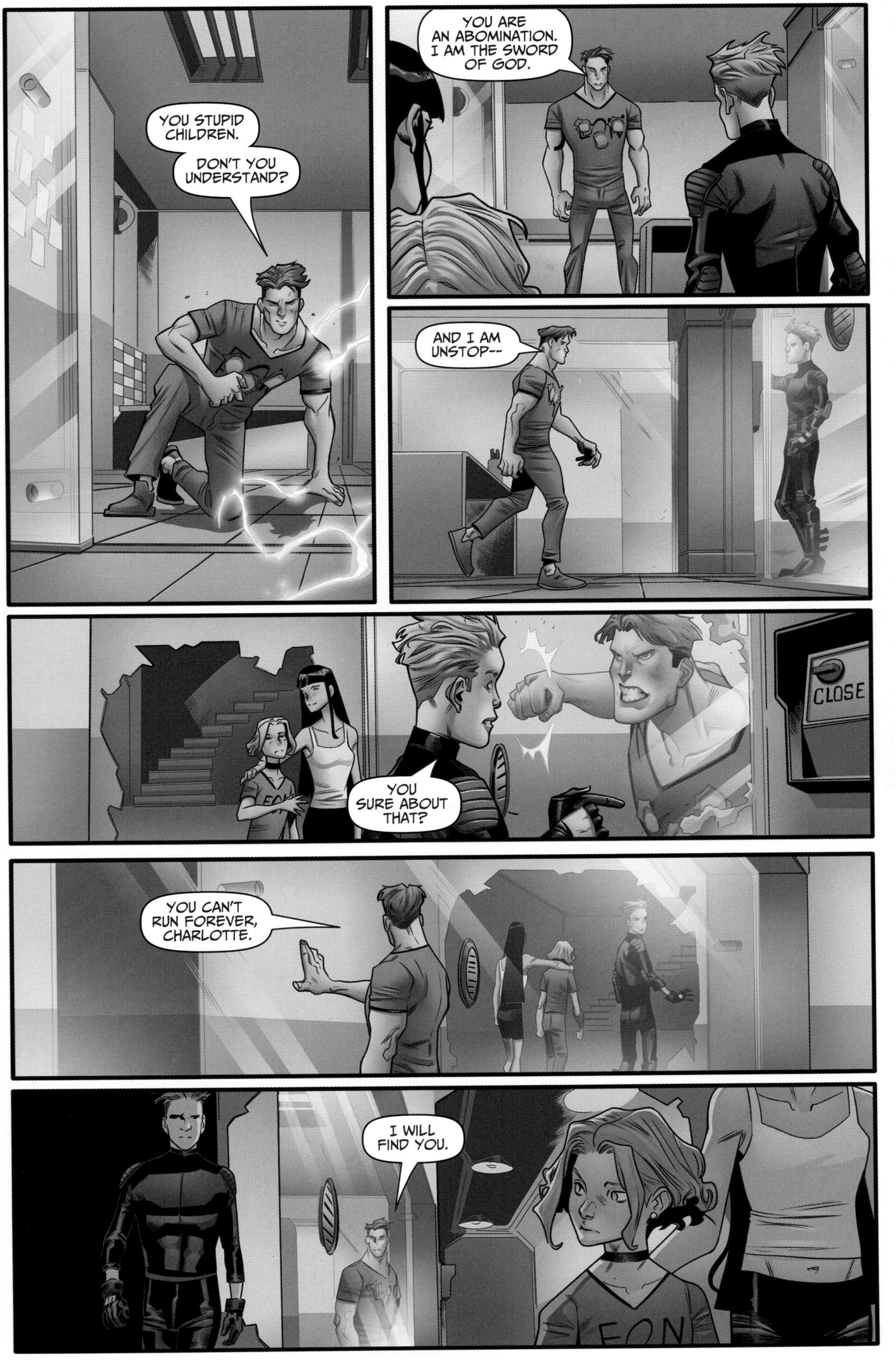
YOU STUPID CHILDREN.
DON'T YOU UNDERSTAND?
YOU ARE AN ABOMINATION. I AM THE SWORD OF GOD.
AND I AM UNSTOP--
CLOSE
YOU SURE ABOUT THAT?
YOU CAN'T RUN FOREVER, CHARLOTTE.
I WILL FIND YOU.

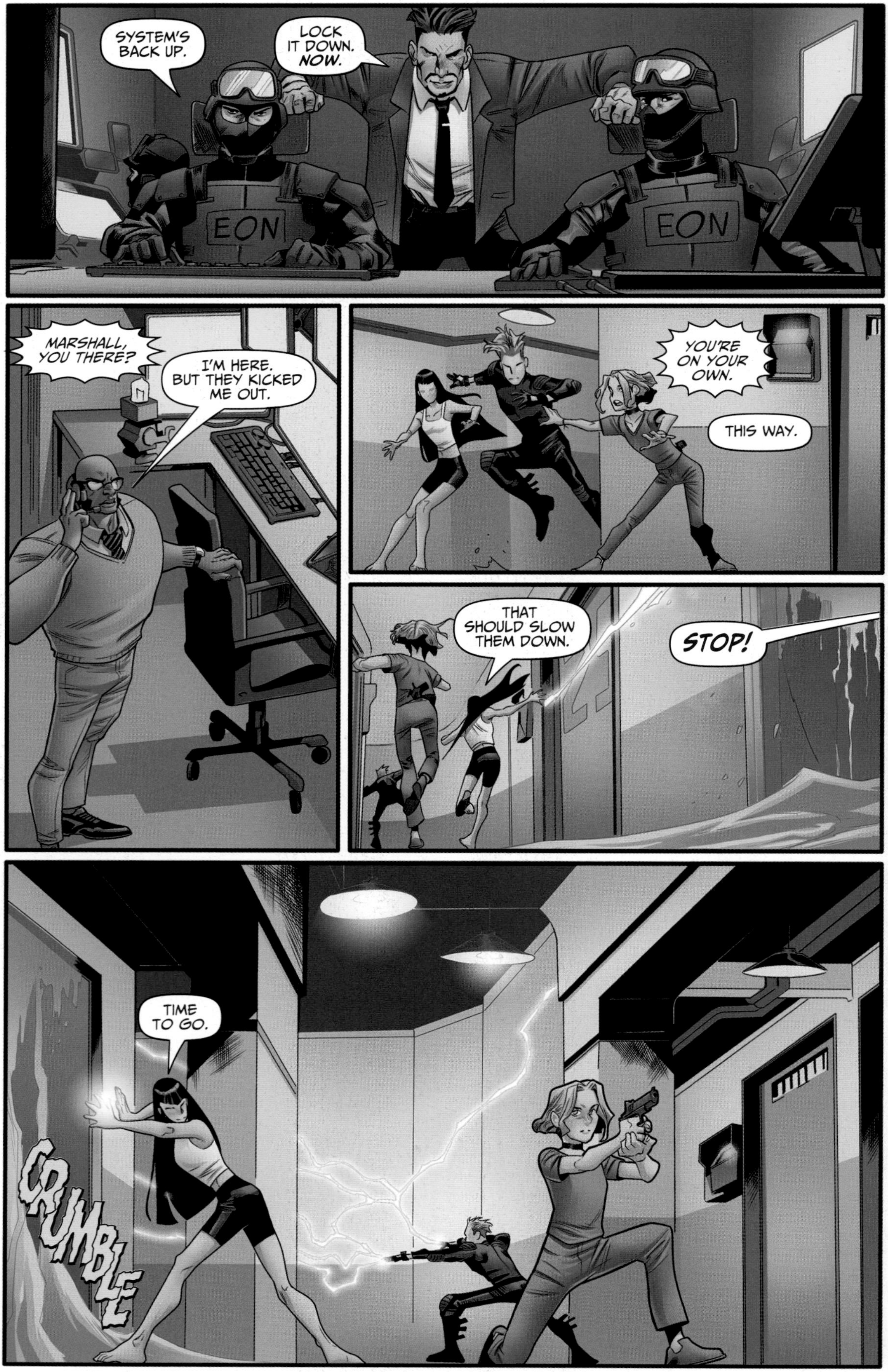
SYSTEM'S BACK UP.
LOCK IT DOWN. NOW.
EON
EON
MARSHALL, YOU THERE?
I'M HERE. BUT THEY KICKED ME OUT.
YOU'RE ON YOUR OWN.
THIS WAY.
THAT SHOULD SLOW THEM DOWN.
STOP!
TIME TO GO.
CRUMBLE

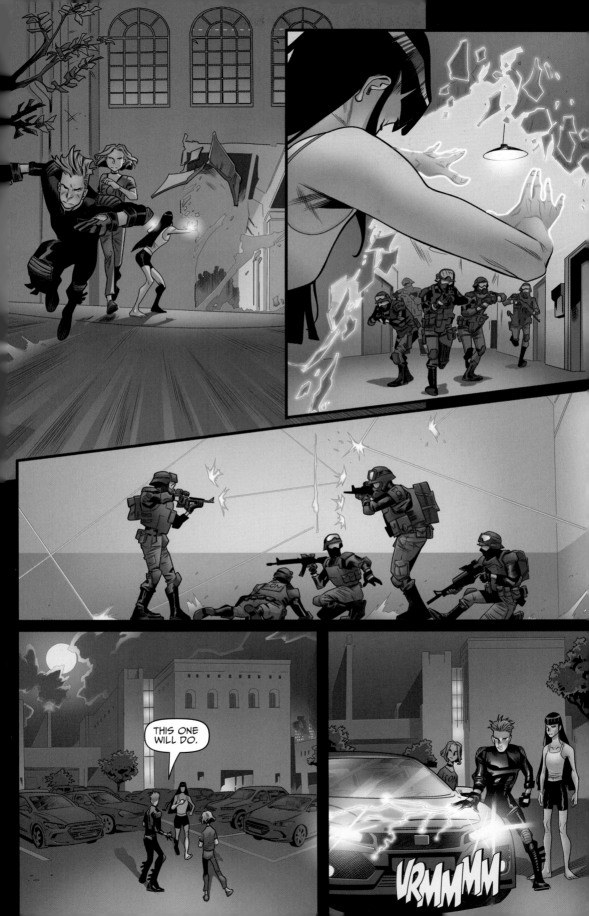

THIS ONE
WILL DO.

VRMMMM

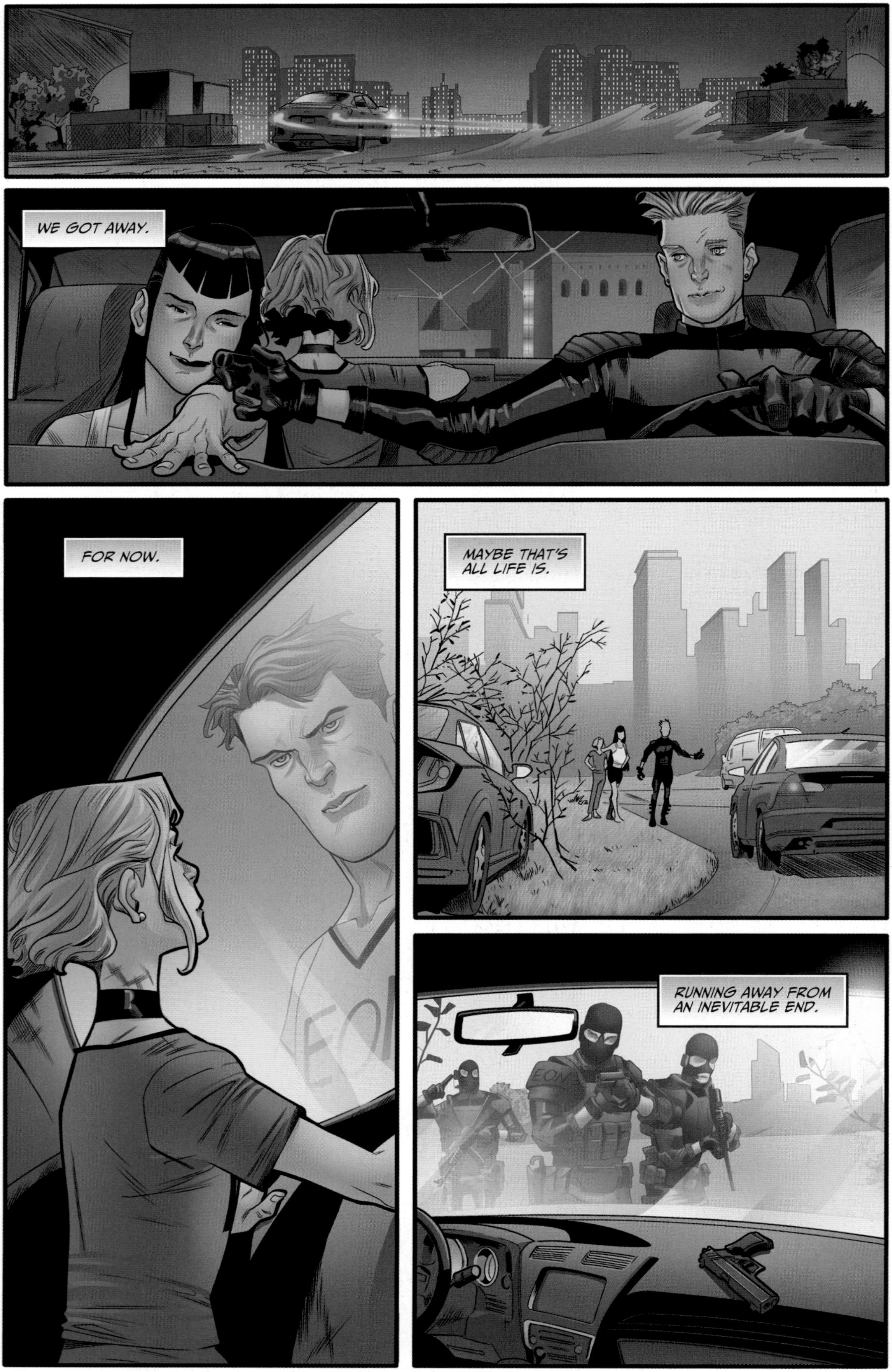
WE GOT AWAY.
FOR NOW.
MAYBE THAT'S ALL LIFE IS.
RUNNING AWAY FROM AN INEVITABLE END.

BUT WHAT DO I DO NOW?

I CAN'T GO BACK HOME. THEY'LL FIND ME.

BUT IS THERE A PLACE FOR ME HERE?

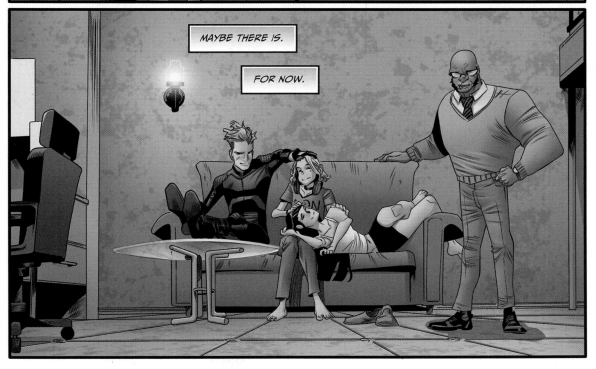

MAYBE THERE IS.

FOR NOW.

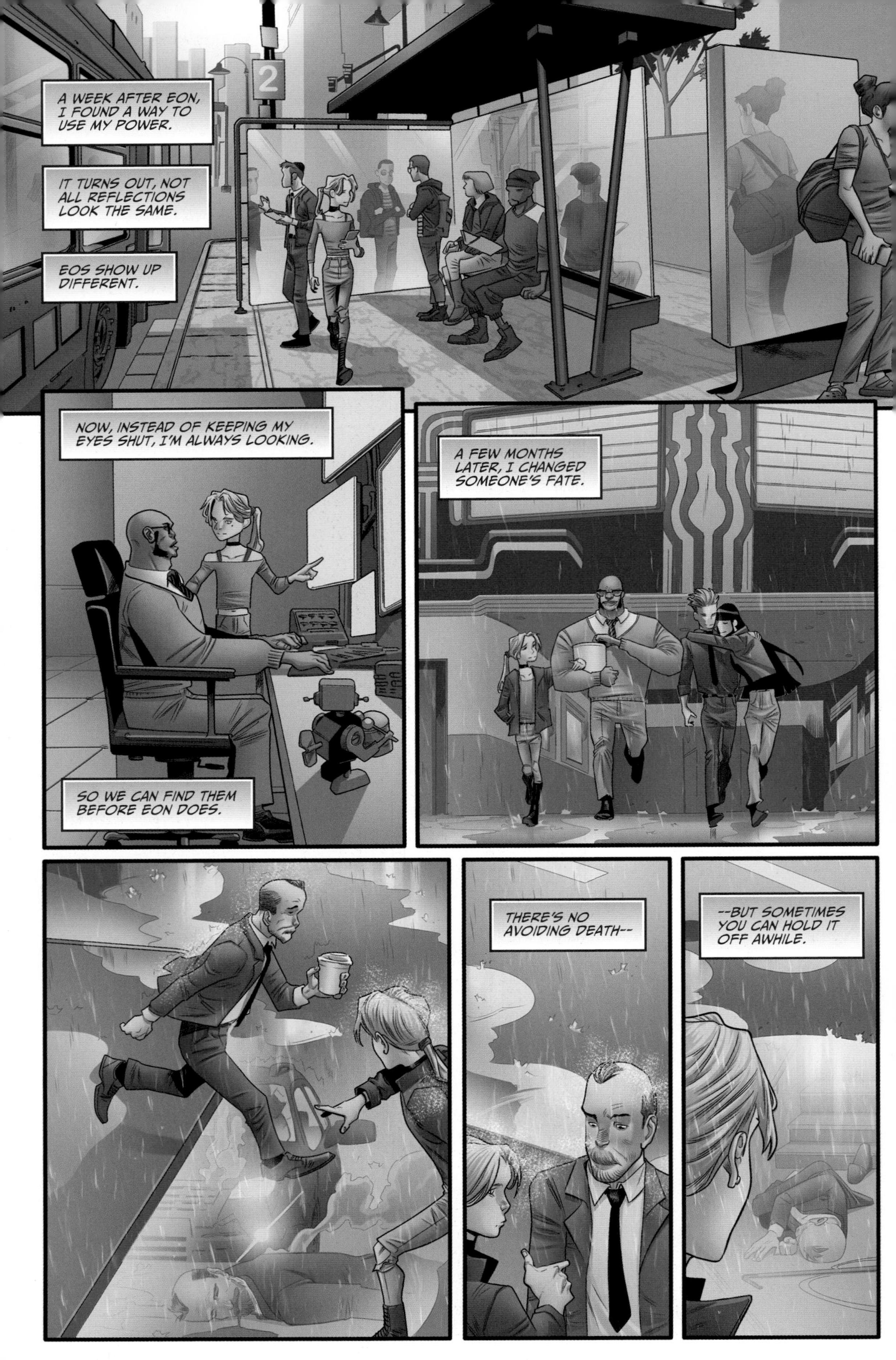
A WEEK AFTER EON, I FOUND A WAY TO USE MY POWER.
IT TURNS OUT, NOT ALL REFLECTIONS LOOK THE SAME.
EOS SHOW UP DIFFERENT.
2
NOW, INSTEAD OF KEEPING MY EYES SHUT, I'M ALWAYS LOOKING.
SO WE CAN FIND THEM BEFORE EON DOES.
A FEW MONTHS LATER, I CHANGED SOMEONE'S FATE.
THERE'S NO AVOIDING DEATH--
--BUT SOMETIMES YOU CAN HOLD IT OFF AWHILE.

AS FOR ELI...

FOR TWO STRAIGHT YEARS, I SAW HIM. EVERYWHERE I LOOKED.

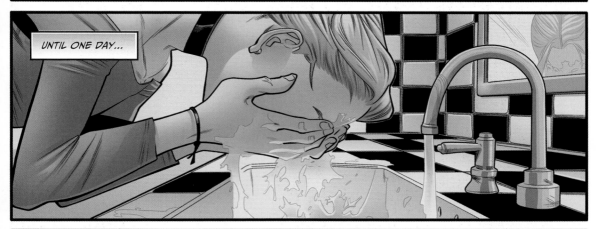

UNTIL ONE DAY...

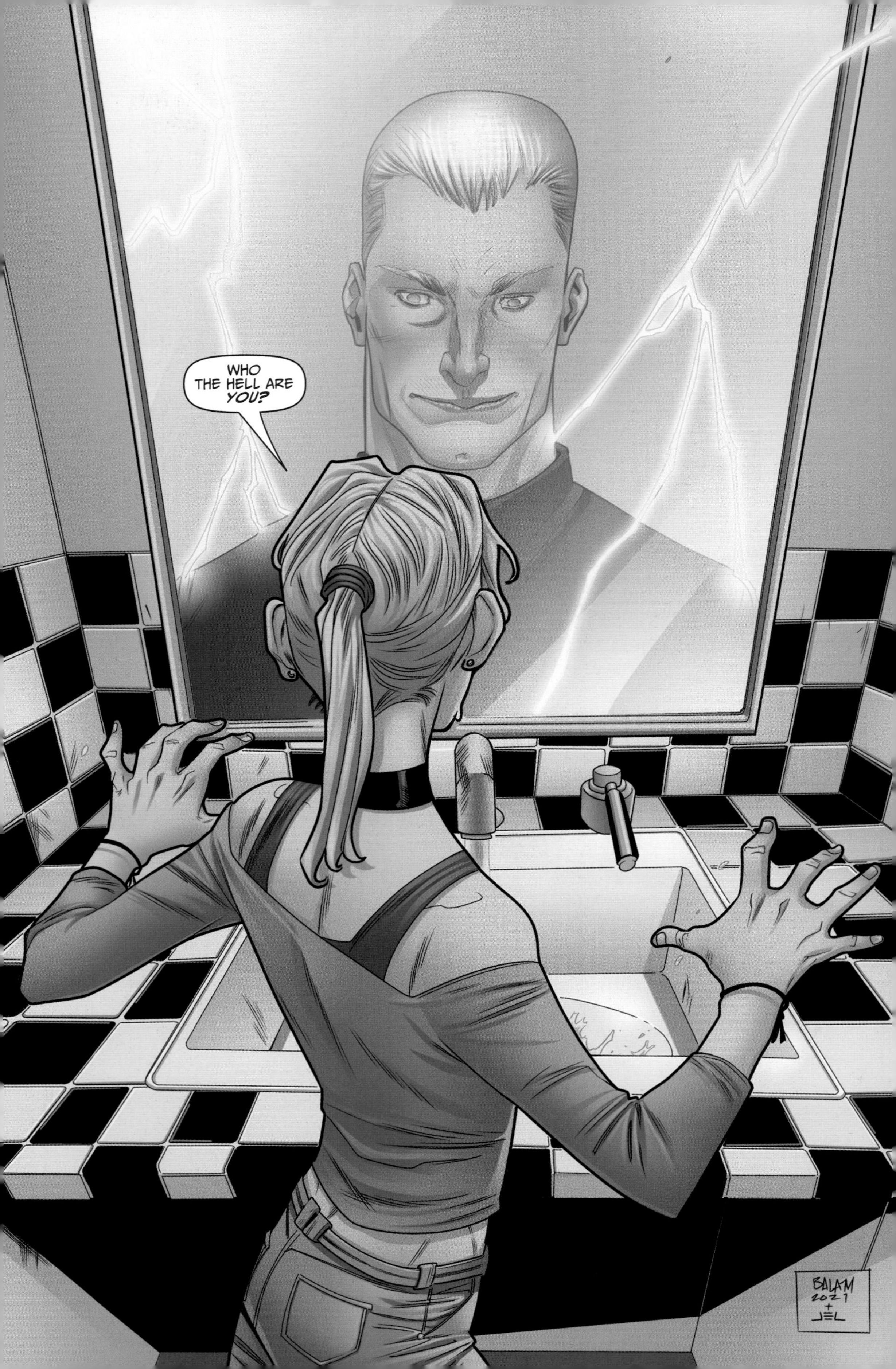
WHO THE HELL ARE YOU?

V. E. SCHWAB

Discover the world of V. E. Schwab with her original novels, published in the USA and Canada by **Tor Books** (covers on the left) and in the UK/Eire/R.O.W. by **Titan Books** (covers on the right). **Titan Comics** available worldwide.

A DARKER SHADE OF MAGIC
(SHADES OF MAGIC BOOK ONE)

A GATHERING OF SHADOWS
(SHADES OF MAGIC BOOK TWO)

A CONJURING OF LIGHT
(SHADES OF MAGIC BOOK THREE)

VICIOUS
(VILLAINS BOOK ONE)

VENGEFUL
(VILLAINS BOOK TWO)

THE NEAR WITCH

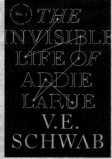 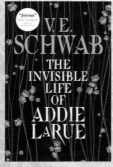   

THE INVISIBLE LIFE OF ADDIE LARUE

SHADES OF MAGIC VOLUMES 1-3
(SHADES OF MAGIC COMIC COLLECTION)

FOR MORE INFORMATION, VISIT: TOR BOOKS tor-forge.com
TITAN BOOKS titanbooks.com | TITAN COMICS titan-comics.com

WARM UP - A SHORT STORY

It's been 297 days since David died—and came back. He may have survived the avalanche, but the aftermath has been far worse. His wife moved out, taking his son with her, and a devastated David hasn't left his house since, terrified of the mysterious new power that followed him home from the ill-fated expedition. After months in seclusion, David's ready for a fresh start, and ventures out, determined to keep his power in check. But David's power isn't the one he needs to worry about.

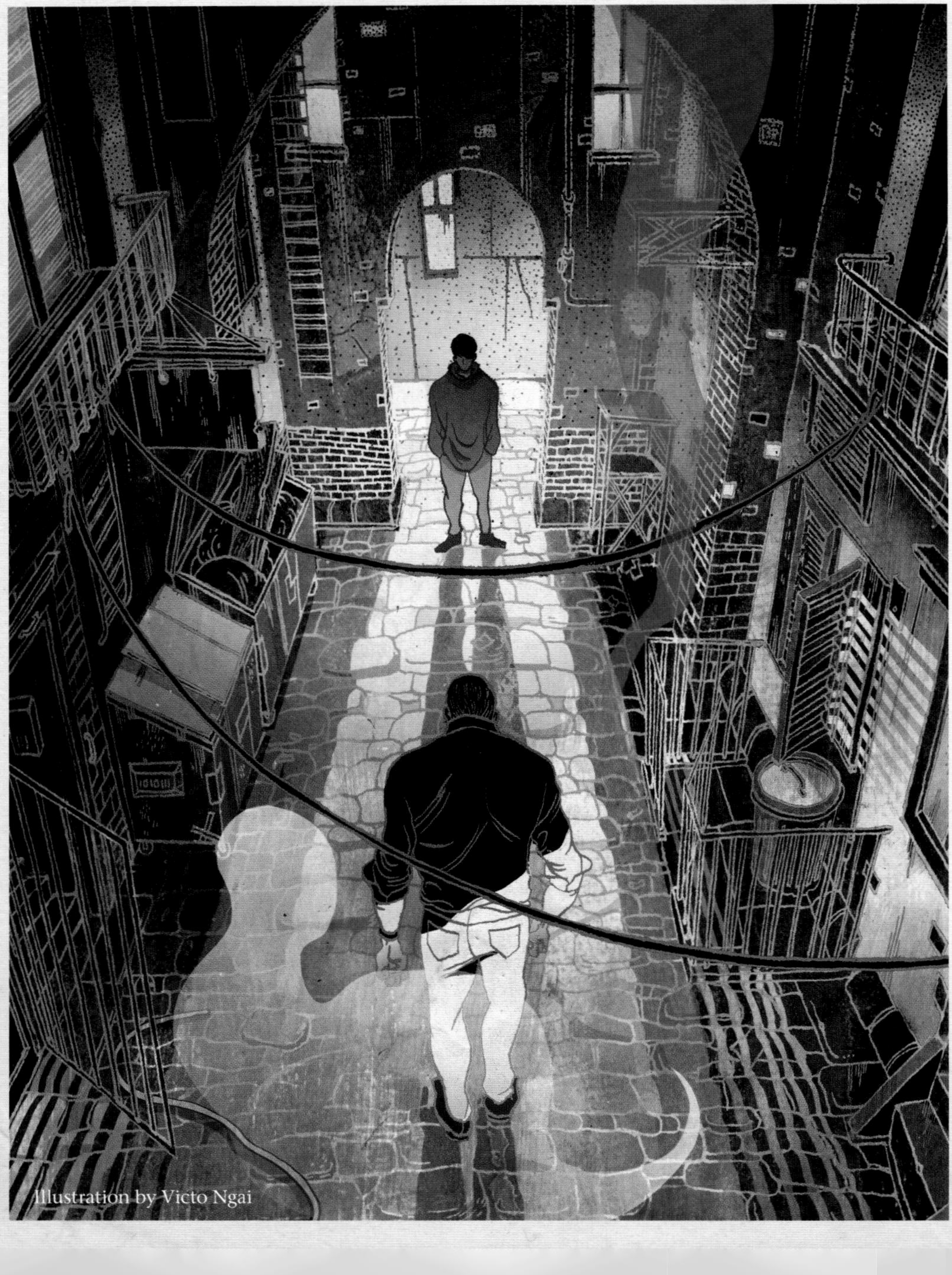

Illustration by Victo Ngai

It had been 297 days since David died.

294 days since Samantha left.

293 days since he locked himself in the house that had been his and then theirs and was now his again.

And he had finally made a decision.

He wasn't quite sure when he made it, somewhere between turning on the shower and stepping in, perhaps, or pouring the milk and adding the cereal, or maybe a dozen tiny decisions had added up like letters until they finally made a word, a phrase, a sentence.

Either way, he'd made the decision, and now he stood very still at the kitchen counter, holding his choice in his hands with his coffee, afraid that if he moved, his resolve would crumble. He stood there until the coffee went cold, and he was still standing there when Jess came in, arms full of groceries.

"Jesus, David," she said, dropping the bags on the counter, "it's like an oven in here."

His sister went for the thermostat. He swallowed. Three small words, a phrase, a sentence.

A *decision*.

"I'm going out," he said.

Jess's hand froze above the AC. "Don't joke about that."

She'd pleaded with him for weeks—months—to leave the house, before finally giving up.

Now her eyes brightened with a kind of guarded hope.

"I'm not," said David. "I'm going out."

The words felt more solid the second time. Jess gave him a long, hard look. "What changed?"

"Nothing," he lied. "I just think it's time."

Jess turned the temperature down and came to him, resting her elbows on the kitchen counter between them. "How long has it been?" she asked casually, as if they weren't both counting.

297.

294.

293.

He didn't know how to choose the right number. The instant of impact or the aftermath?

"Two hundred ninety-seven," he said at last, because it had all started there in the snow.

"Sure you don't want to wait for three hundred?" Jess managed a thin smile when she said it, but the joke was too careful, too light, like she knew they were on cracking ice. The smallest misstep would send them under. David felt it, too. That's why he'd been standing so still.

"I'm ready," he said, looking down at the still-full cup, the coffee long since cold. He tightened his grip on the porcelain, and a moment later fresh steam rose from the dark surface. A small, conscious effort. The line between accidental and intentional meant everything. I'm going out tonight."

"Okay. Great," said Jess, rousing. "This is great. I get off work at seven. I'll swing by and we can—" David shook his head. "I need to do this."

Alone. The word hung in the air, unsaid but understood. Control was all about focus, and he couldn't do that, not with Jess hovering, studying him like a puzzle she could piece back together. She hadn't yet realized that the picture had changed.

David had thought about telling her. Hell, he'd acted out that conversation a hundred times. Maybe tonight, he would finally do it. He'd come home, and he'd call her, and he'd tell her why Samantha had left, and why he'd spent 293 days in his house, and why he kept shivering no matter how high he turned the thermostat up. It would all make sense, and she'd know he wasn't crazy. He was just scared.

And cold. Tonight, he decided, setting aside the coffee cup and turning toward the groceries. He handled the items gingerly, manoeuvring the carton of milk, the apples, the steak, like they were grips, outcrops, footholds, ones that might give way if he weren't careful. That first week, every single piece of food had turned to ash in his hands. Now he cupped a Granny Smith in his palm, marveling at the way the green skin glistened.

He was ready.

Behind him, Jess scooped up the discarded mug.

"Fuck," she swore, fumbling the cup. It hit the floor and shattered, spilling coffee across the tiles. "Fuck, fuck, fuck," she murmured, shaking her fingers.

"You okay?" David knelt and gathered up the broken shards.

"Careful," she said, running her hand under the tap. "It's hot."

David nodded absently as he piled the broken pieces in his palm before dumping them in the trash. Dulled nerves, he'd told her. From years of climbing ice.

You should really get that checked out, she'd said.

You're probably right, he'd replied.

"Sorry," he said now, sponging up the coffee with a towel.

"It's not your fault," she said. She didn't know. "Sorry about the mess." She glanced at her watch. "Crap, I'm going to be late." Jess taught second grade at an elementary school. David's son, Jack, was in kindergarten there. It had been 294 days since he'd seen him.

"Go," said David, wringing out the towel. "I've got this."

Jess didn't move. She just stood there and stared, squinting at him like he was written in another language. "I'm proud of you,

"HE REMEMBERED THE LONG MOMENT OF SILENCE BEFORE THE SNOW HIT, AND THE LONGER MOMENT AFTER."

Dave," she said, reaching out and touching his shoulder. He didn't touch her back. "Call me when you're home, okay?"

David nodded. "Sure thing," he said as if the very act of leaving the house wasn't a strange and terrifying prospect.

It had been 297 days since David died.

Aside from the constant count in his head and his new . . . affliction, the only reminder was a photograph. It sat in a frame on the chest of drawers by his bed, a beaming version of himself, bundled up and ready for the climb, sunlight winking off snow. The rest of the group—six climbers in all—milled in the background. David was holding up three gloved fingers. It was a milestone. His thirtieth climb.

David never bothered with photos, but one of his teammates, Jackson—a partner at David's firm—took his camera everywhere. That's how they'd found his body after, the lens winking in the sun.

Gotta capture the moment, Jackson had said, snapping a shot. Memories fade.

So do pictures, David had thought, but he'd smiled and posed anyways.

Now he picked up the photograph, and ran a finger over the frame, steam blossoming on the glass.

Some people forget, he thought. A bad thing happens to them and their mind sweeps in and buries the bad thing deep, and all that's left is a stretch of white in their heads, like fresh snow. Looking at it—at them—you wouldn't even know anything was trapped beneath.

Some people forget, but David remembered everything.

He remembered the light-headed thrill of the climb. The wind-stripped voices of the others in his wake. The crunch of the icy crust on the snow. The sound and shape of his breath in the air. And somewhere, between an exhale and an inhale, a far-off sound like a hush but heavier. He remembered looking up and seeing the wall of white, as big as the sky.

He remembered the long moment of silence before the snow hit, and the longer moment after. The horrifying cold that ate through every layer of clothing, bit into his skin, clawed at his bones. All David could think of was that cold, and how badly he wanted to warm up.

Warm up warm up warm up, he'd thought, the plea like a pulse, soft and slowing until the air ran out, and his thoughts froze, and his heart stopped.

It had been 297 days since David died. And 297 since he'd come back, gasped and sat up in a base camp hospital tent covered in warming pads, the defibrillator still buzzing in the medic's hands, his teeth chattering with cold.

Jackson didn't make it.

None of them did.

An envelope showed up in David's mailbox a few weeks later—he'd made Jess open it—from Jackson's wife, Anita. Inside was the photograph, and a note.

All that's left, it said.

Now David unfastened the metal clasps that held the frame together and pulled the photograph free. He pinched the bottom of the paper. For a moment, nothing happened. And then the photo began to blacken and curl.

It didn't catch fire. Nothing ever actually caught fire.

No, it all simply *burned.*

The photo—the broad smile, the wind-chapped face, the three gloved fingers—crumbled to ash in his hand.

What changed? Jess had asked. The truth was, David had. He'd fallen so far, and the climb back up had been slow, agonizingly so—some days inching forward, others slipping back—but little by little, he'd fought his way back to the summit. He could see a life from here. Not his life, that was gone, but a life.

It was time for a fresh start.

It had been 294 days since Samantha left.

If any of David's colleagues or Samantha's old friends had come to visit, the first thing they would have noticed about the house was the shocking absence of stuff.

David had never been a fan of stuff, but Samantha loved acquiring it. She had spent a small fortune collecting trinkets and knick-knacks, tapestries and prints and other random oddities. She treated every inch of empty surface—countertop, table, shelf—like an affront, something to be scrubbed out.

Nothing wrong with negative space, Sam, he'd said, tossing the latest bauble from hand to hand. That's how he saw climbing, a physical exercise in positive and negative space. The vast expanse of white drawing the small, person-shaped speck into sharp relief.

At least my hobbies won't get me killed, she'd said, plucking the ornament out of his hand and pecking him on the cheek.

After the accident, and after the fight, when Samantha left him in the middle of the night, she didn't take any of the clutter with her. No, she took Jack and two suitcases and left David and the house full of stuff behind. He'd ruined most of it in those first weeks, a few select things out of spite (that damn lamp, those ugly bookends, the statue on the patio) but the rest were merely victims of his desperate search for control—sacrificed as he tried to relearn how to touch, how to hold, how to live. How to warm up.

After the accident, they'd airlifted him off the mountain.

As they loaded him into the helicopter, the EMTs had given him a blanket. It didn't help. When he tried to pull it tighter, the fabric went ember-red under his touch, and then crumbled. David stared down at the smear of ash across his palms as the EMTs piled in. They gave him another blanket. He didn't touch it. Instead, he clutched a metal

"SOME PEOPLE FORGET, BUT DAVID REMEMBERED EVERYTHING."

rail beside his stretcher. The silver began to glow beneath his fingers. He felt nothing, no heat, but when an EMT leaned against it mid-flight, it burned the skin from the man's arm.

A *malfunction*, they called it. When the chopper landed, the doctors couldn't convince David to unclench his hands. They gave up. *Trauma*, they wrote in their books. They told him they'd come back in the morning.

But in the morning, he was gone.

David paid off two nurses and a front desk clerk and checked himself out—terrified that if he stayed, he'd be dissected as some kind of freak—and went home. Afterward, he wished he hadn't, wished he'd had the strength to run away. From his family. His life. Anything that could be burned. Instead, he stood at the gate where the cab dropped him off and stared up at the oversized, overstuffed house, desperate to see his family again. To have the chance to say good-bye.

Samantha threw her arms around him. Jack clung to his leg, begging to be picked up. He kept his hands balled at his sides, terrified of touching them. Samantha said he looked tired. They went to bed. He only wanted to be near her. One last time. He lay there in the dark, hands

away. A few of them were truths. Most of them were lies.

And then a horrible thing happened.

She went to slap him and he caught her wrist.

He hadn't meant to hurt her. It was reflex, self-defense, a hand raised against a hand. But the moment his fingers met her skin, she screamed. He let go at once, but it was too late. The flesh had bubbled and burned, raised welts in the shape of his hand.

Samantha pulled away, horrified.

A malfunction.

He tried to apologize, tried to explain, but he couldn't make her understand. He didn't understand.

She left right after, in the middle of the night, Jack and two suitcases in the car, David and his trauma left behind in the house.

Some days David told himself that if he found control—when he found control—he'd make it right. Piece that part of his life back together. But he knew he wouldn't. No matter how good he got, it would never be good enough to embrace his wife, to hold his son.

The only papers in the house that he hadn't burned were the divorce papers. He hadn't signed them, not yet, but he would.

After tonight, he told himself.

It had been 293 days since he locked himself in.

his fingers to rest on the handle— it remained cool beneath his touch—and turned. He stepped through. Closed the door. Locked it. Took one step, then another. David made it to the end of the drive, through the gate, up the quiet road. Every block he paused and asked himself if he wanted to turn back or keep going.

He kept going.

The Lanes' house sat only a mile or so from the city center, and as David walked, the street and path—both empty when he set out—began to fill. It happened quite suddenly, this populating of the world, and David soon found himself standing at an intersection crowded with people. His pulse quickened, and he hung back to let them cross while he composed himself, flexing his hands, reassuring himself that he was all right. A hedge decorated the corner behind him, and he plucked a leaf and held it in his palm. It didn't burn. He dropped it with relief and crossed the street.

As he did, David had the feeling he was being watched. He scanned the other corners and found a handful of people—an older woman, a pair of teen girls, a young man—but none of them were looking his way, and he shook it off; nearly a year without prying eyes was bound to make the world seem full of them.

"BUT THE REST WERE MERELY VICTIMS OF HIS DESPERATE SEARCH FOR CONTROL."

wrapped around his own ribs—the heat never reached him—to keep her safe, but it wasn't enough.

She tried to embrace him. He shook her off.

That's how the fight started. They'd had so many, over the years, everything from minor quarrels to screaming matches— he worked too late, she spent too much—but this one was different.

David knew what it was: the chance to set her free. To let her go. An awful, dull ache spread through him as he said things— cruel things—any and everything he could think of to push her

Now, as David stood facing the front door, he checked himself— keys, wallet, phone—savoring the small measure of control he felt at confirming each thing, and the small comfort at delaying the vital moment a few seconds longer. Shoes. Pants. Shirt. Jacket. He'd showered and shaved—not that he hadn't continued those rituals daily under his self-imposed seclusion; David had always been a creature of routine—and combed back his hair, which Jess had cut for him the week before.

I'm ready.

He reached out and brought

He kept going.

David passed half a dozen shops, a handful of restaurants, a bar. At the last, his steps slowed.

McKillan's read the sign over the doors. Samantha despised bars, couldn't stand the noise and the smoke and the sticky floors. David went in.

The world got smaller. The people got closer. He tried not to think about how easily the wooden shell of the place would burn as he made his way to the counter and climbed up onto the stool, lacing his fingers in front of him. He ordered a gin and tonic.

"AND THEN A HORRIBLE THING HAPPENED."

And then another. And a third. He went to the bathroom. When he came back, a fresh drink was waiting at David's stool. A beer.

"From the lady at the end," said the bartender, pointing to the edge of the counter. "Said you looked like you could use it."

David twisted in his seat to see the woman. She had red hair and redder lips, and the darkest brown eyes he'd ever seen. Everything about her seemed . . . warm. David hesitated. And then he took his drink, and went to join her.

Her name was Christa. She touched his arm when she talked, and he leaned into her heat. After the first beer, he'd forgotten about the crowded bar. After the second, he'd forgotten about the days—weeks, months—of meticulous planning. After the third, he'd forgotten about his fear, and his power.

By the time David left, he could barely see straight enough to read Christa's number on the napkin. On the way out, he thought he recognized the young man in the corner booth. But he couldn't place him.

He ambled down the sidewalk, feeling better than he had in 297 days. The bar had been loud, but in the relative quiet of the street, David heard his phone beep. He had a message. He tugged the cell gingerly from his pocket and pressed the button, holding it lightly to his ear as he walked.

"Hey Dave," Jess's voice said, "just your baby sister here. I hope you made it past the driveway. Don't forget to check in. Love you. Be safe."

When he put the phone away, and looked up, he realized his feet had carried him down a side street. He turned back and made his way toward the main road, and was halfway there when he snagged his shoe on a bit of alley debris and stumbled forward. Without thinking, he threw out his hand, and caught himself against a restaurant's back door.

It only took a second. The surprise of the fall and the pain of the impact caught him off guard, and his control wavered. He pulled back as quickly as he could, but by then he'd singed a handprint into the wood.

Clumsy, growled David to himself as he straightened. He'd been doing so well.

He took another step toward the main road before he realized someone was standing in his way. The light in the alley was lower than that on the main street and at first the figure was nothing more than a fuzzy silhouette in David's far-from-sober vision. And then the shape moved toward him, sharpening, and David frowned.

It was the young man from the corner booth. And the street corner, David realized. He was dressed in dark jeans and a long-sleeved shirt. He barely looked old enough to drink.

"Can I help you, kid?" asked David.

The stranger continued toward him with slow, measured steps, and David found himself retreating, even as he said, "Hey, I'm talking to you."

"THE SHAPE MOVED TOWARDS HIM, SHARPENING, AND DAVID FROWNED."

The young man reached the burned door, and stopped.

"The son of man," he said softly, bringing his hand to the wood, "shall send forth his angels, and they shall gather out of his kingdom all that offend." His hand fell away from the door. "And cast them into a furnace of fire."

The stranger's eyes glittered in the dark.

"What the hell are you talking about?" said David.

"David Lane," said the stranger.

David's blood ran cold. "How do you know my name?"

"You have sinned against God."

"Who are you?"

A knife appeared in the stranger's hand. "One of his angels."

David stumbled backward several feet, but his shoulders fetched up against a trash bin, and before he could get away, the stranger was there. "Wait, please—"

He didn't get the chance to finish. The knife slid between David's ribs. Pain, bright and hot—hotter than anything he'd felt in 297 days—tore through him as his knees buckled.

He grasped at the stranger's arm as he sank, tightening his fingers around the man's sleeve. The fabric burned instantly, and the flesh beneath began to char, and the stranger gritted his teeth, but didn't let go. David's grip began to weaken, until his fingers finally slipped from the stranger's arm. The knife slid free. Everything got quiet. Even the sound of his own body falling forward to the street seemed far away. He felt the cold then, not blistering as it had been beneath the snow, but steady, spreading through him as he lay there.

Warm up, he thought, but his hands rested uselessly against the pavement. Warm up, he willed, but only the cold was there to meet him. The cold and the quiet. They took hold and dragged him down, and the last thing David saw was the stranger crossing himself, the ruined flesh of his arm knitting back together.

And then the darkness came, and buried David Lane in a blanket of ash.

COVER GALLERY

Presented here are all four 'A' covers for the mini-series.

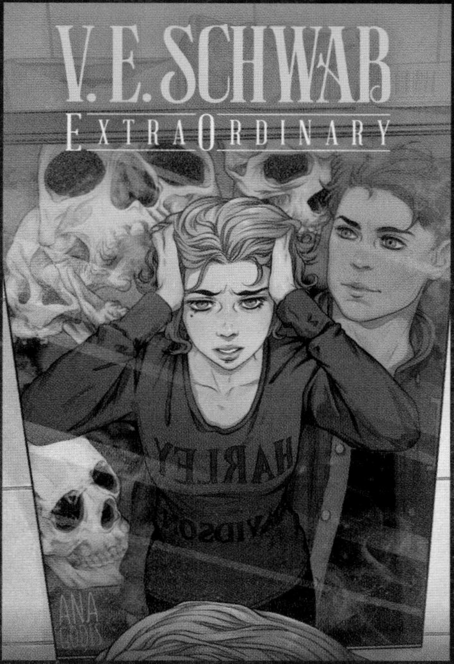
V. E. SCHWAB
EXTRAORDINARY
ANA GODIS

ISSUE 1 COVER A
ANA GODIS

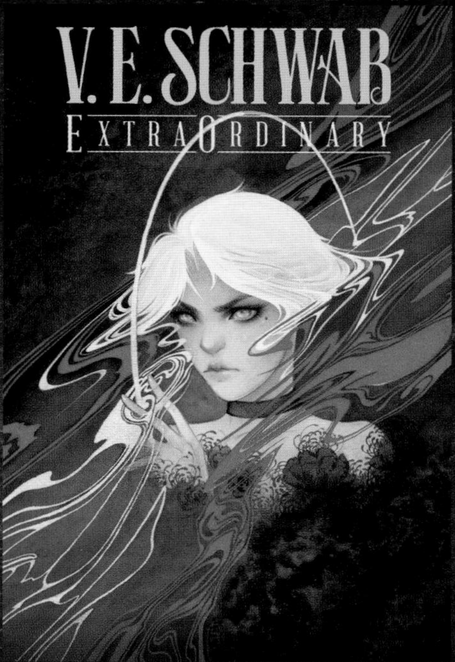
V. E. SCHWAB
EXTRAORDINARY

ISSUE 2 COVER A
NEN CHANG & LIZ TECCA

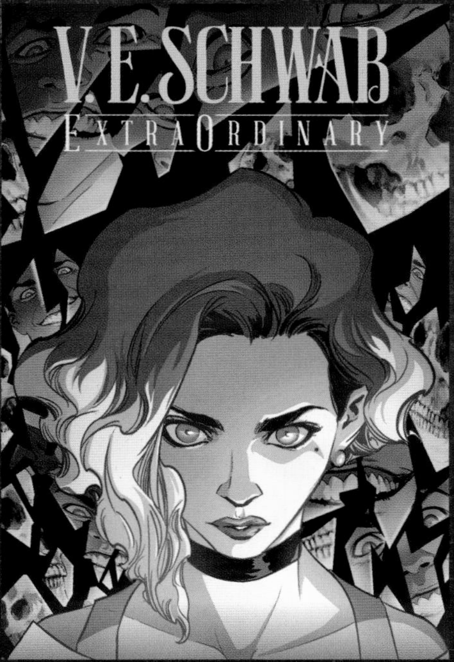
V. E. SCHWAB
EXTRAORDINARY

ISSUE 3 COVER A
PRISCILLA PETRAITES & MARCO LESKO

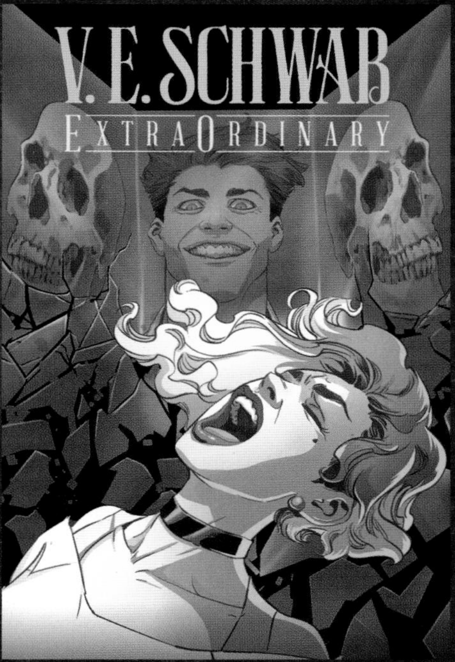
V. E. SCHWAB
EXTRAORDINARY

ISSUE 4 COVER A
PRISCILLA PETRAITES & MARCO LESKO

BIOGRAPHIES

V. E. SCHWAB

Victoria "V.E." Schwab is the #1 *NYT*, USA, and Indie-
bestselling author of more than a dozen books, including
Vicious, the *Shades of Magic* series, and *This Savage Song*.
Her work has received critical acclaim, been featured
by *Entertainment Weekly* and the *New York Times*, been
ttranslated into more than a dozen languages, and has
been optioned for TV and Film. *The Independent* calls her
the "natural successor to Diana Wynne Jones" and touts her
"enviable, almost Gaiman-esque ability to switch
between styles, genres, and tones."

ENID BALÁM

Enid currently lives in México City where he studied art on
the MaPA art program at the Autonomous University of the
State of Morelos. He graduated in 2016 with a Masters in
Artistic Production and established his own screen-print art
shop. In 2015, he started his professional comic art career
working for a French publisher as a colorist on *Cutting Edge*.
In 2018, he wrote and drew his first graphic novel, *Someday
Comes Paradise*, and in 2020 he drew the four-book
miniseries *OMNI* for an L.A. publishing house.
Currently Enid is drawing the *Reptil* miniseries
for a leading American publisher.

JORDI ESCUIN LLORACH

Jordi Escuin Llorach is a Spanish comic book colorist, whose
work can be seen in *The Lion King*, *Dan Dare*, *M.A.S.K.*,
Aladdin, *Skylander*, *Rivers of London: Monday Monday*,
Dungeons and Dragons: Evil at Baldur's Gate, *Fathom*,
as well as in books for various other publishers.

ROB STEEN

Rob Steen is an experienced letterer, whose skilled
calligraphy has enlivened the works of many publishers,
from *Wolverine* and the *X-Men*, *Arrowsmith* and *Astro City*,
Harbinger and *Bloodshot*, and Titan's own *Rivers of London*
and *Warhammer 40,000* series.